D0856746

DANIEL IN HIS TIME

Studies on Personalities of the Old Testament
James L. Crenshaw, Editor

DANIEL
in His Time

André LaCocque

UNIVERSITY OF SOUTH CAROLINA PRESS

Published in Columbia, South Carolina, by the
University of South Carolina Press

Manufactured in the United States of America

Library of Congress Cataloging-in-Publication Data
LaCocque, André.
  Daniel in his time.

  (Studies on personalities of the Old Testament)
  Translation of: Daniel et son temps.¹
  Bibliography: p.
  Includes Index
  1.Bible. O.T. Daniel—Criticism, interpretation,
etc. I. Title. II. Series.
BS1555.2.L3313 **1988**   224'.506   87-13590
ISBN 0-87249-481-0

¹*Daniel et son temps*, Geneva, Labor et Fides, 1983.

Contents

CONTENTS

Abbreviations

AB	Anchor Bible
'Abot R. Nat.	*'Abot de Rabbi Nathan*
Adam and Eve	Books of Adam and Eve
AJSL	*American Journal of Semitic Languages and Literatures*
ANET	*Ancient Near Eastern Texts*, ed. J. B. Pritchard
Ant.	Josephus *Antiquities of the Jews*
APOT	*Apocrypha and Pseudepigrapha of the Old Testament*, ed. R. H. Charles
As. Mos.	Assumption of Moses
b.	Babylonian Talmud
BA	*Biblical Archaeologist*
Barn.	Barnabas
BASOR	*Bulletion of the American Schools of Oriental Research*
B. Bat.	*Baba Batra*
Ber.	*Berakot*
B. Mes.	*Baba Mesi 'a*
B. Qam.	*Baba Qamma*
BHH	*Biblisch-Historisches Handwörterbuch*, ed. B. Reicke and L. Rost
Bib. Ant.	Pseudo-Philo, Biblical Antiquities
BibOr.	Biblica et orientalia
B.J.	Jerusalem Bible (Bible de Jerusalem)
BKAT	Biblischer Kommentar: Altes Testament
BR	*Biblical Research*
BWANT	Beiträge zur Wissenschaft vom Alten und Neuen Testament
CAT	Commentaire de l'Ancien Testament
CBQ	*Catholic Biblical Quarterly*
CD	Cairo (Genizah text of the) Damascus (Document)
CSBR	Chicago Society for Biblical Research
DBSup	*Dictionnaire de la Bible, Supplement*

ABBREVIATIONS

Hag.	*Hagiga*
HAT	Handbuch zum Alten Testament
HKAT	Hand Kommentar zum Alten Testament
Hul.	*Hullin*
HUCA	*Hebrew Union College Annual*
IDBSup	Supplementary volume to the Interpreter's Dictionary of the Bible, ed. G.A. Buttrick
JAOS	*Journal of the American Oriental Society*
JBL	*Journal of Biblical Literature*
Jos.	Flavius Josephus
Jos. *B.J.*	Josephus: Bellum Judaeorum (*The Jewish War*)
Jub.	Jubilees
m.	Mishna
Meg.	*Megilla*
Mid.	*Middot*
Mo'ed Qat.	*Mo'ed Qaṭan*
Ned.	*Nedarim*
Pes.	*Pesahim*
P	The *Priestly Source*
Pss. Sol.	Psalms of Solomon
1Q, 2Q, etc.	Numbered caves of Qumran; followed by abbreviation of biblical or apocryphal book
1QDan.	Daniel
1QH	*Hôdāyôt* (Thanksgiving Hymns) from Cave 1
1QHab	Habbakuk
1QM	*Milḥāmāh* (War Scroll)
1QS	*Serek hayyaḥad* (Rule of the Community, Manual of Discipline)
1QSa	Appendix A (Rule of the Congregation) to 1QS
1QSb	Appendix B (Blessings) to 1QS
4QEnᶜ	Enoch, Ms C, Cave 4
4QFlor	*Florilegium* (Eschatological Midrashim) Cave 4
4QJN	Description of the New Jerusalem
4QPrNab	Prayer of Nabonidus

ABBREVIATIONS

4QpPs	pesher Psalms
4QDibHam	*Diberei Hameōrōt* (Words of the Luminaries)
11QPsa	Psalms
Rab.	*Rabbah* (following abbreviation for biblical book: Gen. Rab. = Genesis Rabbah)
RB	*Revue biblique*
RechBib	Recherches bibliques
RevQ	*Revue de Qumran*
RGG	*Religion in Geschichte und Gegenwart*
RSR	*Recherches de science religieuse*
Šabb.	*Šabbat*
Sanh.	*Sanhedrin*
Sib. Or.	Sibylline Oracles
t.	Tosepta
T.	Testament (of Levi, Benj., etc.)
T. 12 Patr.	Testaments of the Twelve Patriarchs
Tg. Isa.	*Targum of Isaiah*
TOB	Traduction Oecuménique de la Bible (Paris)
TRu	*Theologische Rundschau*
TSK	*Theologische Studien und Kritiken*
TWNT	*Theologisches Wörterbuch zum Neuen Testament*, ed. G. Kittel and G. Friedrich
UF	*Ugarit-Forschungen*
VD	*Verbum domini*
VT	*Vetus Testamentum*
VTSup	Vetus Testamentum, Supplements
y.	Jerusalem Talmud
Yal	*Yalquṭ*
ZAW	*Zeitschrift für die alttestamentliche Wissenschaft*
ZDPV	*Zeitschrift des deutschen Palästina-Vereins*
ZTK	*Zeitschrift für Theologie und Kirche*

Foreword

Jewish (and even Christian) apocalyptic has prompted contrary reactions ranging from total rejection to delirious enthusiasm. It is, in point of fact, a complex phenomenon. Specialists in the field are far from agreeing on a definition of its origins, its spokesmen, or even its characteristics. One of the many questions that arise is that of its legitimacy in the context of biblical revelation. With its armies of angels, its strange visions, its obscure symbols, its cryptic language, and its radical statements, does the apocalyptic movement show a remarkable fidelity to Scripture or a dangerous deviation from biblical faith?

Jewish apocalyptic circles, the chief writings of which lie between the second century B.C.E. and the second century of the common era, have stood trial time and again, and official theology has all too often left to the sects the task of deciphering pages in which the fantastic vies with the enigmatic. While the prophetic message has at last been received by the church, the apocalyptic message is still left to one side and still regarded with persistent suspicion.

Here and there, however, a voice speaks out for Jewish apocalyptic. Scholars in recent years have spoken of its decisive importance for all apostolic witness and, eventually, for all Christian theology. Its political implications and its influence on its contemporaries have been pointed out. Some have declared that its spokesmen, far from embracing a sort of resigned fatalism, dared to hope, at a tragic moment for the Jewish people, and to live according to their hope. It is true that the apocalyptic writers sought to respond to the challenge of their times by expressing the faith of their fathers in a language imposed on them by their misfortunes. They were not satisfied to repeat what preceding generations had proclaimed; they took the risk of reinterpreting what their elders had passed on to them in a form that they thought appropriate to the spiritual and cultural context of their epoch. Even if from time to time they made mistakes, still their intention was legitimate, and we are to some extent their heirs.

One work that speaks for Jewish apocalyptic is the book of Daniel. It is one of the oldest examples of this literature and, for that reason, a paradigmatic work, now chosen for further study by André LaCocque, who has taught for many years at the Chicago Theological Seminary, and who directs its Center for Jewish-Christian Studies.

Foreword

André LaCocque is also the author of a well-received study on the book of Daniel that appeared in the Commentaire de l'Ancien Testament Series (vol. 15b, 1976). Further, he has published a study of the book of Zechariah, certain chapters of which have apocalyptical overtones (*Zacharie 9–14*, in the same series [vol. 11c, 1981]). In the present study he develops themes touched on previously and introduces the reader into the milieu that gave rise to the book of Daniel; he discusses the many difficulties inherent in this text, and he clarifies its interest for today's reader. Both LaCocque's knowledge of the critical literature of Jewish apocalyptic, particularly in the United States and Great Britain, and his long-standing familiarity with Jewish thought enable him to treat the delicate problems raised by the book of Daniel. Long but erroneously classified as a prophetic book, Daniel is one of the results of the grave crisis experienced by the Jewish people in the second century B.C.E., when Judaism was torn between the supporters of an "updating" of tradition, who could count on the backing of the Seleucid dynasty, and those who defended the old ways of living the Mosaic faith, who were prepared to face martyrdom or to break into rebellion in order to save what they held to be the essence of their forefathers' heritage. This book, one of the last in date in the Old Testament, shows signs of two sorts of confrontation. First, those who demanded the Hellenization of Jerusalem were locked in a merciless struggle with those who were equally passionately opposed to Hellenization. Second (and more important, as André LaCocque points out), the apocalyptic author was in conflict within himself, torn between his faith and the denial of history; and he raised a vibrant "No!" against tyrants, against violence, and against men's lies while he proclaimed the "death of God" to be impossible.

Everything about this apocalyptical presentation of God's truth is complicated. The author uses two languages, Hebrew and Aramaic—the former a sacred language particularly appropriate to the eschatological chapters that end the book. The book is divided into two parts differing in both form and content: the first six chapters follow the Midrashic model and were written before the Maccabean era; they are recast by whoever was responsible for the last chapters, which are apocalyptic in the strict sense. Furthermore, there is use of a symbolic and even mythic language that raises its sights to the cosmic and the universal and that contrasts with the usual views of Israel, for whom "salva-

FOREWORD

tion history" concerned essentially the people of God. The temporal framework of this pseudepigraph is telescoped or inverted: it transports the reader to the time of Babylonian imperialism, whereas in reality it concerns the fate of the Jews under Antiochus IV Epiphanes (175–164 B.C.E.).

André LaCocque also calls attention to other problems of a more purely theological nature, such as the return to a concern with the origins of the world, some elements of which are integrated into the final vision of human destiny. He points out the importance of chapter 7, the key to the entire book, with its foundation in the cult and its central figure of a "son of man" who embodies several complementary significances—priestly, collective, Adamic—and in whom humanity is called to find some sort of assumption. Furthermore, LaCocque notes the novel, and even the revolutionary, affirmation of resurrection, which, according to him, follows logically from the apocalyptic. It opposes man's death as punishment to his death as an offering—a pathetic sign of his weakness but also of his transcendence, which calls for a divine response that is none other than the continually renewed gift of life.

LaCocque's study breathes with a life of its own; it is anything but a dry enumeration of the difficulties that the book of Daniel presents. We can sense that its author not only is well informed on the problems posed by this model of the Jewish apocalyptic, but that he has thought long and hard about the many aspects of this biblical testimony. He has taken to his own the faith of the Hasidim, among whom these pages were written; he has accepted their struggles and their hope. His knowledge has not led him to a cold dissection of the text of Daniel, taken as an inert object: he has let himself be won over by the flame that inhabited the faithful witnesses of the God of Israel at a time at which the very future of biblical revelation was at stake. *Daniel in His Time* is thus an excellent initiation to the best aspects of Jewish apocalyptic.

Robert Martin-Achard

Editor's Preface

Critical study of the Bible in its ancient Near Eastern setting has stimulated interest in the individuals who shaped the course of history and whom events singled out as tragic or heroic figures. Rolf Rendtorff's *Men of the Old Testament* (1968) focuses on the lives of important biblical figures as a means of illuminating history, particularly the sacred dimension that permeates Israel's convictions about its God. Fleming James's *Personalities of the Old Testament* (1939) addresses another issue, that of individuals who function as inspiration for their religious successors in the twentieth century. Studies restricting themselves to a single individual—e.g., Moses, Abraham, Samson, Elijah, David, Saul, Ruth, Jonah, Job, Jeremiah—enable scholars to deal with a host of questions: psychological, literary, theological, sociological, and historical. Some, like Gerhard von Rad's *Moses*, introduce a specific approach to interpreting the Bible, hence provide valuable pedagogic tools.

As a rule, these treatments of isolated figures have not reached the general public. Some were written by outsiders who lacked a knowledge of biblical criticism (Freud on Moses, Jung on Job) and whose conclusions, however provocative, remain problematic. Others were targeted for the guild of professional biblical critics (David Gunn on David and Saul, Phyllis Trible on Ruth, Terence Fretheim and Jonathan Magonet on Jonah). None has succeeded in capturing the imagination of the reading public in the way fictional works like Archibald MacLeish's *J.B.* and Joseph Heller's *God Knows* have done.

It could be argued that the general public would derive little benefit from learning more about the personalities of the Bible. Their conduct, often less than exemplary, reveals a flawed character, and their everyday concerns have nothing to do with our preoccupations from dawn to dusk. To be sure, some individuals transcend their own age, entering the gallery of classical literary figures from time immemorial. But only these rare achievers can justify specific treatments of them. Then why publish additional studies on biblical personalities?

The answer cannot be that we read about biblical figures to learn ancient history, even of the sacred kind, or to discover models for ethical action. But what remains? Perhaps the primary significance of biblical personages is the light they throw on the imaging of deity in biblical times. At the very least, the Bible constitutes human perceptions of deity's relationship with the world and its creatures. Close readings of biblical personalities therefore clarify ancient understandings of God. That is the important datum which we seek—not because we endorse that specific view of deity, but because all such efforts to make sense of reality contribute something worthwhile to the endless quest for knowledge.

James L. Crenshaw
Duke Divinity School

Preface to the English Edition

The English version of *Daniel in His Time* is basically a translation from the French by Lydia Cochrane, whose care and accurateness are beyond laudation.

I have reworked this version of my book, if only to honor critiques and suggestions of scholarly friends whom I here thank wholeheartedly. The pattern of the work has been changed according to a more logical sequence of ideas. Furthermore, in reply to recent onslaughts against the attribution to the "Hasidim" of apocalyptic documents, including Daniel, I have appended to the chapter 2 a discussion of the arguments. This appendix affords me the opportunity to give to the Enochian literature and to the Qumran documents a weightier importance in the whole. Thus, I believe, the book is better balanced.

Less important improvements from the French edition are numerous, and will hopefully result in a more pleasurely reading of the book. Not the least of these is a thorough reworking of the index, for which again I am deeply in the debt of Max J. Havlick, Jr.

A.L.

ONE

Historical Introduction

PRESENTATION

The book of Daniel divides quite naturally into two parts of nearly equal length: Daniel A includes chapters 1–6 and is made up of narrations for the most part centering on the person of someone named Daniel. These six chapters are popular narratives. Daniel B, chapters 7–12, narrates the apocalyptic visions of this same personage, who now speaks in the first person singular. Chapter 7, at the heart of the book, serves as a pivot between its two parts and has aspects of both of their literary genres.

The book is unique in its genre. This is one of the reasons for which it has been so "sadly misunderstood."[1] To be sure, its author relied heavily on his predecessors, and we can, with Gerhard von Rad, wonder, "Might not the presentation in Daniel II [Daniel B] actually be described as a *pesher* of Isaiah?"[2] The fact remains, however, that Daniel, generally speaking, has no parallel in Scripture.

Anyone opening the book of Daniel for the first time is immediately struck by the change of atmosphere between it and the other books of the Bible. To be sure, it is tempting, at first glance, to see in it a prophetic text, for it speaks of dreams, visions, signs, predictions, and it explains them in an oracular tone. Moreover, Hellenistic Judaism placed Daniel after Ezekiel and before Hosea among the *nebiim*

3

(prophets). An attentive reader will note certain details that might cause hesitation, however. Here we are no longer, as with the prophets of the classical epoch, in a time of pure creation, but in a period of the exploitation of scriptural materials either already "canonized" at the time of the writing of Daniel or at least already imbued with authority. The midrash, for example, a genre to which Daniel 1–6 is akin, is none other than the expansion of a tradition, written or oral, that was already known. It is a series of variations on a central biblical theme considered still relevant to present history.

As for the apocalypse—a genre represented in chapters 7–12—it is the prolongation of prophecy[3] and, in a sense, its replacement by a suprahistorical speculation on the basis of contemporary events. In either case, it is clear that one biblical period has ended and a new era has begun, and that the first has laid the foundations of the second. This second tradition refers to the first as to a recognized and incontestable authority, unique and divine, and situates itself in relation to the first. Not by chance was Daniel placed by Palestinian tradition not among the prophets but among the writings—that is, in the series of books that Judaism considers as a third level, resting on the group of the *nebiim*, which in turn has the Torah as its foundation.[4]

The problems that the book of Daniel poses to criticism are many and complex. Not only is the apocalyptic language purposely obscure and the historical allusions deliberately cryptic; the work is also pseudepigraphal, antedated, bilingual, and influenced by literary and spiritual contributions of various foreign origins; its text in Greek versions has a greater amplitude and is often different in character from the Semitic text; and so forth. As for the message, it too is presented in a form that bristles with snares and traps for reader. The author makes use of existing materials, which he reworks to bend them to his purposes; he attempts both to be obscure—for this is how he conceives the prophetic form—and to allow his meaning to be guessed,[5] particularly since it is urgent that Israel grasp the lesson of a history that is soon to reach its end. He is a man of his times, and he adopts the language appropriate to the culture of his contemporaries to proclaim his "prophetic" message.[6] In a sense, the shift from Hebrew to Aramaic, then back to Hebrew, is already an indication on the technical level of the difficulties he has undergone. Is it better to speak the holy tongue and risk seeming affected, or the vernacular, at the risk of imitating foreign works?[7]

HISTORICAL INTRODUCTION

Daniel contains even more decisive choices. Has history a meaning, as the prophets were persuaded? Why, then, did contemporary events seem to give the lie to this certainty? Was the meaning of history a secret jealously guarded by God, in which case human liberty is denied and men and women are but toys in the divine hands? Was Israel in the second century B.C.E. the helpless victim of a cosmic struggle between two powers of opposed significance? Had the prophets been wrong to rise up against Babylonian dualism (cf. Isa. 45:7)? And if they had been right, what was the role of evil in the dialogue between God and people? Up to what point did God intend to make use of evil? How would he lead us out of these straits? Was the end of tribulations in sight? Under what form would this end come? Would it be eschatological? Messianic? A new life after death?

As we can see, the book of Daniel raises a set of problems that are influenced by the epoch in which it was written. Here, more than ever, the question of the historical setting must be resolved, and its resolution must serve as a constant reference throughout the reading of all twelve chapters of the document. Because they have neglected this elementary procedure, commentators (but not exegetes) both ancient and modern have attempted to speculate on supposed predictions of the future mysteriously contained in the book, giving themselves over to calculations as vain as they are muddle-headed in order to learn the date of the "end of time."

PSEUDEPIGRAPHY

Daniel is the name of a mythical personage mentioned, along with Noah and Job, in Ezekiel 14:14, 20[8] as one of the wisest men the earth has ever known (Ezek. 28:3).[9] This tradition can be traced back to the Canaanite Ugaritic literature, one of the heroes of which was a wise king named Danel,[10] who was also at the origin of the tradition echoed by 1 Enoch 6; 7; 69:2.[11] When he sets up the fiction that the book was written by this ancient Middle Eastern patriarch known for his universal knowledge, the biblical author immediately indicates the spirit in which he is presenting his work and its orientation. As Martin Hengel writes, "The supposed great age of these writings was a demonstration of their truth. The *pseudepigraphic form* necessarily becomes a firm rule for Jewish apocalyptic, since the apocalyptists' unheard-of claim to revelation could only be maintained by reference to those who had been

5

endowed with the spirit in ancient times."[12] This is why all of the "literature of revelation" of the Hellenistic world is pseudepigraphic in character,[13] as, for example, the Sibylline, Hermetic, and Orphic texts, all of which are closely connected to the international wisdom literature. This fact should arouse our attention. It suggests the presence of a foreign influence, at least on the form of Jewish apocalyptic literature. We will find further confirmation of this in the course of this study. We should remember, however, that the technique of the pseudonym is extremely old in Scripture and is used as early as the Pentateuch. Thus Genesis 49, written between 1000 and 932, claims to go back to the fourteenth century.[14] Similarly, many of the psalms are called "of David," many proverbs are "of Solomon," the discourses of Deuteronomy "of Moses," and so forth.

It is true that Daniel is a name found fairly frequently in the Bible.[15] In 1 Chronicles 3:1 it refers to a son of David and Abigail; in Ezra 8:2 and Nehemiah 10:6 it is the name of a priest returned to Jerusalem from exile. Its punctuation (vocalization) is uniformly odd, as it obscures the theophoric element in the name, giving *daniye'l* instead of *dany'el*.[16]

In Akkadian the name "Danilu" is attested from 2000 B.C.E. on.[17] In Hebrew the name means "God is the defender of my right" (as in Gen. 30:6, concerning Dan). It seems evident that the author of our book took advantage of the legends in circulation concerning Danel the incomparably wise, combining this with Daniel the priest, one of the Judean exiles in Babylon (sixth century B.C.E.).[18]

The pseudonymic method answers two conditions. On the one hand, the prophetic spirit seemed exhausted after Haggai, Zechariah, and Malachi, a conviction that remains to this day in rabbinic Judaism.[19] For G. H. Box, moreover, the absence of prophets, which coincides with the conquests of Alexander the Great and with Greek influence, constitutes the most important event of the age. Box writes: "The old control exercised by the High Priest and the priestly Soferim was no longer possible. . . . Thus, for some seventy or eighty years—from about 270 to 190 B.C.—there seems to have been a break in authoritative teaching."[20] On the other hand, in conformity with the mentality of the ancient Middle East, Israelite authors always considered it perfectly legitimate to put writings to express their thoughts—even fictional writings—under the name of a hero of the past, occasionally of the distant past.[21] This is a literary phenomenon of greatest importance

6

for biblical criticism. Later Jewish tradition was to say, in the same spirit, that all true teachings of a "disciple of a sage" only repeat what Moses received in revelation on Mount Sinai.[22] The principle is an ancient one: it explains, for example, how there can be two or three works by different authors all placed under the name of Isaiah or Zechariah. Above all, it affirms the unity of divine inspiration among authors of different epochs.[23]

The procedure of pseudonymity implies a certain esoteric quality. Eschatological secrets have been known during the course of history only by a few particularly enlightened saints. They are revealed (*apokalupsis*) now, openly and publicly, only to effect, within humanity and within the holy people, the final winnowing of the elect from the rejected. It is in this sense that revelation remains 'hidden," impenetrable to eyes that have not been opened (Dan. 8:26; 12:4,9).[24] This is what makes the book of Daniel not only an apocalypse but also the first known example of an apocryphon—that is, according to Montgomery's definition of this word, "a volume of alleged antiquity that had been purposely 'hidden away' until the emergency arrived for its publication."[25]

THE PROBLEM OF AUTHENTICITY

The book of Daniel opens with a chronological note: "In the third year of the reign of Jehoiakim king of Judah,[26] Nebuchadnezzar king of Babylon came to Jerusalem and besieged it." As early as the third century C.E., however, the pagan critic Porphyry attacked the authenticity of this chronology. He saw Daniel as the work of a forger written at the time of Antiochus IV Epiphanes (175–164 B.C.E.).[27]

This interpretation requires qualification, but it is correct in essence. There are many elements to prove this so. Briefly: not only was the book not included among the prophets,[28] but we have to wait until the Sibylline Oracles (bk. 3) to find any trace of it (between 145 and 140). First Maccabees 1:54, still later (between 134 and 104), offers a text that parallels Daniel 9:27 and 11:31. Similarly, we find Daniel mentioned in the book of Jubilees (around 110 B.C.E.). It is not cited in Sirach (190–180), as one might expect, for example in 48:22 or in 49:7, 8, and 10. Only on the most recent literary levels of the book of Enoch (end of the first century B.C.E.) do we find some trace of it, as in 104:2 and in the "Book of Parables" (even later).

External criticism is confirmed by internal: the vision of chapters 10 and 11 takes us, step by step, up to the events of 165 (11:39), and it stops before 164. The author is aware, in fact, of the profanation of the temple of Jerusalem by Antiochus IV (7 December 167; Dan. 11:31). He alludes to the revolt of the Maccabees and to the first successes of Judas (166; Dan. 11:34). But the death of Antiochus (autumn 164) as he narrates it is fiction (Dan. 11:40–45), and he is unaware of the purification of the temple by Judas on 14 December 164.[29] At least the second part of the book of Daniel (7–12) can be dated, with a comfortable margin of certainty, between 166 and 164, more probably 166. As for chapters 1–6, they present another texture and belong to the literary genre of popular narrative. Nonetheless, their final composition cannot under any circumstances have come much before that of the final chapters. There are allusions in the early chapters to the problems Judaism was facing in the second century B.C.E., such as the keeping of the Levitic dietary prescriptions (Dan. 1:5–8; cf. 2 Macc. 6:18–31), the resistance to idolatry imposed by coercion (Dan. 3:1–12), the deification of a human king (6:6–10),[30] and martyrdom (3:9–21; 6:17–18). Little wonder, then, that the theme of feverish expectation of the tyrant's death runs through the entire book: 5:21, 30; 7:11, 24–26; 8:25; 9:26–27; 11:45.

A more thorough discussion of the nature and the respective dates of composition of Daniel A and Daniel B can be found in chapter 2.

BILINGUALISM IN THE BOOK OF DANIEL

One of the most difficult problems in the study of the book of Daniel is the sudden change from Hebrew to Aramaic in 2:4, then back to Hebrew in 8:1. The passages in Aramaic are quite certainly not translated from the Hebrew—quite the contrary, the Hebrew seems to be based on an original in Aramaic. This point is decisive; to misinterpret it is to arrive at an impasse.

Thus, for Otto Eissfeldt, no satisfactory solution to this question has yet been proposed.[31] Emil Kraeling thinks that this phenomenon can be explained by "the difficulty of finding a complete copy of the Hebrew book when it was decided to include it among 'the Writings.' It seems certain that Daniel played a role at the time of the Jewish revolt in A.D. 68 and that copies of it were destroyed by the Romans wherever they were found."[32] Jean Steinmann points out that the ABA order of the book (Hebrew, Aramaic, Hebrew) corresponds to that of the Code of Hammurabi (verse, prose, verse) and the book of Job (prose, verse, prose).[33] According to the solution H. H. Rowley proposes, the stories of Daniel A (2–6) are the work of an anonymous Maccabean author.[34] Their aim is to encourage the victims of the persecutions of Antiochus Epiphanes. Later, the same author added chapter 7, also in Aramaic, and then the apocalyptical visions. But since the visions were of a totally different nature, he composed them in Hebrew. He "topped off" the whole with an introductory chapter (1) also in Hebrew. The pseudonymity of the work is a sign of its unity.

For Otto Plöger, the languages employed correspond to the fundamental structures of the book.[35] The "Aramaic" mentioned in 2:4b, at the point at which the book abandons Hebrew, symbolizes the foreign language that Daniel learned at the royal court. The relationship between chapters 2 and 4, 3 and 6, 2 and 7, explains why these chapters were written in a common language. To be sure, chapter 7 is intimately connected with chapter 8; but in the latter, for the first time actually, Israel comes to the foreground, hence Hebrew is appropriate.

In my opinion, this solution of Plöger's, combined with the results of H. L. Ginsberg's *Studies in Daniel*,[36] points in the right direction.

Steinmann's theory explains nothing and Kraeling's cannot be confirmed. Rowley's can be rejected; John Gammie was right to see it as a tour de force that ignores too many factors to be convincing—among others, that power is considered in Daniel A with too much sympathy for this portion to have been written at the time of the persecution under Epiphanes.[37] We will return to this important point later. I believe that a solution to the problem of the bilingualism of the book can be found in the following manner:

1. The *agadoth* of Daniel A are old traditions from a "Daniel cycle" in circulation during the Persian period, expressed in Empire Aramaic,[38] the origin of which goes back—at least in their oral phase—much further. The author of Daniel B made use of these for his apologetic and parenetic purposes by transforming them as little as possible, both in language and in content.

2. That same author, although his native language was Aramaic, made the effort to write in Hebrew the part of his creation (Daniel B). Chapters 8–12 are "translations" from the Aramaic, either because the author thought in Aramaic (as it happens when we speak a foreign language without complete mastery of it), or because he really did compose in Aramaic and then translate what he had written.[39] His desire to use

9

the sacred language is understandable, given the majesty of the eschato-logical subject to which Daniel A merely serves as a preface.

3. He introduced the entire book with a chapter in Hebrew, not—as it has been repeated all too often—so that his work would find a wel-come in the canon of the Scriptures,[40] but for the following and decisive reason:

4. The chapters—or, more accurately, the literary units—of Daniel correspond harmoniously. The parallels between chapters 2 and 7, 3 and 6, and 4 and 5 have often been pointed out, but there is more: Chapter 1 (in Hebrew) corresponds to the conclusion, chapters 11–12.4; the first chapter ties the past to the present of Daniel and his con-temporaries, while the conclusion joins the present to the future. A com-mon ideological and semantic element links them: the notion of wisdom or of intelligence (of dreams and of secrets). The term *maskilim* can be found here and there (1:4; 1:17 [*haskél*]; cf., 1:20; 11:33, 35; 12:3, 10). These chapters, which belong respectively to Daniel A and Daniel B, are of course in Hebrew. One might object that the root *skl* can also be found in Daniel 9 (vv. 13, 22, 25), but these usages should be seen as the divine response to the *sèkèl* (skills) of Antiochus IV in Daniel 8:25; the terms in Daniel 8 and 9 are not technical, whereas in chapters 1 and 11–12 they are. Chapters 8 and 9 correspond. Evil reaches its highest point in the coming of Antiochus IV: "He shall even rise up against the Prince of princes; but, by no human hand, he shall be broken" (8:25); "Upon the wing of abominations shall come one who makes desolate, until the decreed end is poured out on the desolator" (9:27). There is a corre-spondence between chapter 10, the prologue to the section 11–12:4, that corresponds to 12:5ff., its epilogue.

Thus the Hebrew of Daniel 1–2:4 and the Aramaic of Daniel 7 can be explained. The argument can be schematized thus:

Hebrew and Aramic in the Book of Daniel

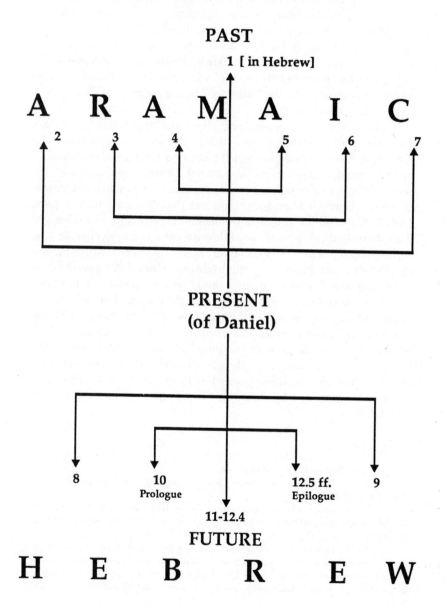

PAST

1 [in Hebrew]

A R A M A I C

2   3   4   5   6   7

PRESENT
(of Daniel)

8   10   12.5 ff.   9
    Prologue Epilogue

11-12.4

FUTURE

H E B R E W

II

One remark is imperative: If this schema is workable, this means that literary structure decidedly prevails over chronological succession. For most certainly, from the chronological point of view, Daniel 7 should come between 4 and 5, since it is dated as from the first year of the reign of Belshazzar. Daniel 6 would also change place, since it refers to events of the reign of Darius the Mede, Belshazzar's successor.[41] But the author had more urgent needs of a structural nature, and it is thus not legitimate to argue the "disorder" of the chapters of Daniel A to draw critical conclusions.[42]

There is nothing astonishing about the importance of literary structure in an apocalyptic work such as Daniel. This is customary in the genre. Later works, such as 2 Baruch or 4 Esdras,[43] come immediately to mind, but there are also earlier writings—for example, the seven visions of 1 Zechariah[44] or the magnificient fresco of 2 Zechariah, in which geometric hyperbole dominates the organization of its parts (ABCB'A')[45] Did the author of Daniel find his structure in Zechariah? This thesis finds support in the enthronement scene in Zechariah 4, in correspondence with the "son of man" scene in Daniel 7. My opinion is that the structure follows the "candelabrum" scheme that was in vogue in the postexilic Jewish community, and I base my preference to a large extent on the centrality of the question of the temple. This structure is developed majestically in the Christian book of the Apocalypse of John. Elisabeth Schüssler Fiorenza comments that this was a pattern widely employed "in the literature of antiquity" and in "temple images." She adds that it can be traced to "the golden candelabrum which appears on the arch of Titus in Rome [and which] consists of a centerpiece paralleled on either side by three pieces and thus exhibits the pattern ABCDC'B'A'."[46]

NOTES

1. John Bright, *A History of Israel*, 183.

2. Gerhard von Rad, *Old Testament Theology*, 2:314 n. 29. J.-L. Seeligmann is of the same opinion (*VT Sup*, 1:171).

3. Otto Plöger is a better guide in this than von Rad, who sees in the apocalypse the heir not of prophetism but of wisdom. See Plöger, *Theocracy and Eschatology*, 27, and von Rad, *Old Testament Theology*, 2:301 ff.

4. Cf. the judgment of Maimonides: There are, he says, eleven degrees in prophecy, the lowest of which is a (simple) communication of the Holy Spirit. "For this reason the nation desired to place the book of Daniel among the Hagiographa, and not among the prophets. . . . They [Daniel and Solomon] belonged to the class of men that spoke,

inspired by the *ruaḥ ha-kodesh*, 'the holy spirit,' " which often manifested itself by dreams, proverbs, psalms, etc. "The authors of all these books (Prov., Eccl., Dan., Ps., Ruth, Esth.) are called prophets in the more general sense of the term" (*The Guide for the Perplexed*, 241, 243–44.). Furthermore, Daniel never uses the authoritative formula of the prophets: "Thus saith the Lord."

5. There are precedents on this point as well. Cf. Deut. 8:3: History teaches a lesson that Israel must learn. There is a "mystery" to be discovered under the veil of history, unlike the opinion of literary Jahwist (J) and Elohist (E) schools, for which the presence of YHWH was in the reality of the event itself.

6. In the sense indicated above of faithfulness to models such as Isaiah, Jeremiah, Ezekiel, or Habakkuk.

7. The author gets out of this difficulty by suggesting that the discourse of the "Chaldeans" was in Aramaic. I consider Dan. 2:4, "in Aramaic," as authentic and not as a gloss; See my Commentary, *The Book of Daniel*, ad loc.

8. Always spelled "Danel" in Ezekiel.

9. See Martin Noth, "Noah, Daniel und Hiob in Ezekiel XIV." For a totally different—midrashic—reading see *Midrash Beréshit Rabba* (in the Mann edition), p. 151: "Noah saw a world completed, destroyed, completed [again]; Job saw his house/family built, shattered, rebuilt; Daniel saw the Temple founded, devastated, founded [anew]."

10. See *Syria* 12 (1931); 21–22, 77, 193; W. F. Albright, JBL 51 (1932): 99–100; BASOR 46 (1932): 19; BASOR 63 (1936): 27. All of these articles deal with the Canaanite hero-king Danel.

11. According to Norman W. Porteous (*Daniel*, 17), we should perhaps think less of the Danel of Ras Shamra–Ugarit (2 Aqhat V: 7–8) than of the Danel of Jub. 4:20: Enoch the chief sage married Edmu, "the daughter of Danel." We shall return to this point.

12. Martin Hengel, *Judaism and Hellenism*, 205.

13. See "The Oracle of the Potter," a Greek papyrus from Oxyrhynchos dating from the second-third centuries C.E. The Potter was a sage who lived a thousand years earlier, under the reign of Amenophis III.

14. R. de Vaux, *La Genèse*, ad loc.

15. According to C. D. Ginsburg the word appears 81 times, 30 of them in Hebrew (*Introduction to the Massoretico-Critical Edition of the Hebrew Bible*, 397).

16. But it agrees with the Masoretic rule according to which "the *tséré* must be under the *jod*, according to the famous codex of the land of Eden" (Orient 2350 fol. 27a British Museum; Ginsburg, *Introduction*, 397 n. 2).

17. J. de Fraine in *VDo* 25 (1947): 127.

18. Note that traditional Jewish literature holds Daniel to be of royal and even Davidic descent. To prove this, Saadya Gaon cites Dan. 1:3, e.g. He was claimed to be related to the king Zedekiah (Jos. *Ant.* 10.10.1). Isa. 39:7 is interpreted as a prediction of his career (*Sanh.* 39b); his wisdom is greater than that of all the wise men of the nations put together (*Yoma* 77a). He transmits his powers to Zerubbabel.

19. According to Sir. 49:10, e.g., the Twelve Prophets constitute a closed category. Cf. 1 Macc. 4:46; 9:27; Pr. Azar. 3:28; Jos. *C. Apion* 1.8; *Pirke 'Abot* 1.1. Cf. *Meg.* 3a: "They [Haggai, Zechariah, Malachi] are prophets, but he [Daniel] is not a prophet." Rashi comments: "They are prophets because they have prophesied for Israel like envoys of prophecy." According to *Meg.* 14a and *Seder Olam R.* chs. 20–21, there were 48 prophets

13

and 7 prophetesses in Israel. When the last prophet died, the Spirit went away from Israel (*t. Sota* 13.2; *Sanh.* 11a). Y. Kaufmann remarks that Daniel keeps his revelations to himself (7:28) until the events take place (8:26; 12:4, 9). He himself works no miracles. Daniel is an extraordinary man, but only by his wisdom (1:17, 20). In chapters 1–6, he does not himself dream. In 2:19 he does nothing but repeat in his dream the dream of the king. Even in chs. 7–12, he is seeking comprehension (*bînah*) (7:16; 8:15; 9:22–23; 10:1, 11–12). There is no parallel in biblical prophecy. Kaufmann concludes from this that classical prophecy ended with Mal. 3 and that apocalyptic prophecy begins in Dan. 7. The tales narrated in chs. 1–6 make the transition between the two genres. (*History of Israel's Faith,* 8:409ff.).

20. G. H. Box, *Judaism in the Greek Period,* 51–52.

21. See D. S. Russell, *The Method and Message of Jewish Apocalyptic, 200 BC –AD 100,* 127–39: The apocalyptists were conscious of belonging to a heritage, or to a corporate personality, that included Enoch, Moses, Ezra, and Daniel. They were the heirs and representatives of their predecessors.

22. See *Ber.* 26b; *Deut. Rab.* 8. 6 (on Deut. 30:12); *y. Meg.* 1.7. 70d; *b. Hul.* 124a; *B.Mes.* 58bf.; *Exod. Rab.* 28.4 (cited by S. Baron; *A Social and Religious History of the Jews,* 2:383 n. 14).

23. All of this is evidently of importance for the underlying concept of time.

24. According to 4 Ezra 14, the apocryphal books seem better than the canonical books. They are destined only to the elite. See J. B. Frey, "Apocalyptique."

25. J. A. Montgomery, *A Critical and Exegetical Commentary on the Book of Daniel,* 76.

26. That is, in 606, unless we should read "Yehoyakin," which would take us to around 594.

27. Augustine called Porphyry "the wisest of the philosophers." This disciple of Plotinus had theorized that the author of the Pentateuch was Ezra rather than Moses. He also declared that the Old Testament recognized the existence of other gods and that the Judeo-Christian belief in angels was proof of this. This last point is not lacking in interest for the reader of Daniel. See Baron, *A Social . . . History,* 2:158–59.

28. Which indicates, according to Kaufmann, that the canon of the *nebiim* had been formed before the appearance of pseudonymic prophecy *(Toldot,* 8:405–08).

29. After the publication of the chronology of the Seleucids in cuneiform by Sachs and Wiseman, we now know that Antiochus IV did not die at the beginning of 163 but soon before the dedication of the temple of Jerusalem by Judas Maccabaeus, 14 December 164 ("A Babylonian King-list of the Hellenistic Period").

30. The title "Epiphanes" means "divine apparition." By derision the adversaries of Antiochus called him "Epimanes" (madman, maniac). Cf. Polybius 26. 10; 31. 3–4; Livy 41. 19–20; Diodorus 29. 32; 31. 16, 1–2.

31. Otto Eissfeldt, *The Old Testament,* 516–17. Bo Reicke and Leonard Rost, (*BHH* 1: cols. 318ff.).. are of the same opinion (*BHH* 1: A. Bentzen, *Daniel,* 9, speaks of unresolved enigmas.

32. Emil Kraeling, *Commentary on the Prophets,* 2:20.

33. Jean Steinmann, *Daniel.*

34. H. H. Rowley, "The Bilingual Problem of Daniel."

35. Plöger, *Das Buch Daniel,* 26–27.

36. H. L. Ginsberg, *Studies in Daniel.*

37. John Gammie, "The Classification, Stages of Growth, and Changing Intentions in the Book of Daniel," esp. p. 195 n. 25.

38. Aramaic became an international language as early as the eighth century B.C.E. in the Middle East, from India all the way to southern Egypt (Elephantine) and from Asia Minor to the north of Arabia, including the kingdoms of Assyria and Persia. In the Bible there are other passages in Aramaic besides those in Dan. 2:4–7: Ezra 4:8—6.18; 7:12–26; Jer. 10:11; Gen. 31:47 (two words).

39. This situation was far from unique. The Iranian Shahrokl Meskoub writes, concerning a religious text: "The structure of the language, the syntax of the sentences, the vast majority of the words, and some of the grammatical constructions are Arabic, as if the book had been written in Arabic and translated into bad Persian" (cited by Shaul Baklash in an article on the situation in Iran after the seventh-century Islamic conquest; *The New York Review of Books*, Feb. 1985).

40. As if there were "inspectors" or customs people, satisfied with a summary inspection of the merchandise! Even H. L. Ginsberg falls into this trap (*Studies in Daniel*, 38–39). Furthermore, the author of Daniel would have to have had the notion of a "canon of Scriptures" in the second century B.C.E., and would have to have deliberately written his book for the purpose of becoming a part of this canon.

41. Unless the chronology of the book of Daniel had its own strictly biblical logic and, consequently, its own rigor, as E. Bickerman explains, concerning "Darius the Mede" (Dan. 6:1). See Bickerman, *Four Strange Books of the Bible*, 93, based on Theodoret.

42. *Pace* Gammie, "The Classification."

43. On 2 Bar. see P. Bogaert, *Apocalypse de Baruch*; the division of the work into seven parts is discussed in 1:58ff. On 4 Ezra see A. L. Thompson, *Responsibility for Evil in the Theodicy of IV Ezra*. Thompson finds a model in 3 + 1 + 3 "episodes."

44. On 1 Zech. see S. Amsler in Amsler, Lacocque, and Vuilleumier, *Aggée, Zacharie, Malachie*, esp. p. 58.

45. See A. Lacocque on 2 Zech., ibid., esp. p. 131.

46. Elisabeth Schüssler Fiorenza, "Composition and Structure of the Book of Revelation." The book of Revelation is permeated with the symbolism of the number seven. Chs. 1:4—3:22 speak of the seven churches of Asia Minor. Their symbols are seven stars (2:1), seven angels (1:4), and seven candelabra (2:1). In Rev. 6:1–8:1 one finds seven seals; there are seven trumpets and seven claps of thunder in 8:2ff.; seven bowls in 15–16, and so forth.

TWO

The Social and Spiritual Milieu of the Early Jewish Apocalypses

DANIEL IN HIS TIME

At his death in 323 Alexander the Great left an immense empire that his generals, who were called *diadochi* (successors), immediately set to disputing. Egypt fell to the lot of Ptolemy, who gave his name to the dynasty that followed him. Syria, which included a vast territory embracing Babylonia and Persia, was governed by the Seleucids. Palestine,[1] lying between the two rivals, constituted a region of utmost strategic importance; it was a veritable lance in the flank of either power.

In 312 Palestine became part of the Ptolemaic kingdom, and it remained under this jurisdiction for more than a century, until 198. Under Ptolemy II (282–246 B.C.E.) the Egyptian penetration into Palestine was intense, bringing an Egyptianized Hellenism into that part of the world with a regime that was to last for sixty years or so. The Greek "new order" was first imposed in totally secular domains. Its "missionaries" were above all Hellenic mercenaries established in *cleruchies*[2] or *katoikiai* (colonies) that enjoyed special economic privileges. When they came into contact with these Greeks—in Egypt, for example—Jewish mercenaries began to adopt the Greek language and this economically profitable assimilation soon spread among others.

In Jerusalem authority was in theory exercised by the high priest, who was vested with both religious and political powers. The Ptolemaic

16

regime, however, which has been characterized as "a state capitalism without parallel in the ancient world,"[3] had taken the precaution of flanking the pontiff with a *prostatès tou hiérou* (inspector of the temple) who had final powers of decision in financial matters. Moreover, an aristocratic assembly called *gerousia*[4] was charged with supporting the high priest, but in practice it opposed him on many occasions. These "elders" played a determining role in the creation of a *polis* in Jerusalem in the second century.

Although it was a conquered territory and, by this fact, the property of the king of Egypt by "the law of arms," Palestine under the Ptolemies enjoyed substantial autonomy and a remarkable economic prosperity. The moral price to be paid for this was to the Jews extremely great, however. Materialism was all the more attractive for bringing notable political advantages along with individual economic power. It was among the wealthy social classes that the free citizens of the "polis Antioch-in-Jerusalem" would later be recruited.

After the Greek mercenaries came a constant stream of Greek merchants and immigrants, which continued to flow through the breach that Alexander had opened in the Persian Empire. They came with an irresistible program and conception of the world, based on the *oikoumènè*. All peoples were invited to unite to assure the harmony of the universe. All that was needed was for everyone to seek and to find his or her place in a world that had become a human habitat. Will Durant has written that Harmony "was literally worshipped by the people as a god."[5] Thus western Asia became spiritually Hellenistic even while it maintained certain local traits such as absolute monarchy and religious practices centered on the ancestral gods.[6]

Profound convulsions shook the Middle Eastern world, however, due to the rivalry between the Ptolemies and the Seleucids. The end of the third century saw the decadence of Egypt, governed by a Ptolemy Philopator (221–203 B.C.E.) of dissolute habits and an extreme attachment to the orgiastic cults of the Great Mother and of Dionysos. At that same time an energetic man was governing in Syria: Antiochus III. He took advantage of an internal revolt against Philopator to penetrate into Palestine. He fought to a major victory at Paneion in 200 B.C.E., and Palestine became Seleucid in 198.

"Egypt apart," Pierre Jouguet writes, "the Seleucid empire embraced the most ancient and the most glorious cradles of human civilization: Babylon, Susa, and Jerusalem. It included the ruins of Troy and the ruins of Nineveh. It turned out, oddly enough, to be the common homeland of the most diverse forms of poetic and religious inspiration: David's canticles, Zoroaster's preaching, and Homer's epic were born under this brilliant sky."[7] What this empire lacked was a unity of spirit that the king could perhaps have embodied, but the structure of the kingdom was feudal and the sovereignty of the monarch was more theoretical than real. Seleucid power rested in reality on the infrastructure of the Greek cities implanted in Asia Minor.[8]

Thus the giant had clay feet. Some in Israel sensed this well:

There was only one tradition in the Mediterranean world which did not go down under the predominance of Greece and Rome, which met power with equal power and showed a unique stubbornness of resistance—the tradition of Israel. Judaism might indeed enter into various combinations with Hellenism, in which the Jewish tradition underwent notable modification, but it always gave as well as received, and in the end, Greek intellectual culture and Roman imperial sagacity had to accept the supremacy of a Hebraic religion.[9]

As in the time of the Ptolemies, the spectacle that Seleucid society offered to "orthodox" Jews was nothing short of shocking. The empire included vast domains that belonged to veritable religious principalities, "with their population of hierodules, of the devout, of the possessed (*théophorètoi*), of sacred prostitutes; their periodic feasts and the fairs that accompanied them."[10] As for the Hellenized cities, the way of life they fostered encouraged widespread sexual immorality. Athletic competitions, public baths, and contests of oratory had become institutions. At the risk of anticipating, we should note immediately that some young Jews in Jerusalem had operations to hide their circumcision, which the Greeks considered a sort of castration (see 1 Macc. 1:15).[11]

The Jewish masses remained adverse to this Hellenization—a phenomenon all the more remarkable for being unique at that time. This resistance, which was latent under the Ptolemies, became more accentuated after 198, under the Seleucid domination. Indeed, after very liberal beginnings the regime hardened its positions, ultimately turning to persecution to force the recalcitrant Jews to adopt Hellenism. In Jerusalem it relied upon the support of a collaborationist party made up of members of the priestly and aristocratic classes and under the leadersip of the Tobiad family. It is quite possible that their allegiance to the Syrian government was not without duplicity and that they entertained the secret hope of facilitating a victory over the foreigner and a rejection of his yoke.[12] Whatever the case might be, the Tobiads encountered stiff opposition among the influential family of the Oniads, who backed the Ptolemies of Egypt.

This is the background of the events we are about to examine; events that were to have a decisive influence on contemporary Judaism and, beyond that, on the apocalyptic Jewish sects, including Hasidism, Essenism, and Qumran, and on Christianity.

In 191 the Seleucid Antiochus III (the Great) was defeated by the Romans in the defile of Thermopylae. This was the first time that Romans had interevened in this part of the world, and they put a definitive end to Mediterranean expansion from the east. Antiochus became the vassal of Rome under the terms of the peace treaty of Apamea (188), and he was forced to deliver over his son, Antiochus IV, as a hostage. In 187 Antiochus III was assassinated, and another of his sons, Seleucus IV Philopator (187–175) succeeded him.

Daniel 11:20 tells how Seleucus sent his chief financial advisor, Heliodorus, to Jerusalem with the mission of seizing the treasure of the temple. Apparently the high priest Onias III, who backed the Ptolemies, had failed to pay the tribute due the Seleucid kings, and a certain Simon,[13] who coveted the office of high priest, had reported to Seleucus that Onias was hiding a treasure in the temple at Jerusalem. Heliodorus was unable to complete his mission, however. According to 2 Maccabees 3, he was prevented from doing so by a supernatural apparition.[14] Onias III was in a difficult position. He resolved to go to plead his cause in person before the king, but Seleucus died, poisoned by Heliodorus (176). As all this was taking place, Antiochus IV returned from Rome, having promised to restore the temple of Olympian Zeus in Athens. His return and the death of Seleucus provided an occasion for the Hellenistic party in Jerusalem to carry out a sort of palace revolution with the support of Jason, the brother of Onias III. Jason succeeded in persuading Antiochus, to whom he had promised enormous sums of money, to name him high priest in his brother's stead, and with Jason the Hellenistic party came to power in Jerusalem (174–171).

In 172 Menelaus, the brother of Simon "the Tobiad," managed to strip Jason of the high priesthood by promising even greater sums of money to Antiochus. Since he was not of a Zadokite priestly family, Menelaus aroused spirited opposition, even among the supporters of the Hellenistic party.[15] He reached new heights of infamy by dipping into the treasure of the temple and by having Onias III assassinated.

The people had considered Onias a saint, perhaps even a messianic figure (see Dan. 9:25–26;[16] 11:22). Second Maccabees 3:1 praises him for his piety and his "hatred of wickedness." His death galvanized the energies of the opposition party and had as a direct or indirect consequence the formation of the sect of the Hasidim (the Pious, the Faithful to the true Faith), to which we owe the book of Daniel.

When the rumor of the king's death spread through Jerusalem, a rebellion against Syria broke out and independence was proclaimed. In reality, as the Roman historians Polybius (29.1) and Livy (44.19; 45.12) tell us, the Roman consul Gaius Popilius Laenas had come to meet with Antiochus IV, who had become too powerful in the eyes of Rome after his victory in Egypt. The two men met near Alexandria, and Gaius delivered the Roman Senate's ultimatum to retire—backed by the presence of the Roman fleet off the Syrian coast.[17] Antiochus was forced to capitulate.

During this time grave events were taking place in Jerusalem. Despite some confusion in our sources,[18] the chronology of these events seems to have been as follows: Jason, the high priest who was ousted in favor of Menelaus, headed the opposition in Jerusalem. He gained control of the city during a civil war (2 Macc. 5:6). When Antiochus returned from Egypt, however, he won back Jerusalem in a lightning-swift campaign (2 Macc. 5:11ff). He massacred 40,000 persons and sold off as many again as slaves. But no sooner had he left the city than rebellion broke out once more (2 Macc. 5:22ff.).

Apollonius, the general of the mercenaries, took control of the city on a sabbath day in 167. He constructed the citadel of Acra, which became the center of the Greek *polis* (1 Macc. 1:23–34; also v. 53 for crowds of city dwellers abandoning the city). It is of the Hellenized citizens of the *polis* that Daniel 11:30 is speaking when it calls them "those who forsake the holy covenant"[19] (see 1 Macc. 1:11–15, 43, 52). Even the temple became the common property of the Judeo-pagan citizens.[20]

Daniel 11:32 is witness to the dissensions among the Jewish people. Parties crystallized in Jerusalem that were to be at the origin of the Sadducees and the Hasidim, and later the Pharisees, the Herodians, and others. Daniel's sympathies are obviously with the members of his own party, the Hasidim.[21] They "will act with firmness," for are they not called the "mighty warriors of Israel" in 1 Maccabees 2:42? They are "wise"; they "shall make many understand" (Dan. 11:33), and there were indeed many scribes among them (1 Macc. 7:12).

Their adversaries are described in Daniel as "those who violate the covenant" (11:32), an expression also found in Qumran (1QM 1.2; see also CD 20.26) to designate, as here, the Hellenistic party. Antiochus "will make them apostates by intrigues" (11:39; cf. 1 Macc. 1:52).[22] This comparison with Qumran is interesting: the hypothesis of a Hasidic Daniel, which I will defend in the present work, already finds confirmation there, and we can better understand how Antiochus IV appears to a "fundamentalist" author as the personification of evil. He is even the most highly refined and the ultimate product of the wickedness of human empires in revolt against God (see Dan. 2; 7; 11; and *passim*). The summit of blasphemy against the Lord is reached by the king's self-deification (cf. 1 Macc. 1:50; 2 Macc. 5:7ff.). The king places himself over all the gods (Dan. 7:8, 20). He pronounces, Daniel 11:36 tells us, *niphlaôth*: "astonishing things," revolting slander.[23] For Daniel, this rebellion against God had to reach this peak, for only thus would divine wrath be complete.[24]

In a more objective vein, Adam C. Welch reminds us that "the horde led by Alexander was not made up of Greek philosophers. . . . There was nothing left which such an Emperor could play in order to unite his kingdom except his own personality."[25] This is equally true of Antiochus IV. He found himself discredited by tendentious factions for having replaced the Syrian gods of his fathers with Olympian Zeus, to whom he gave his own features (Dan. 11:37–38).[26] First Maccabees 1:41ff. even insinuates that Antiochus attempted to establish a pagan monotheism: "a thing unparalleled in the Graeco-Roman world before the third century C.E.," according to Victor Tcherikover, who rejects this hypothesis.[27] He adds that the unification of the whole population of Antiochus' empire is simply "not credible" (p.398). However that may be, the temple of Jerusalem received the name of Temple of Zeus Olympios, and the Jews were forced to celebrate a monthly royal ceremony in it and to participate in the ritual procession in honor of Dionysos.

Tempting as it is, I still refuse the explanation of Lucien Cerfaux and Julien Tondriau that "in order to make the cult of the sovereigns a reality, it was not only necessary to have raised the prestige of mortals to the skies (Alexander had contributed much here), but also to have depreciated the immortals (and the religion of Olympos suffered from just this 'depreciation.')"[28] For Zeus is certainly the god designated by "the god of fortresses" in Daniel 11:38.[29] Antiochus also had a magnificent temple built to him at Antioch, according to Livy (45.20). This manifestation of piety toward the traditional gods was, furthermore, a common trait among the Hellenistic sovereigns. In Syria and Egypt alike, the various cults joined and fertilized one another. Already the Seleucid Antiochus I, one of the successors of Alexander, was assimilated to Zeus, and Apollo was declared the founder of the dynasty. Later Seleucid kings would even be deified during their lifetime. Similarly, in Egypt, where the deification of the pharaohs had always been at the center of religion, the Ptolemies considered themselves as gods from 270 on. Here once again the dynastic cult enriched a religious base in which the traditional pantheon more or less kept its place. It was to respect these various religious traditions—and to take advantage of them—that the state cult adapted to local particularities and took on their form.[30]

It seems that the indignation of the author of Daniel was provoked by the attribution of a *name* (Zeus Akraios) to the "anonymous" divinity of the temple, who nonetheless continued to be the revered god there. This action on the part of the king should be regarded as an "action of 'non-essential' designation, what the ancient grammarians called 'denominatio.' "[31] Moreover, the cult in Jerusalem continued to allow no images. Daniel 11:35 demonstrates that the divinity had not become "Greek": he was Zeus-Baal Shamim. As for the installation of the "abomination that makes desolate" in the temple, mentioned three times in Daniel (9:27; 11:31; 12:11), this refers, according to Bickerman, to an alteration of the altar of holocausts in the temple courtyard (see 1 Macc. 1:54, 59; Jos. *Ant.* 12.253). Underlying this conception there is the Syro-Phoenician "bomolatry," (worship of the altar) mentioned by Porphyry (*De Superst.* 2. 56): "[the Arabs] worship the altar like an idol." In other words, the altar of the holocausts "was turned into the base for a fetish,"[32] and it served as a model for a proliferation of similar altars in Judea (2 Macc. 10:2; 1 Macc 1:51, 54–55; 2:23, 45). Hence Antiochus did not attempt to impose another divinity on the Jews, but rather a new religious conception and another cultic structure to which the Hellenized Jews of the Diaspora and of Jerusalem were ready to accommodate themselves.[33] It was only after the revolt of 169–168 that Antiochus took to persecution to impose a religious uniformity on the

Jews (see 1 Macc. 1:41) that was all the more rigid because "liberal" measures had failed.

The pro-Seleucid party in Jerusalem was willing to back Antiochus even in this last extremity. Daniel 11:23 gives historical verity its due by avowing that responsibility for the easy triumph of the tyrant ultimately rested with this collaborationist party. As Norman Bentwich wrote some time ago: "[Antiochus IV] was less the promoter than the instrument of the policy which had its roots in the corruption of a part of the Jewish people."[34] Emil Schürer adds: "A section of the people [of Israel], including the upper classes and the educated, readily gave their consent to the Hellenizing projects of Antiochus Epiphanes, and even went beyond him in carrying them out." As for the character of the king, Schürer's judgment gives a good idea of him (and one in conformity with Polybius 26. 10) when he says: "[Antiochus] was by nature a genuine despot, eccentric and undependable, sometimes extravagantly liberal, and fraternizing with the common people in an affected manner; at other times cruel and tyrannical."[35] He has been compared to Caligula and to Nero for his contradictory moods. However, Eduard Meyer and Mikhail Rostovtsev, for example, see in Antiochus IV a man of parts, full of energy and activity, and one of the most important personalities in the dynasty.[36] Auguste Bouché-Leclercq and Joseph Klausner, on the other hand, see him as a degenerate.[37] He was in any event an enthusiastic Hellenist, and this was enough to arouse the scorn of "orthodox" Jews of the time. In a letter that he sent to Nicanor concerning the Samaritans, the king explains his repressive measures against the Jews by their lack of interest in living "according to the Greek customs" (see Jos. *Ant.* 12. 263; also 2 Macc. 6:9; 11:24). Antiochus was ambitious to be the spiritual successor of Alexander, who had held "the grandiose plan . . . to found a world empire that would be held together, not only by unity of government, but also by a unity of language, customs and culture."[38]

It is in this perspective that we can return to the question of the self-deification of Antiochus "Epiphanes." Daniel 11:36 says clearly: "He shall exalt himself and magnify himself above every god." In a somewhat uneven article, Julian Morgenstern sees the conception of a divine Antiochus as going back to the traditions of the city of Tyre, where already in the eleventh century, as a result of the commercial expansion of the island, there was a change from the lunar to the solar calendar—that is, to a sun religion, a condition basic to the creation of an empire.[39] Baal-Hadad became Baal-Shamem, "Lord of the Heavens" or the Zeus Olympios of Josephus; Tammuz-Adon became Melqart, "King of the City-State," or the Heracles of Josephus. In like fashion the king of Tyre was identified with this divinity, as appears in Ezekiel 28:1–19. When games were organized in honor of Heracles/Melqart at Tyre in 172 (2 Macc. 4:18–20), Antiochus took on the royal and divine role inasmuch as he was *Epiphanes*. This is why, according to Josephus (*Ant.* 12.5) the Samaritans addressed a letter "To King Antiochus, the God, Epiphanes," and why we find the title of *Theos* on coins bearing his name.

On the other hand, since Antiochus had more than his share of duplicity, the sources lead us to think that with some people he insisted on these divine honors, but knew how to present them as purely "symbolic" to others. Menelaus and the Hellenophile party in Jerusalem obviously chose the second interpretation (e.g., Dan. 11:30*b*, 32*a*).

In any event, even Antiochus' allies were to regret their cooperation. Antiochus was no better as a friend than as an enemy. The king, in fact, saw only his own particular interests and those of his powerful courtiers, next to whom the collaborationist Jews carried little weight.[40] In vain the Jews constructed altars "behind the door and the doorpost" (Isa. 57:8) in order to unseat the Jerusalem temple as the only place where one could sacrifice; they were powerless to conjure away the sad fate of the city. It was there that the Syrian installed his own soldiers, and they carried out a radical transformation of the Jewish city. As Tcherikover writes: "Every *cleruchy* or *katoikia* in the Hellenistic period was military in its membership and organization . . . (Jos. *Ant.* 12, 159)."[41] This involved, according to Thucydides (1.114.3; 2.70. 4; 4. 102.3), the confiscation of property, acts of harassment and violence toward the original inhabitants, the imposition of taxes, and even expulsion from the city.

In Palestine as in the other territories of Alexander's empire, "Greeks"—that is, immigrants from Hellas and the heterogeneous mass that had become Hellenized through contact with them—had become settled and had created communities that responded to their conceptions of society and philosophy. The natives' communities seemed to these colonists like vestiges of a barbarous age gone by. In the colonists' own eyes they were the pioneers of civilization; the others were subhumans without culture, leading a savorless life.[42]

By preference, but also in opposition to the obscurantism of the neighboring peoples, the "Greeks" gave themselves over to an Epicurean mode of existence. Each *polis* had its indispensable Greek institutions, its temples to the Hellenic gods and goddesses, its schools and academies in which the arts and sciences were cultivated just as in Athens or in Corinth, its gymnasia in which young men stripped nude to measure their strength and their skill, its agora in which municipal and individual liberties were discussed.[43]

Beauty and harmony were their ideals. As for the "salt of life," it could be found in gatherings to sing and to dance, in refined banqueting, and in totally amoral orgies. Skepticism was triumphant; any reference to the transcendent was considered the fruit of a noncivilized superstition. Hellenistic religion had become one aspect of culture; what was important was no longer to obey the will of the gods but to live in tune with the times. Anything in a people's tradition that constituted a puritanical barrier to bringing on the new world was met with scorn and sarcasm.[44]

One highly important aspect of this culture, which must be added to the picture, occasionally acted as a corrective: Hellenistic culture was "the civilization of the paideia," to repeat Henri-Irénée Marrou's expression.[45] The gymnasium was an institution central to it. A boy entered it at the age of seven and remained in it until the age of twenty, passing from schoolboy, to ephebus (fourteen to sixteen years of age), then to "young man." He read Homer, was initiated into Greek mythology, participated in physical exercise and practiced military arts, observed the innumerable feast days, and worshiped the king. He enrolled in sporting competitions of a religious nature.[46] Stoicism, on this "pedagogical" basis, went beyond all national and social distinctions. What mattered was wisdom, and that had no frontiers. Isocrates (*Panegyric* 4.50) claims; "The designation of 'Hellene' seems no longer to be a matter of descent, but of disposition, and those who share in our education have more right to be called Hellenes than those who have only a common descent with us."[47] Moreover, one could become a "naturalized" Greek by enrolling in a *politeuma* and by taking a Greek name.

This refreshing liberalism was not enough to win the sympathies of the Hasidim. Not only was the nudity of the gymnasts shocking to them (see Jub. 3:31 on Gen. 3:21),[48] but the authorities made it a duty of all citizens to worship a local Hellenistic deity, with any transgression being taxed with atheism, a crime in the eyes of the law. Add to this the deification of the king, the triumph of mysticism in the mystery cults promising salvation, Dionysian orgies, and so forth. Small wonder that 2 Maccabees returns the insult of the Hellenists, who spoke of the *perioikoi*[49] (those beyond the pale) in the *chora* (back-country) by calling the Seleucids' supporters "barbarians" (2:21; 4:25; 5:22; 10:4). In contrast, the faithful Jews were citizens of a holy *polis*, and they were combatting for the establishment of the *politeia* granted them by God himself (4:5, 11, 50; 5:6, 8, 23; 8:17; 9:19; 13:14; 15:30).[50]

This quite Augustinian choice made it possible for the Jews to opt for the city of God rather than the Hellenistic *polis*. According to 3 Maccabees 2:30–31 (see also 3:21), the Jews in Egypt who permitted themselves to be initiated into the Dionysian mysteries received Alexandrian citizenship.

The temptation was just as strong in Jerusalem as everywhere else to cede to this flood of new ideas. Not only did these ideas seem able to "liberate" the ancestral tradition from its bonds, they also infused life into the renewed body of a world become the universal habitat of humankind. Who could know, at that point, whether the Living God was not perhaps at the origin of such an unheard-of development? Who could be sure that this was not a unique opportunity for Judaism to become truly universal?

The Tobiad clan, as we have seen, supported the Seleucids. They lacked neither religious learning nor religious interests. One of their fervent supporters and perhaps a member of the family, Menelaus, became high priest. That this post was coveted for political reasons is undeniable. We can at least presume, however, that the exercise of power went hand in hand, for the Tobiads, with a typically Jewish dream: to contribute to bringing about the messianic era. It is true that we have precious few historical elements with which to form even a roughly accurate idea of the arguments put forth by the various Jewish parties. It seems logical to think, however, that the "collaborators" answered the spiritual and traditional remonstrances of the Hasidim and the other adversaries of Hellenization with counterarguments of the same order. It was only when Menelaus became high priest in 172 that YHWH became openly identified with Zeus and that sacrifices were ordered to Greek deities. Even the priests were to participate—nude—in the games in the stadium.

Nevertheless, all of these efforts to Hellenize the Jewish population only galvanized its deep resistance. When Antiochus IV was forced to withdraw from Egypt in 168 under the threat of armed intervention from Rome, the king, humiliated and thirsting for revenge, set off the first pogrom in Jewish history. Seleucid persecution passed from the political plane to the religious.[51]

Thus it is on this religious plane, which turned out to be so crucial, that we must now pose the historical question of the priests' collaboration with Hellenism. How is it possible that the high priest and his clergy adopted a thought so foreign to Judaism and became the instruments by which the Holy City was transformed into a Hellenistic *polis*? To answer these questions, we need to focus our attention on the idea of *law* in Israel during this epoch.

THE HASIDIM

The theocratic party in Jerusalem at the time of the Second Temple was not without opposition. It is to these malcontents that we must turn to seek the milieu out of which Jewish apocalypse arose as a literature of protest and resistance. As Solomon Schechter said, "It is among the sects severed from the general body of Judaism in which we have to look for the origin of . . . works [like Daniel] . . . and *not* in Pharisaic Judaism."[52] The question is, then, which Jewish sect had a religious philosophy of history in which universal events had their assigned place in God's cosmic design,[53] and in which the present—always a dramatic time—is the summit of this history, since it prompts the appearance of a "son of man" or a messianic figure whose empire will last forever.[54]

One thinks immediately of the Essenes, especially now that we know them better, after the discovery of what seems to have been their library in the desert of Judea. Their speculations on angels and on the hereafter are well known, as is their mysticism, their quasi-magical interpretation of ritual, their asceticism, and their esoteric teachings.[55] In point of fact, there is an undeniable relationship between apocalyptic literature and the writings of Qumran; the desert sectarians had an apocalyptical vision of the world and of history. Nonetheless, with Daniel and the earliest texts of the sort,[56] we are at an epoch that precedes Essenism, for the Essenes inherited the genre and did not initiate it. The milieu responsible for the apocalypses of the second century B.C.E. was that of the Essenes' forefathers.

In the book of Daniel itself we find a term to designate these people: they are the *maskilim*, "those who are wise" (11:33, 35; 12:3, 10), who have been charged to instruct the *rabbim,* or the multitude. These two terms should be kept in mind. According to 1 Enoch 93:10, "the elect righteous"[57] are those who will be chosen "to receive sevenfold instruction concerning all His creation."[58] The term *maskil* does not designate a constituted party any more than the term *multitude.* But the sociological import of this should not be neglected, for at Qumran *rabbim* referred to the community of the elect, to the exclusion of the novices (1QS 6:20–23),[59] and the *maskilim* were the instructors of the community.[60] Daniel is halfway to a technical use of these terms, since Qumran certainly represents a point of arrival in this evolution. The linguistic parallels found here permit us to identify more precisely who were these "wise" people. In 1 Maccabees 2:42 we find the designation *hekousiazomenoi,* the "consecrated" (to the Torah). The word is used in the Septuagint as equivalent to the Hebrew *ndb,* a term characteristic of Qumran to designate the members of the community (1QS 1.7, 11; 5.1, 6, 8, 10, 21, 22; 6.13). They form a *synagoge,* according to 1 Maccabees 2, an *'edah,* according to the Qumran correspondent, which, among other terms, refers to the community itself (4QpPs 37.2, 16; 1QS 5.20)

This socioreligious category on which our inquiry focuses was also called in Greek the *asidaioi* (Assideans), in Hebrew, *Hasidim.*[61] The word signified the pious, the faithful, in contrast to those touched by Hellenization, who had abandoned the faith of their fathers and had compromised themselves by embracing an idolatrous modernism.

The origin of the Hasidic movement is unclear, but its general outline can be traced. From the beginning of the revolt of the Maccabees in 167–166, the Assidean party is mentioned among the "freedom fighters," "guerrillas," or "revolutionaries" (1 Macc. 2:42; 7:13; 2 Macc. 14:6–7; Pss. Sol. 16). Thus we need to look to an earlier age. The Maccabean origin of the movement is confirmed by the Damascus Document (1.5–12), which speaks of a "remainder" in Israel during the second century B.C.E., some twenty years before the coming of the Master of Justice, or around 175–170, at the very moment that Antiochus IV was trying to Hellenize Palestine.[62] Out of fidelity to the Torah the Assideans went over to the resistance, although they were not totally closed to foreign influences, as is seen in the apocalypse, which contains a good number of non-Jewish elements.[63] Like them, Daniel shows his fidelity to the Levitic rites (Dan. 1; 6) and his attachment to the priestly function (Dan. 9:25; 11:22; see my Commentary on chs. 7–12; also 1 Macc. 7:12).

SOCIAL AND SPIRITUAL MILIEU

Such an origin is perfectly logical. Hasidism probably crystallized as a party in reaction to Antiochus' persecution. Its program was a total fidelity to the law of Moses. But political and religious movements generally do not have a beginning that can be dated with precision.

> There are some grounds for the supposition that the sect was first organized under Simon the Just— at the beginning of the second century B.C.E. . . . Simon the Just himself belonged, apparently, to the Hasidim, and, as he was chief and leader of the theocratic commonwealth, the scribal interpretations were accepted by the priesthood, and the Oral Law fostered by the scribes was declared by the Jerusalem community to be the official authoritative interpretation of the Mosaic Law.[64]

Be that as it may, 1 Maccabees 2:42 gives us two valuable indications of the characteristics of the movement: it was a popular movement and it rallied those who resisted Hellenization. Mattathias assembled around him "a company of Hasidim, mighty warriors of Israel, every one who offered himself willingly for the law." These two points are fundamental. The defense of the Torah was taken on increasingly by laymen, backed up by members of the lower priesthood. First Maccabees 7:12 speaks of "a group of scribes." That they were in fact Hasidim is proven, for Tcherikover, by the comparison of this text with 2:29 on the basis of their common denominator, a thirst for justice. In the first case, it is the congregation of scribes that is seeking justice; in the second, it is all those who had fled to the desert under the persecution of Antiochus.

It would be a mistake to consider this group as pacifist no matter what. As we have just seen, the Hasidim gathered around the "freedom fighter" Mattathias, and 2 Maccabees 14:6 makes Judas, Mattathias' son, their chief. It is evident that this group contributed much to rallying the people around the Maccabees, even if their own involvement was not unconditional. National independence was for them a means, not an end. They were interested in creating the conditions necessary for the reestablishment, then the maintenance, of the purity of both religion and ritual in Zion. When the Hasmoneans took on other and more politically ambitious tasks, the Hasidim dissociated themselves from the undertaking. Their concerns were exclusively spiritual.

In the book of Daniel the situation presented is somewhat in contradiction to the one portrayed in the books of the Maccabees in this regard. As we have seen, Daniel 11:33 describes the pious as *maskilim*.

29

The verse reads: "The thoughtful ones among the people will instruct a multitude but they will stumble before the sword, the flames, the captivity and the looting, for some days."

This text (to which the verse that follows should be added, as it is extremely important)[65] shows either an evolution in Hasidic doctrine or divergent tendencies within the movement, in which some had recourse to armed force and contributed to the ejection from Jerusalem of the unworthy high priest Jason (172), and others—the group to which the apocalyptist Daniel belonged—preferred martyrdom to active resistance. This attitude was perhaps new in Israel, but it was not to remain an isolated case, as subsequent history has shown even into our own days. In this perspective it is interesting to note that the group represented in Daniel did not seem to advocate the ostracism of the other branch of the Hasidim. In fact, Daniel 11:34 may mean that the pious who were waiting for a direct and miraculous intervention of God retired into the desert and the mountains of Judah. This is a difficult verse. Tcherikover's reading of it may be the correct one. He sees in the "detours" mentioned at the end of the verse not "intrigues," but the twisting mountain roads that the resistants were to take (Ps. 35:6 and Jer. 23:12). Hence the Hasmoneans' partisans were not being taxed with hypocrisy here.

On the other hand, if we opt for a chronological evolution of the Hasidic attitude toward the Hasmoneans from the beginning, we can see a certain wait-and-see attitude at the time of Daniel, or even a clearly negative reaction. But this was followed by a general rallying to Judas, probably when the first success of the Maccabees was interpreted as emanating from God himself (1 Macc. 2:28–38, 42–43). To their basic virtue of being the "people who know their God" (Dan. 11:32; Dan. 8:24, 25, 27; 1 Macc. 1:65; 2 Macc. 6:9; CD 6.2; 20.27; 1QpHab 5.7; 12.3–5) the Hasidim added the virtue of being "mighty warriors of Israel" (1 Macc. 2:42).

This evolution seems to me to continue as follows: the group set itself apart from the Hasmoneans and left them to their political appetites. Their dearest wish was to serve as a spiritual model for the rest of their compatriots.[66] This led the people to range them with the righteous and the perfect (Pss. 34:2, 17; 37:11, 17, 18, 29, 37).[67] Finally, they grouped together, like their later spiritual descendants, the Essenes, in brotherhoods (1 Macc. 2:42 *Synagoge asidaiôn*). These monasteries, as we can see from the Hasidic Psalm 149, were of a military type (v. 6: "Let the high praises of God be in their throats and two-edged swords in their hands,"[68] which should probably be understood as a state of purely defensive military preparedness). This is confirmed, not only at Qumran, but also later at Masada (C.E. 73).[69] There were a great many learned men among them, scribes and priests (1 Macc. 7:12), and Daniel, significantly, insists on the necessity of practicing the Levitical rites (1; 6:11; 10:3). This does not mean that they shared the theocratic optimism of the high clergy. This is, furthermore, one of the elements that enable us to shift from diachrony to synchrony to explain the difference within Hasidism between the militant activism of some and the quietism (to the point of martyrdom) of others. We can imagine perfectly well that the humbler classes might have been attracted by action and the cultivated circles by reflection and passive resistance. We should not forget that the literary works of the latter "were attempts of the educated clerks to make sense of major changes in society within the universal scheme of history provided by apocalypticism."[70]

The Hasidim were moved by a radically pessimist view of history. The circumstances that led to the exile in Babylon had really not changed with the reconstruction of the temple in 515. The sacrifices that were offered at the time were "polluted and not pure" (Enoch 89:73). Nothing appeared to redeem this "time of trouble, such as never has been since there was a nation" (Dan. 12:1). But history is two-faced: to some it bears the odor of death; to others, the odor of life. For the latter—for the pious—history has a "secret." It is punctuated, not with powerful kings and emperors like Nebuchadnezzar or Alexander the Great, but by pious sovereign pontiffs. This is what Daniel 9 shows, for example. The anointed prince of Daniel 9:25 should be seen as the high priest of the restoration, Joshua. This is probably the best interpretation of this allusive passage, for the preceding and the following verses also speak of "messiahs" (anointed ones): the high priest Onias III (also referred to in 11:22), and "the priestly consecration of Aaron and his sons."[71]

A theology of history of this sort explains the strictly limited participation of the Assideans in the resistance to the Seleucids (1 Macc. 6:59). After the peace of Lysias (163), the Hasidim left it to the Hasmoneans to win the independence of the nation without their aid (see 1 Macc. 7:4–18).[72]

31

DANIEL IN HIS TIME

QUMRAN

Comparison with Qumran is manifold and illuminating. Daniel was much read among the sectarians. Seven different Qumran manuscripts of the book have been found. One seems to have been written only a century or less after the original reached its final state.[73] However, it is not sure that the book was considered a canonical text. The format of the written columns and occasionally the materials employed (caves 1 and 6) are different from those the Essene library usually used for biblical books.[74]

Be that as it may, the spiritual and literary points of contact between the sectarians and Daniel are interesting. The Judean recluses called themselves "the men of the vision" (1QH 14.7) or "those who see the angels of holiness; those whose ear is open and who hear profound things" (1QM 10.10–11) The Qumran War Scroll 1.3–7 is obviously based on Daniel 11:40–45. Furthermore, in one work from cave 4, three fragments "presumably report revelations of Daniel."[75] Also from cave 4, five fragments make up the Prayer of Nabonidus, which parallels Daniel 3:31–4:34. Daniel is presented in this passage as a Jewish exorcist.[76] The text is apocalyptic. The Qumran library contained a good number of apocalyptical writings, such as Enoch, Jubilees, Testaments of the Twelve Patriarchs, and others previously unknown to us.[77] We thus have indirect confirmation of certain affirmations of Josephus that the sectarians of the Dead Sea interpreted dreams and performed divinations (1QH 14.7; 1QM 10.10-11).

Consequently, we are not suprised to find the Hymn to Zion (11QPs a) an appeal to the inhabitants of Jerusalem to believe the announcement in Daniel 9 of the restoration of Jerusalem and of its temple.[78]

The points of comparison between the book of Daniel and the Zadokite document[79] are revealing:

CD 4.4: "those who rise up at the end of days"

Daniel 12:13: "you shall arise to receive your lot in the end of the days"

CD 6.21: "by his holy anointed one"

Daniel 9:24ff.: "to anoint a most holy place," "an anointed one," etc.

CD 20.8: "the saints of the Most High"

Daniel 7:18, etc.: "the saints of the Most High"

CD 20.25: "all those who have made breaches in the wall of the Torah"
  Daniel 11:14: "the men of the breaches of your people"
CD 20.26: "all the corruptors of Judah in the time of the purification by
  fire"
    Daniel 11:32: "the corruptors of the covenant" (about "corruptors
    of the alliance" and "purification," See Dan. 11:34; 12:10)
CD 20.28: cf. Daniel 9:5

These parallels are not merely technical. On both sides, we can feel
there is an evolution in the consciousness of election. The sectarians
have a dramatic conception of history in general and of the moral and
spiritual state of their own people in particular. This is why, in their
own eyes, they are the last, the final bastion of faith and sanctity. They
are all Israel, its spirit and its institutions; they have become, spiritually, the Temple of the Presence. The expressions they use to designate
themselves are bold, and they appear in nearly the same terms in
Qumran and in Daniel: "the holy people" (Dan. 12:7); (the people of)
"the saints of the Most High" (7:18, 25, 27); "the people of the saints"
(8:24; cf. 1 Macc. 1:15); "the holy covenant" (11:28, 30, cf. verse 22; see
Dan. 3.34 [in Greek]) "do not destroy your Covenant"; cf. Judith 9:13:
"those who have planned dire things against your covenant, your holy
temple" and Psalm 74:20: "Have regard for thy covenant," which is
perhaps a Maccabean stanza.[80]

The scribes, as we have seen, were found in great numbers among
the Assideans and the sectarians of the Judean desert. It follows that in
both cases we see a similar attachment to the sons of Aaron and a devotion to the Torah. They share a characteristic vocabulary. Aside from
maskil[81] and its pendant *(ha)rabbim* (Isa. 53:11, 12a, b), which had
become technical terms, the word *pesher* took on a sense in both litera-
tures that went beyond its usual utilization. "All Scripture was considered as a mystery for which the interpretation (*pesher*) needed to be
found," Annie Jaubert writes, speaking of the Qumranians.[82] In this
sort of exegesis every detail of Scripture is equally important. In Lou H.
Silberman's felicitous expression, the question is to "unriddle the riddle."[83] Silberman shows that the transition from "the interpretation of
dreams"—which was what pesher originally signified[84]—to "the interpretation of a previous revelation" is made through the intermediary of
an affirmation like that of *Sifré* on Numbers 12:6: "God has spoken to
the prophets, with the exception of Moses, *be-halom u-be-hazion*, in
dreams and visions." Silberman cites the example of 1QpHab 7.1–5 on

33

Habakkuk 1:1–2: "God has made known to the Master of Justice the *pesher* of the *razim* (secrets) of the words of his servants the prophets." This finds echoes in Daniel 2:18–19, 27, 28–29, 47; 4:6. Furthermore, the term *pesher* appears no fewer than thirty times in Daniel.

Many other secondary elements figure in the list of things common to Daniel and to Qumran—the explanation of mysteries by angelic interpreters, for example. Jaubert gives a good summary of how the age thought about the matter:

> The powerful beings on high were by definition the masters of knowledge. They possessed the secrets of the cosmos, the elements of which they governed; they participated in the divine secrets that they could reveal to men with God's permission. Sharing the knowledge of the angels was for man of flesh and blood an extraordinary destiny: it was the supreme goal (1QS 4.22). The collection known as Hymns calls the angels "Knowers" (11.14) and never ceases in its astonishment that men have been called to share in the knowledge of such mysteries: 3.22–23; 13.12–14.[85]

Finally, we should note, regarding the extant manuscripts of the text of Daniel, that there is usually agreement between the Qumran and the Masoretic texts. The same transition from Hebrew to Aramaic takes place, and at the same place (2:4; cf. 1QDan. 2.2–6). In 1QDan. 3. 22–28,[86] the Canticle of the Three Youths is absent, as it is in the Masoretic Text. We can thus legitimately subscribe to Martin McNamara's judgment that "the text of Daniel was already fixed in the first century B.C.E."[87]

In conclusion, I would say, in agreement with Jaubert, that there is no hiatus on the line from Daniel as a point of departure and the Essene writings as a point of arrival. The same current runs through them both; it even swells at Qumran.[88]

THE BOOK OF DANIEL AS A JEWISH BOOK

With the apocalypse we oscillate curiously between a rigor where the contents are concerned with a fluidity in forms of expression. The Hasidim and their successors, the Essenes, were resolute enemies to the process of Hellenization, but they adopted—consciously or, more probably, unconsciously—Hellenized forms for the communication of their Semitic ideas. Their case is far from being unique: New Testament literature is another example, some two centuries later. The Septuagint and

Philo are literary representatives of the Jewish Diaspora, but a Saul/ Paul, although he came from Tarsus, is much more traditionally "Palestinian." Martin Hengel protests vehemently the widespread illusion that only the Jewish Diaspora was contaminated by the modernist ideas of the epoch.[89] As he remarks, there was in all Judaism a clear intellectualization of piety that affected the perception of such concepts as knowledge, comprehension, revelation, and mystery. We are at the beginning of an intellectual movement that was ultimately to give rise to Gnosticism. Stoicism in particular was a great attraction, and it imposed its views, to a certain extent, even in rabbinic thought. Judaism, however, was far from being swept off its feet by the Hellenistic avalanche. Hengel writes: "On the other hand, the fundamental difference should not be overlooked. Despite its predestinarian basis, what happened in the world did not rest on impersonal fate, which simply expresses a strict causality within a world understood along monist lines, but on God's plan as to the free disposition of his personal transcendent power."[90]

To be sure, we can see Hellenistic influence in the conception of *sympatheia* between what occurs on the earth and in the heavens. We can see it in the conception of the angels or the stars, which demonstrated, even according to the Qumranian integrists, the existence "of an immutable order that proceeds from the mouth of God and is testimony to being" (1QH 12.9). We might, for example, with Josephus (*Ant.* 15.10.4), be struck by the resemblances in form between the Essene and the Pythagorian communities. But "all in all . . . these alien influences affect the detail rather than the totality of the apocalyptic picture of the world and history, which fundamentally still rests on an Old Testament conception of salvation history."[91] For, contrary to the surrounding Hellenistic philosophy, which aimed exclusively at success and the "great life," the affirmation of the pious in Judea was that God lay at the origin of all historical phenomena, even the most painful or the most mysterious ones.

If we take another example, that of the individualism imposed by pagan humanism, it is clear that here once again apocalyptic Judaism did not remain untouched. To be sure, in the book of Daniel we cannot find texts that give formal evidence that the category of people of Israel had been abandoned in favor of the category of the individual. But the fact remains that the concept of Israel runs into some problems. Daniel B speaks of the saints; Daniel A shows us Daniel and his three companions. Their actions are remarkable, but when exclusive attention is paid to them, they come dangerously close to eclipsing the actions of the people as a whole. Daniel is far from being another Moses (cf. Exod. 32:10–11, 32).

Jewish individualism had other bases than Greek alienation, however. What we see is not skepticism but a personal and intimate relationship with God. It is remarkable that when the Hellenistic kingdoms totally collapsed, polytheism was incapable of furnishing a new raison d'être to individuals who had just discovered that they were unique and irreplaceable.[92]

TORAH AND CONSTITUTION

The conception of the Torah reached an important turning point in the fifth century, when Ezra and Nehemiah were sent by the Persian government to Jersualem to ensure the respect of the Torah as state law. This was the first time in history that the Torah had this function.[93] It shifted to the level of a legal code recognized by the powers and applied to an entire local population by designated magistrates. It is legitimate to wonder whether the Persian conception of the law was indeed shared by the Jewish leaders and the Jewish people in the fifth century. It is possible that some Judeans saw in this a fiction useful to regain a degree of independence from the occupying forces.

With time, however, this "fiction" undoubtedly became less and less sustainable. In the fourth century Judea passed from Persian jurisdiction to the Alexandrine empire. The Torah became *Nomos*, the fundamental principle in the cosmic structure as it was practiced in Jerusalem.[94]

This conception according an intrinsic value to the law and detaching it completely in its application, if not in its origin, from the divine legislator was confirmed in 200, when Antiochus III conquered Palestine from the Ptolemies and granted the Jews a charter, or "letter of emancipation," that recognized the law of Moses as the legal code of the *ethnos* of Judea. If there ever had been any question of a fiction fostered by the inhabitants of Jerusalem concerning the double nature of the Torah as viewed either from the exterior or the interior, this fiction had now dissolved and the Torah had become a state constitution.

In this manner, during the period of the Second Temple, the Torah underwent a progressive secularization, due, paradoxically, to the fact that it was becoming more absolute. This process put increased emphasis on the intrinsic value of the law, whereas originally its authority was mediated by and depended on the authority of God, who had given it. This means that it became possible, at least in theory, to obey the Torah without believing in YHWH; in any event without necessarily making the connection between the law and the legislator. The guarantor of the Torah was no longer God but the sovereign.[95] The Torah was *one* possible law in a Hellenized world; it was *one* expression of the cosmic law, standing beside other expressions specific to the various peoples, each of which had its own character.

If certain conservative Jews persisted in recognizing a divine origin to their law, then, they were not necessarily in the wrong in the eyes of the Hellenizers, for cosmic law was so transcendent that it must be divine in its essence. However, these orthodox Jews were confusing one manifestation of the law with the idea of the law. To the extent that their particularism made them intransigent, it was "barbarian" and contained dangers for all concerned. Even the high priest of the Jews, Menelaus, was in agreement on this point: his desire was for measure in all things. Moreover, when the Oniad faction in Jerusalem, for political reasons but probably also through religious conviction, placed the survival of the Jewish *ethnos* in danger in 168, Menelaus obtained the "privilege" of a change in the city constitution and its promotion to the status of a Hellenistic *polis*.

With the backing of such a pontifical guarantor, Antiochus IV razed the walls of Jerusalem and built the citadel-*polis* of Acra. To be sure, he was not at first aware that he was attacking the Word of God when he oveturned the previous Judaic constitution. Quite simply, what Antiochus III had recognized in 198 as the legal code of Judea was reduced to the status of popular custom and, as such, was susceptible to substitution by an authentically Hellenistic constitution. A Jerusalem elite was established, called *politeuma* or *demos*, with the guardian of the constitution, the high priest Menelaus, at its head.

One of the principal consequences of this thoroughgoing shake-up was that the population subject to the new order lost its authentically Jewish character to become "universalized" in the taste of the times. Implicitly, the Torah of Moses had failed to live up to its universalist pretensions. It was now no more than a faded witness to an age gone by. The "primitive" oriental tribe had reached its maturity and was now judged worthy of being assimilated into the *oikoumènè* inaugurated by

37

Alexander the Great. Menelaus was a citizen of the world first; a Jew next. He was the first by choice; the second by accident of birth. He felt closer to the "pagan" citizens of the Acra or to the *ephebi* of the gymnasium than to the "backward" Jews of the popular sections of the city. We could even speculate that the high priest—unless, of course, he had lost all professional conscience and all sentiment of belonging to the Jewish people, which is within the realm of the possible—shared with the Greeks a "scientific" conception of the law. Hellenistic science, in fact, saw the most perfect expression of a thought in its primordial form and its progressive corruption in its development. Hence the Torah of Moses, which had come four centuries after the blessed age of the patriarchs, was but an imperfect form of a religion once pure, without exterior form, without ceremonies, without laws, etc. Bickerman writes:

> Just like the incorrupted children of nature of Greek theory, the "sons of the Acra," *i.e.* Menelaus and his partisans, thus worshipped the heavenly god of their ancestors without temple and images, under the open sky upon the altar which stood on Mt. Zion. They were free from the yoke of the law, and in mutual tolerance they were united with the Gentiles. What could be more human, what could be more natural, than their desire to force this tolerance also upon those of their coreligionists who were still unenlightened? That was the persecution of Epiphanes.[96]

If Menelaus had had any illusions about the irresistible nature of his proclamation of enlightenment, he soon lost them. Popular resistance to the Hellenization of Jerusalem was such that the Acra found itself isolated in the middle of a hostile city. It is conceivable that under the new constitution there was no veritable prohibition of the ancestral Jewish customs. The alimentary regulations, for example, probably could have been followed in the name of a tradition without religious significance. One might even find reasons a posteriori to follow them for dietetic reasons and to praise the physiological wisdom of the ancient legislator.[97] But now these same traditional regulations were followed in a spirit of resistance, in the name of a "retrograde" conception of religion; now, instead of bringing peoples together in a common search for moral and physical health, sheer habit, based in custom, separated the Jews from other men.[98] Then those wielding power had no other alternative than to forbid circumcision, ritual foods, respect of the sabbath, the reading of the sacred texts, and in general all that recalled the old religious tradition.

It is inaccurate, therefore, to make Antiochus entirely responsible for the religious persecution because of his syncretist ideal. In reality, as Hengel writes, "explicit religio-political measures to subject unruly populaces are without parallel in antiquity."[99] The ultimate responsibility of the Hellenistic party in Jerusalem seems well established, particularly since, according to Josephus (*Ant.* 12.262, 263), the Samaritans continued in free observance of the laws of Moses; they had had the "simplicity" to address Antiochus as *theos*. Moreover, the Jewish response to the process of Hellenization came in a variety of forms. At the opposite end of the scale from the party of the high priest could be found the movement of the Maccabees. This movement was in itself complex, however, and the restoration that it succeeded in establishing in Palestine was ambiguous from the start (see 1 Macc. 2:48; 3:21; 13:3; 14:29). One particular group stood out among them from the beginning: the Hasidim (spoken of in texts such as 1 Macc. 2:42; 7:13; 2 Macc. 14:6–7; Pss. Sol. 16, discussed above). The Hasidim (or Assideans; the pious, the faithful), spiritual ancestors of the Essenes and, like them, resistant to the Hellenization of Judea, at first participated in the adventure of the Maccabean army because they saw in it a return to the Torah, "purified" of all narrowing interpretations. But when the Hasmoneans established a state in which the "religion"[100] was civil—that is, in the service of a higher reality—the "pious" seceded (and we might note that the Talmud later significantly passed over the revolt of the Maccabees in silence, with the exception of *B.Qam.* 6,6 and *Šabb.* 21b).

Even the "pietist" (Hasidic) faction of the movement did not remain impermeable to outside influences, however. The best example is given by the "periodization" of history as it is systematized in the Hasidic writings or, more specifically, in the apocalyptic writings. As Hengel writes, "The materials used to depict these new outlines of 'universal history' culminating in the time of salvation were largely drawn from the mythological conceptions of the Hellenized oriental environment."[101]

Thus Greek influence was considerable, even on the faction the most openly hostile to the Hellenization of Judea. For example, the Pharisees (also successors to the Assideans), created a Beth-Din-ha-Gadol (a supreme court) on the model of the *boulè* of the Greek cities. Moreover, for Ellis Rivkin the Pharisee revolution was "exposed to the

Hellenistic *polis* culture on all sides"; he cites, for example, the rabbis' insistence on individual conscience.[102] It should be noted in this connection that the book of Daniel comes in a period of transition. On the one hand, to be sure, no text can be found that bears formal witness to the transition from the collectivity of the people to the individual; but, on the other hand, we do wonder where is Israel while Daniel and his three companions pass before our eyes in Daniel A. And the references to the "saints" in Daniel B, we must admit, remain very general indeed. In short, as Hengel writes, "From about the middle of the third century BC *all Judaism* must really be designated '*Hellenistic Judaism*' in the strict sense."[103]

But let us not stray from the book of Daniel. It represents a qualified, elitist position, at some distance from both the Maccabean popular fervor at its origins and the aristocratic order represented by the high priesthood.[104] We might say that from the rivalry between a Jason and a Menelaus as representative of the modernist party, on the one hand, and a Mattathias and his sons as representative of the traditionalist party, there was born a third order, the evolution of which takes us from the Hasidim to the Pharisees. Daniel was written by a Hasid, and his attitude toward institutions shows both a sincere attachment to them and often a sharply critical spirit. The best example is what amounts— as I shall show in ch. 6—to an enthronement of the "son of man" in the celestial temple as royal high priest for ever more. Thus is kept the eternal promise made to David (2 Sam. 7), but the promise is interpreted in a new spirit that was to find its highest expression 150 years later: "God is able from these stones to raise up children to Abraham" (Matt. 3:9; Luke 3:8).

It is remarkable that Daniel no longer cites one single word of the Pentateuch, no longer alludes to the Exodus,[105] and no longer refers to the great master, Moses, or the priest par excellence, Aaron. The term *Torah* is used rarely (6:3; 7:25) outside of chapter 9. For the Hellenists, "modernity" made the law obsolete; for the Hasidim, the law applied to the new times, but not without qualifications. This is why, when Daniel cites a Word of God, the author finds it in Jeremiah, Ezekiel, and Habakkuk. It was not the author's intention to confirm—even indirectly—the hegemony of the priestly caste, the status of which was declining in the second century (and which was to give rise to the Sadducean party). On the other hand, however, there was no conceptual opposition between the apocalyptic and the "Pharisaic" legalism.[106] As

W. D. Davies says, "Apocalyptic was the outcome of a profound ethical seriousness which was no less concerned with the observance of the Torah than was Pharisaism."[107]

Antiochus, in absentia (which explains "forces from him" in Dan. 11:31), had the temple profaned by his troops 7 December 168 and its precious objects removed. An idol was set up and consecrated to Olympian Zeus, and an altar was superimposed on the old altar, the "horns" of which were removed from its four corners. This is the "devastating abomination."[108] Pigs were sacrificed on this altar. As Giuseppe Ricciotti says, this animal was selected "because it offered the double advantage of being particularly odious to the Jews, as especially impure, and (without even speaking of its consecration to Demeter) of being an important element in the purification rites of the Eleusinian mysteries. It was a delicious humiliation to impose what had until then been impurity itself as an element of purification, or at least as a symbol of purity."[109]

For three years the practices connected with the Jewish cult were forbidden. The sabbath, the feast days, circumcision, were all outlawed. On pain of death, the Hellenistic rites had to be followed by all. The holy scrolls were burned. Jews by the thousand were sold into slavery. The synagogues and the schools were closed. Jews were forced to decorate themselves with ivy leaves in honor of Dionysos during the Bacchanalia. Many, however, fled the city and hid in the grottoes of the Judean mountains. The books of the Maccabees tell the tale of their resistance, then of their exploits, under the leadership of Mattathias and his five sons. With their armed revolt, however, we move into a period later than that of Daniel that was also, for a certain time, "postapocalyptic."

It is a remarkable fact that the profanation of the temple of Jerusalem by Antiochus IV raised popular indignation throughout the Hellenistic world, for which sacrilege, even regarding a foreign temple, was a crime. Seleucid propaganda, in order to justify the actions of its party, spread defamatory ideas concerning the Jewish people. It was then that the accusation of ritual murder was made for the first time. Antiochus IV had supposedly discovered in the Jerusalem temple a Greek, "kidnapped" to be sacrificed to the god of the Jews. He also supposedly discovered, in the Holy of Holies, the true object of Jewish worship: an ass.[110]

Under these circumstances the great majority of the population of Judea resolved to resist desperately. This rejection of Hellenization, nearly without parallel in the world of the time, was, as P. Jouguet has said, "so inconceivable for the kings and their Greek subjects that it inspired in them even more hatred toward those whom they accused of hatred toward the entire human race." It was also, he adds, Hellenization's "most serious failure."[111]

This, then, was the age of Daniel. There seemed to be no way out of the situation, unless God chose to intervene in an unheard of and miraculous manner. The apocalypse is situated precisely at the point of juncture of these two "impossibilities." On the one hand, for the Hasid, it was impossible that God would continue to let his people be mistreated in this manner and himself be denied by the miscreants. On the other hand, it was impossible that the situation which evil had so cleverly created would be resolved by a simple historical evolution. The author of Daniel 11, writing toward the beginning of 166, had no expectation whatsoever that the surprising events of the second half of the same year would occur; that Mattathias would be succeeded by his son Judas, who would rout the generals Lysias, Nicanor, and Gorgias (1 Macc. 3–4). The final pericope of Daniel 11 opens on a note of imprecision: "At the time of the end" (v. 40), and it continues with a recital of events that never took place in history. There is no historical documentation of a total conquest of Egypt by Antiochus. The campaign described beginning with 11:40 is a projection into the future of the author's convictions. The invasion is described there as a veritable inundation, recalling Isaiah and Ezekiel. Moreover, the eschatological dimensions are borrowed from still other texts of Isaiah and Ezekiel (Isa. 10:5ff.; 31:8–9; Ezek. 38–39 on Gog and Magog). It is possible that the death of Antiochus, described in 11:45, was based on the prophecy of the enemy, who would "fall upon the mountains of Israel" (Ezek. 39:4; see also Zech. 14:2; Joel 3:2; Isa. 14:25). This eschatological aspect did not escape the sectarians of Qumran: the War Scroll (1QM) is a midrash of our text.[112]

The death of the historical Antiochus occurred before the dedication of the temple of Jerusalem by Judas Maccabeus 14 December 164; more precisely, he died between 20 November and 19 December 164, in Tabae, in Persia.[113]

APPENDIX: THE HASIDIM FROM ENOCH TO QUMRAN

The problem of the Hasidim's identity is notoriously difficult.[114] I have opted here for an understanding that has been recently vigorously opposed from different quarters. It is thus not superfluous to scrutinize the counterarguments of two of those critics, viz. J. A. Goldstein in his commentary on 1 and 2 Maccabees[115] and J. J. Collins in *The Apocalyptic Imagination* and, more recently, in an article entitled "Daniel and His Social World."[116]

First, there is a dearth of sources. Collins retains only three texts where the term "Hasidim (*Asidaioi*)" is certainly technical: 1 Maccabees 2:42; 7:12–13 and 2 Maccabees 14:6. In all three the vocabulary is very general and vague. *Synagoge* in 1 Maccabean texts means any ad hoc gathering (e.g. 3:44; 12:28), and *Asidaioi* seems to designate a general spiritual stance rather than a party, something like "the pious ones," without specification. The only characteristic we can be sure of on the basis of these texts is that those called "Hasidim" here are bellicose, in contradistinction to the *maskilim* spoken of in the book of Daniel; this opposition is strongly emphasized by Collins, who sees in this the proof that one should not speak of the Hasidim as responsible for the pacifist book of Daniel. Before I critize this position, let me call attention to what appears to me a contradiction. On the one hand, *Asidaioi* would have no more specific meaning than "the pious ones"; on the other hand, these pietists would never be pacifists. But, with this latter affirmation, we have already attained a specificity of sorts; so much so that the Danielic *maskilim* are not to be counted within their ranks, although sharing with them features common to the opponents to the Gentile rule over Israel.

Goldstein adds to the quoted texts of Maccabees, Jubilees 23:16, 19–20 and 1 Enoch 90:9–11, which also show the Hasidim as militant ones. There is, however, opposition between 1 and 2 Maccabees on that point as well. In 1 Maccabees, at least some of the *Asidaioi* accepted Alcimus as high priest (7:12–13). But Alcimus had sixty pious sages executed and thus alienated the "pious ones." When Judas punished the "turncoat" Jews, Alcimus called upon the Syrian king for support. The king appointed Nicanor as governor of Judea (1 Macc. 7). The narrative is slanted, showing how foolish the *Asidaioi* were to break with the Hasmoneans. To the contrary, Jason of Cyrene, author of 2 Maccabees, turns the *Asidaioi* into stern opponents to the Seleucid regime (and thus to Alcimus; 2 Macc. 7:6–7; 14:6).

In fact, without denying the deep differences of philosophy between 1 and 2 Maccabees, their pictures of the *Asidaioi* are not necessarily contradictory. Their inner contradiction can be eliminated if they

43

reflect, for example, a diachronic succession.[117] The sequence of events then is probably to be seen as something like this: the Hasidim first were pacifists; then, due to circumstances, they made common cause with the Maccabees but withdrew their support (1 Macc. 7.13ff.), granting their allegiance to the Syrian-appointed high priest Alcimus, because the latter was an Aaronide and was to be preferred to Menelaus (ca. 162 B.C.E.; see Jos. *Ant.* 20.235). The sequel of this story is known. Alcimus betrayed their trust and ordered the execution of sixty Assideans, thus showing that the Maccabean party had been right in their opposition.

It is not hard to imagine how the *Asidaioi* reacted. They had wanted peace; they were coerced by events into war. Retrospectively, Alcimus' perfidy sheds light on the wavering attitude of the Hasidim between pacifism and belligerency.

Such is at least one possible reading of the events which fill the gap between two attitudes that some find so contradictory as to be irreconcilable. But it is not the only alternative. Below I shall propose another solution which satisfies me even more.

In short, it seems to me that the flaw in Collins' and Goldstein's position is that it does not allow enough *historical* flexibility in the Hasidim's attitudes. The plural form of this last word is appropriate. Circumstances played a decisive role. Fundamentally pacifistic and preoccupied with otherwordly issues,[118] they found themselves compelled to take arms on different occasions, always with the hope that it would be for a short time.[119]

The skepticism of Goldstein is suprising, for, after all, as scanty as they are, the bits of information we have about the Hasidim (other texts must be added to those selected by Collins, as we shall see) are infinitely more detailed and coherent than the number of hypothetical constructions which run through the two volumes of Goldstein's commentary.[120] To cite just one example among very many, he suggests that Alcimus was the author of Psalms 73; 74; 79; 82; 83, and that he is to be identified with one Yakim of rabbinic legends.

There is, furthermore, no better ground that I can see for the mere feeling that the ancestry of the Pharisees and the Essenes must go back "much earlier" than the *Asidaioi* (*Second Maccabees*, 479). For here again the term *Asidaioi* is used in too narrow a sense, not taking sufficiently into consideration the historical evolution of the sect. At the time of the Hasmoneans the *Asidaioi* appear as a constituted party, but the past history of the sect goes back to the much fuzzier shape of a group still unorganized although sharing some fundamental convictions about the inadequacy of the Jerusalem establishment. This early stage of Hasidism is not too late a phenomenon for constituting, indeed, the common stock for the later developments known as Pharisees and Essenes.

To be sure, the further we go back in time toward the terminus a quo of the history of the movement, the more difficult it is to define the tenets of Hasidism. It is a universal fact that historical doctrines become clearly describable only in their crystallized later forms. This is true, not just for the Hasidim, but for Pharisaism, Essenism, Qumran, and Christianity. The sad paradox is that when such crystallizations are at last analyzable by the professional historian, they already have lost their pristine purity and tend to be dulled. Is there much in common between, say, early Christianity and fourth-century Christianity (not to speak of later metamorphoses, during the Middle Ages for example)?

The *Asidaioi* were first an eschatologically oriented movement, a utopian dream, unified only in their antiestablishment position. They themselves knew certainly more about what they were opposed to than what they agreed on. With time, however, they had to organize and pass from shadowy existence to full concreteness (so much appreciated by the historians). But, as said above, the irony at that point is that the *movement* had become a *stand*, the utopia had passed over to another ideology, and the revolution to another establishment. Of course, this did not remain unchallenged by "purists," so that one finds at this stage of the sect's history simultaneous options as far apart from one another as the belligerency of the Hasidim in the books of Maccabees, Jubilees, and in 1 Enoch, and the pacifism of the *maskilim* in the book of Daniel or of Taxo in the Assumption of Moses. (That Collins can consider the term *maskilim* as designating a sociological group opposed to the Hasidim is beyond me. If he thinks that the latter are hard to define, what is to be said about the former?)

I shall show in a forthcoming work on apocalyptic symbolism and temporality that the Qumran covenanters belonged to an eschatological movement akin to the *Asidaioi*/Hasidim.[121] At this point one finds in Qumran, in a clearly homogeneous community, a similar ambiguity on several levels. First, regarding the issue of marriage and celibacy, there are those who live in total asceticism, while other members of the sect are "marrying and begetting children" (CD 7.6). This ambiguous attitude can only be understood in light of the apocalyptic conception of the "old age" becoming obsolete. Then, it was normal to marry and have a family. It was even the fundamental commandment and the very first given by God to humanity. But, as Frank Cross puts it, now "is a time of trial, and therefore of an 'abnormal' discipline of the flesh."[122]

Transposed to the plane of pacifism versus belligerency, the former attitude belongs to "abnormal" discipline, to asceticism. Paradoxically, this is "holy war" in a totally new interpretation. It entails, as usual, the suspension of all sexual life (Deut. 23:14, 1 Sam. 21:5[6]; 2 Sam. 11:11; Isa. 13:3; Jer. 51:27), the only difference from the previous holy wars being that this one is the ultimate war and therefore the asceticism of the "warriors" at Qumran is constant. This regimen permeated the whole of life in the community (rituals of purity and the Discipline [1QSb 3.22–4.28], the war against the powers of darkness [1QM].)

Similarly, on the doctrine of eschatological expectation itself, there is clearly a hiatus between Qumran messianism on the one hand (Collins goes so far as to call this aspect of the community's hope a "restorative" eschatology[123]), and, on the other hand, the eschatology, let us say, of the *Hōdāyôt* (see 1QH 3). In other words, a this-worldly eschatology runs side by side with a transcendent cosmic one (cf. CD vs. 1QM). Again, from this point of view we are compelled to reassess the problem of pacifism versus militancy. But we will be able, I believe, to exit from the impasse. We shall start with Qumran, then turn retrospectively to early Hasidim, better equipped to fathom its rationale.

The Qumran covenanters had an acute consciousness of being an eschatological community. They were living in the company of the angels, and their purity, both personal and ritual, met heavenly standards. Their rules were celestial, their hymns angelic, their *pesharim* referred to the community's experiences as messianic. So, 1QSa is "the rule for all the congregation of Israel in the last days," and the community meal in 1QS 6.4 is messianic.[124] The hymns in 1QH express the fellowship experienced by the poet with the angels. The commentaries raise the historical happenings in the congregation to the rank of ultimate and decisive developments of the end time (see 1QpHab).

This "realized eschatology" does not, however, prevent the covenanters from effectively expecting an end of time. Their experiences are proleptic. So much so that a Day of Vengeance is expected in 1QM that will mobilize all the militancy the congregation can muster to crush the "sons of darkness," in synergism with the angel legions. Now, such belligerency is in sharp contrast with all we know about Qumran and its quietistic theology. In 1QS the conflict of the spirits is "in human heart" (4.23–24). In 1QSa, in CD, in 4QFlor, in 1QH, the actual community is heaven on earth.

The conclusion is unmistakable. The heirs of the Hasidim at Qumran were also fundamentally pacifistic. But when the Day of Wrath would come, the time for quietism would be over, and, in the image of the formerly peaceful angels, previously singing the praises of God, they would become fierce warriors and participate in the final divine war (1QM). Quite evidently the whole question was then one of discernment. As Collins says, "It is possible that the community felt that that day had arrived with the outbreak of the war against Rome."[125] Transpose this to the time of the outbreak of the Maccabean revolt against Syria, as far as Hasidim were concerned, and it makes as much sense. For, certainly, other earlier "days" were good candidates for being saluted as the Day of Vengeance. As Frank Kermode has shown, it is a common feature in millenarian movements to designate certain dates as marking the "end of time," without discouraging the apocalyptists when it had become clear that the computation was wrong.[126]

It is, I suggest, in this perspective that the conflicting stances of pacifism and militancy must be seen within Hasidism from its origins. It is to be remembered that in the Animal Apocalypse (roughly contemporaneous with the book of Daniel), the vision starts by depicting the pious as harmless "small lambs." But one of them is killed, most probably the high priest Onias III. Then the other lambs grow horns, and they eventually find a leader in a horned ram, no doubt Judas Maccabee (see 1 Enoch 90:6ff.) Similarly, in the Apocalypse of Weeks (before 160 B.C.E.), we see the emergence of the "chosen righteous" (1 Enoch 93:10). They are *given* a sword to punish the sinners at the end (91:12).

It is thus a mistake when Collins states that the groups in 1 Enoch and in Daniel are distinct. One further ground for such a distinction is noteworthy: in Daniel there is a lack of interest in cosmological secrets.[127] But cosmological interests cannot be opposed to eschatological ones, as in many critics. The truth of the matter is that both sets of issues are, on the contrary, convergent. The exploration of the cosmic secrets or of historical secrets is one and the same.[128] Both sets of mysteries have the same background and the same foreground. This present world is only the distorted replica of the true world—the world of celestial powers, angels, divine tablets, predetermination, eternity; in short, that true world is the home of the pleromatic realities, including the pleromatic Israel and the pleromatic Man.[129] All those things are kept secret from average human beings, but some holy people are made privy to them. Now, whether the secrets are described by them along the "spatial axis" in the course of celestial journeys, or along the "temporal axis" through visions and dreams, they constitute the substance of things of which we have here and now only the appearances.[130]

It is fundamentally the same group that would share those kinds of interests, because in both (cosmological and eschatological) there is a disaffection with the "world" and the historical, and the expectation of change not by human forces but by the intervention of God.[131] When one delineates the contours of a sociological group, one does not look necessarily for uniformity in its members. Suffice it that they have a common world view and a general sense of how to reach the acknowledged goal of life and/or history. That is why James VanderKam is probably wrong when he downplays and even dismisses as mere glosses eschatologically oriented texts which crept into "astronomical revelations" in 1 Enoch.[132] The texts in question are 1 Enoch 72.1: ". . . until the new creation shall be made[133] which will last for ever," and 80.2–8, saying that natural laws, which are normally unchanging, will at the End no longer apply (cf. Jubilees 6.22–38). In contradistinction to Collins (*Semeia* 14 [1979]:38) and Stone ("Lists of Revealed Things . . . ," *Magnalia Dei* [1976]:414–52) who accept the authenticity of those passages, VanderKam concludes that the "Astronomical Book" is not an apocalypse.

I cannot concur with such a judgment. The astronomical and eschatological interests are one and the same. Qumran is a living confirmation of my position. This eschatologically oriented community had a keen interest in calendrical, i.e., astronomical, questions.

Let us turn to this problem. It is important on different scores. Goldstein saw in the "sharp differences" between Pharisees and Essenes "on the calendar and other issues" a proof that they did not originate from a common stock that would be the *Asidaioi*. I have already said that this statement is a mistake. The terms *Asidaioi*, Pharisees, and Essenes are all taken in too narrow a sense by Goldstein. Even a relatively late document such as 4 Esdras (ca. 100 C.E.) shows that there was a Pharisaic subgroup much more open to apocalypticism than other subgroups.[134] And, as to the Essenes, suffice it to indicate here in what direction one should look for the warrants of the Essene stance, viz., the apocalyptic dichotomy between the heavenly and the earthly. The present economy, close to reaching its deserved end, is only a caricature of the heavenly and angelic model; true reality is about to replace the shadow of things present. Only an (apocalyptic) elite, such as the Essenes, already has part in that reality. Their calendar gives them the assurance that they are atuned with heaven. So does their ritual, including their frequent purifications, their common meals ("banquets"), their discipline, etc. Now, this is an idea that had been germinating in "pious" circles ever since the return from exile and the invention of an apocalyptic world view.

The thread is unbroken from, at least, the earliest documents that later were inserted into the book of Enoch, to Qumran. Says Cross, "The concrete contacts in theology, terminology, calendrical peculiarities, and priestly interests, between the editions of Enoch, Jubilees, and the Testaments of Levi and Naphtali found at Qumran on the one hand, and the demonstrably sectarian works of Qumran on the other, are so systematic and detailed that we must place the composition of these works within a single line of tradition."[135] He also says, regarding the matter of a common stock with Pharisaism, that those "groups . . . almost certainly have common roots in the Hasidic movement of the Maccabean age. . . . The two groups are related in origin."[136] They seceded when the illegitimate (i.e., non-Zadokite) high priest Simon was consecrated by the people themselves after being appointed by the Syrians (1 Macc. 14:41–47). This situation was held intolerable by the "Essenes," while the "Pharisees" felt able to "go along for a season with the Hasmonaeans."[137]

In conclusion, although scholars such as Schürer, Hengel, and Delcor[138] may have been sometimes too casual in attributing to the Hasidim "the authorship of a wide range of apocalyptic writings, including Daniel,"[139] they were all the same right. There is no compelling reason to see the apocalyptic movement in Isreal as fragmented other than differences in hues and shades. It was indeed "a single movement,"[140] but with a pluralistic outlook—as any spiritual movement has always been in Israel, before and after, may I add. Pacifism and militancy are paradoxically not mutually exclusive. One can see these stances as diachronically in succession, or, synchronically, as coexistent. From this point of view the Day of Vengeance constitutes the totally unique and "abnormal" time when "lambs" must grow horns and wage war against the last enemies.

DANIEL IN HIS TIME

This is not foreign to Daniel's message. The pacifism of the book accommodates itself to descriptions of great violence. Besides, it is to be wondered whether the pacifism represented in Daniel has not been overstressed by critics.[141] In fact, the "One like a man" of chapter 7 is to judge and destroy the beasts. More generally, Michael, the patron angel of Israel, "brings about a sword" and is a transhistorical warrior. The "quietism" of Daniel must not be too hard pressed, especially if and to the extent that the "son of man" is symbolic for a collectivity. To know that God is to intervene personally at the end, and that meanwhile the struggle put on by some against the forces of evil is but "a little help" (Dan. 11:34) does not prevent anyone from actively fighting those forces. On the contrary. One can today feel powerless before the proliferation of nuclear armaments. One can exhort the community faithfully to accept martyrdom with the certainty of God's final victory. One can even believe in divine intervention from heaven before it is too late, and still be very active and militant socially and politically—waiting for the day, perhaps, when opposition must express itself in forms that were objected to before.

NOTES

1. "Palestine" is used here in a purely geographical sense, for lack of a more accurate term. It was the Romans who created this name, which ignored the Jewish inhabitants of the land in favor of the Philistines, whose days of glory ended in the tenth century B.C.E.
2. The name of the Greek colonies in occupied territory. The colonists kept Greek citizenship and each received a parcel of land, taken from the local population.
3. Martin Hengel, *Judaism and Hellenism*, 1:20
4. The *gerousia* later gave rise to the Sanhedrin.
5. Will Durant, *The Story of Civilization*, 2:575.
6. This evolution had begun during Alexander's lifetime. He had, for example, been increasingly tempted by certain Persian notions, above all by the deification of the sovereign. As Durant writes; "The Greeks offered the East philosophy, the East offered Greece religion; religion won because philosophy was a luxury for the few, religion was a consolation for the many" (Ibid., 578).
7. Pierre Jouguet, *L'impérialisme macédonien et l'hellénisation de l'Orient*, 415.
8. In Palestine alone: Samaria, Shechem (Neapolis), Jaffa (Joppa), Ashdod (Azotus), Ascalon, Gaza, Apollonia, Doris, Sycamina, Haïfa (Polis), Acco.
9. Edwyn R. Bevan and Charles Singer, "Hellenistic Judaism," 1.
10. Jouguet, *L'impérialisme macédonien*, 421.
11. This type of surgery, called epispasm, is mentioned in Jos. *Ant.* 12. 5.1 and As. Mos. 8:3

SOCIAL AND SPIRITUAL MILIEU

12.   I admit this point is speculation. When clarity returns to the documentation some years later, it shows a perfect cynicism among the Tobiads and their partisans. I am happy to find expressed a point of view comparable to mine in J. A. Goldstein, *I Maccabees*, 159, and *II Maccabees*, 13. See also the same author in E. P. Sanders, ed., *Jewish and Christian Self-Definition*, 2:67–69, 75–81.

13.   A pawn of the Tobiads, Simon was of the priestly family of Bilga and not Zadokite (cf. *m. Sukk.* 5,8c). He was the brother of Menelaus, who will enter the picture to become high priest. Simon, *prostastès tou hiérou*, (overseer of the temple) was well placed to accuse Onias.

14.   Dan. 11:20 "neither in anger nor in battle."

15.   Priestly authority, which was so effective between the fourth and the second centuries, was founded on the covenant with Pinchas, the son of Eliezer, son of Aaron. In the time of Solomon the chief of the priests, Zadok, was, be it fiction or reality, the descendant of Pinchas. The line continued without interruption to Onias III. It was broken by Jason and then, above all, by Menelaus. In As. Mos. 5 Jason and Menelaus are called "slaves and sons of slaves."

16.   See in particular the version of Theodotion on v. 26. Similarly, Jason of Cyrene (author of a work of which 2 Macc. is an abridgment) makes him a zealot of the law. It is nevertheless odd that Onias takes refuge in a temple of Apollo and Artemis in Daphne.

17.   "Ships of Kittim" (Rome), Dan. 11:30

18.   The confusion is due, in particular, to Josephus, who in *Ant.* 12.5. 2–4 speaks of two visits of Antiochus to Jerusalem. However, we cannot be sure this does not represent mixed sources of information. To be sure, Dan. 11:28–31 also presents events as happening at two times, but this describes two phases of the same act on the part of the king against the "alliance" rather than two visits. 1 Macc. 1 presents only one visit by Antiochus—in 169—followed by sending to the rebel city a *mysarch*, Apollonius, charged with installing in 167–166 what Daniel calls the abomination of desolation (11:31; 12:11). 2 Macc. 5:11–21 corresponds exactly to 1 Macc. 1:20–23. For some, the king's motives were sheer covetousness (Dan. 11:24; Polybius 27.13; Diodorus 30.2; 1 Macc. 1:16). From the same point of view, the version of 1 Macc. states that nothing better is to be expected from pagans. But there is evidence that the imposition of Gentile rituals in Jerusalem was received with favor by the Jewish party in power, if not instigated by them. It is natural to imagine that they called Antiochus from Egypt to their rescue and requested—like the Samaritans somewhat later, according to the testimony of Jos. *Ant.* 12.5. 5—the total Hellenization of the city. On this entire question, see E. Bickerman, *The God of the Maccabees*; V. Tcherikover, *Hellenistic Civilization and the Jews*; M. Hengel, *Judaism and Hellenism*, 1:277ff.; E. Schürer, *The History of the Jewish People in the Age of Jesus Christ*, 1:152 n. 37; Goldstein, *II Maccabees*, 84–123.

19.   It is interesting to contrast with this expression Mattathias' war cry: "Let every one who is zealous for the law and supports the covenant come out with me!" (1 Macc. 2:27).

20.   On the *polis* established in Jerusalem see below.

21.   "The people of those who know their God." See Dan. 11:32. Cf. 8:24; 1 Macc. 1:62–64 (2:20, 29, 42); 2 Macc. 6:9; CD 6.2 (8.5); 20.27; also 3.10; 6.6; 19.9; 1QpHab. 5.7; 12.3–5.

51

22. The term *halaqoth* can be found on several occasions in Qumran, in the expression "the seekers for lighter (legal) burdens." See 4QpNah. 1.7; 2.2, 4; 3.3, 6–7; 4QpIsa. c li. 10.

23. See the Hebraic grammar of Gesenius-Buhl (17th ed.), s.v.

24. See Lacocque, *The Book of Daniel*.

25. Adam C. Welch, *Visions of the End*, 67.

26. The historical authenticity of this self-iconography is now contested (see Hengel, *Judaism and Hellenism*, 1:285; 2:190). Paul uses the text of Dan. 11:37–38 in 2 Thess. 2:4 to describe the Antichrist.

27. Tcherikover, *Hellenistic Civilization and the Jews*, 182.

28. L. Cerfaux and J. Tondriau, *Le culte des souverains dans la civilisation gréco-romaine*, 263.

29. O. S. Rankin ("The Festival of Hanukkah," 198) thinks that it is rather a question of the god Kronos-Helios, whose nature is warlike (see Sib. Or. 3. 97–154). The astral element may have been regarded as a recent importation at the time of Daniel.

Following B. Lifshitz and H. Seyrig, Martin Hengel (*Judaism and Hellenism*, 2:189 n. 169) thinks, as I do, that this concerns not the Capitoline Zeus (cf. R. H. Charles, *A Critical . . . Commentary on Daniel*, 316), but the "god of the Acra." He cites an inscription of Scythopolis dedicated to "Zeus Akraios." See my Commentary on Daniel, ad loc.

30. Worship of the king was evidently particularly strongly established in the cities founded by the kings, such as Demetria, Cassandreia, Seleucia, Ptolemais, Alexandria, Antioch, etc.

31. Bickerman, *The God of the Maccabees*, 63.

32. Ibid., 71.

33. R. Reitzenstein, *Hellenistic Mystery Religions*, 158 n. 27. Cf. B. W. Anderson, *Understanding the Old Testament*, 512: Antiochus "did not object to people having other gods and following local religious customs. But the test of political loyalty was the worship of Zeus, and this meant submission to the absolute authority of the king—'god manifest.'"

34. Norman Bentwich, *Hellenism*, 93, cited in H. H. Rowley, *The Relevance of Apocalyptic*, 37 n. 3.

35. Emil Schürer, *A History of the Jewish People in the Time of Jesus*, 20, 22.

36. Eduard Meyer, *Ursprung und Anfänge des Christentums*, 139ff.; Mikhail Rostovtsev, *Social and Economic History of the Hellenistic World*, 738.

37. Auguste Bouché-Leclercq, *Histoire des Séleucides*, 1:279; Joseph Klausner, *History of the Second Temple Period*, 2:177ff.

38. Schürer, *History of the Jewish People in the Age of Jesus Christ*, 1:143.

39. Julian Morgenstern, "The King-God Among the Western Semites and the Meaning of Epiphanes."

40. See my Commentary on Daniel (11:24).

41. Tcherikover, *Hellenistic Civilization*, 189.

42. Paul Cloché recalls that Callisthenes, one of the chief friends of Alexander and the nephew of Aristotle, believed, as did his uncle, that there was a basic difference in nature between Greeks and barbarians (*Alexandre le Grand*, 139).

43. At the other end of the scale was the native back-country, or *chora*. This was the king's patrimony, as he was master of all that the land bore and all it contained. He was also master of souls (see Jouguet, *L'impérialisme macédonien*, 360). The *chora* was

scorned by the Greeks. The poverty of its inhabitants aroused no pity in their breasts. Hengel remarks that Greek has no word for alms. The Qumran community, in contrast, readily applied the term *ebionim* (the poor) to itself.

44. We can follow Franz Altheim (*Alexander und Asien*), who sees in this bastard form of Hellenism a doctrine that was already dead but was still giving off its last brilliant sparks. When the peoples of Asia were rid of the domination of Alexander, "they realized that they did not know what to do with liberty—then the unpredictable happened: among the newly freed peoples of Asia a growing need of Greek models was felt" (p. 8).

45. H.-I. Marrou, *Histoire de l'éducation dans l'antiquité*, 139.

46. The gymnasium "often was under the patronage of the Greek pantheon, especially Heracles or Hermes" (Baron, *A Social and Religious History*, 1:228).

47. Cited by Hengel, *Judaism and Hellenism*, 1:65. One then became a "cultivated man" (πεπαιδευμένος).

48. According to the Scythian Anacharsis, speaking of the Greeks, "In each city of the Greeks there is a place set apart in which they act insanely day after day" (cited in Baron, *A Social and Religious History*, 1:228).

49. Tcherikover, *Hellenistic Civilization*, 163–65.

50. Texts cited in Hengel, *Judaism and Hellenism*, 1:98.

51. I have emphasized the probably decisive responsibility of the Hellenizing party among the Jews of Jerusalem.

52. Solomon Schechter, *Documents of Jewish Sectaries*, 1:xxvi–xxix.

53. Daniel "was the first to envisage world history . . . as a preparation for the reign of God, [the first] to investigate discreetly this splendid dawn of the hopes of Israel, to lead God's designs for man up to the threshold of eternity" (M.-J. Lagrange, *Le Judaïsme avant Jésus-Christ*, 72).

54. See esp. Dan. 7, but also Dan. 8:19 and 11:36; 8:17 and 11:40; 8:25 and 11:45.

55. Daniel and Qumran will be discussed below. See A. Hilgenfeld, *Die jüdische Apokalyptik in ihrer geschichtlichen Entwicklung*, 253ff.; J. E. H. Thomson, "Apocalyptic Literature"; F. M. Cross, Jr., *The Ancient Library of Qumran*, 195ff.

56. In particular, 1 Enoch. Earlier, it is preferable to speak of preapocalyptic writings (2 Zech. or Joel, e.g.).

57. Or the "elect of justice," as in manuscripts C. D. Y. L. O. See Dan. 12:3, where "those who justify the multitude" are contrasted with "the thoughtful ones."

58. As translated by F. Martin, *Le livre d'Hénoch traduit sur le texte éthopien*, 245.

59. The term appears with no article in Dan. 8:25, (26); 11: (10), 14, 18, (26), 34, 44; 12:2, 4, 10; with the article in 9: (18), 27; 11:33, 39; 12:3 (verses in which the term does not designate the sociological group in question are given in parentheses).

60. See 1QS 3.13; 9.12, 21; 1QSb 1.1; 5.20; K. G. Kuhn, *Konkordanz zu den Qumrantexten*, 134.

61. Hengel, *Judaism and Hellenism*, 1:175: The Aramaic plural equivalent to *Hasidim* with the article is *Hassaya*, transcribed in Greek by Ἐτταιοι. The Essenes were the successors of the older Hasidim.

62. See, e.g., Cross, *The Ancient Library of Qumran*, 133f. Sigmund Mowinckel has identified the mysterious Taxo of As. Mos. (early first century C.E.) with the Staff of CD, arguing that *taxōn* is the Greek work for *meḥôqéq*. It is even possible that we need to look

53

further back in time. As C. Rowland writes, "It seems likely that the rise of the hasidim is hinted at in the animal-apocalypse in 1 Enoch 90.6ff. The lambs who open their eyes and cry to the sheep are the first of the hasidim, whose rise would be dated to the beginning of the Greek period (third century BC). It is apparent from what follows in this apocalypse (1 Enoch 90.13ff.) that the apocalyptist regards the rise of this group as marking one of the last stages of the present age" (*The Open Heaven*, 211).

63. Hengel, *Judaism and Hellenism*, 1:179.

64. Tcherikover, *Hellenistic Civilization*, 125. Thanks to the energetic efforts of Simon the Just (ca. 200), Antiochus III, the conqueror of Jerusalem (198), ratified Mosaic law as the civil law of the Jewish state. Simon's fidelity to the law is cited in Jewish tradition. *Pirke 'Abot* 1.3 quotes one of his adages: "The world rests on three things, the Torah, the cult, and the practice of charity." L. Finkelstein (*The Pharisees and the Men of the Great Assembly*, 40ff.; cited in Tcherikover, p. 457) sees Hasidism as originating even much earlier.

65. "They shall receive a little help" is an allusion, it would seem, to the beginnings of the Maccabean movement.

66. See 1 Macc. 2:34–38: at this point in their resistance, the Hasidim let themselves be massacred, preferring martyrdom to the violation of the sabbath. Later, a *halakhic* decision established that the law of survival was more important than keeping the sabbath a day of rest (vv. 39–42).

67. This is the opinion, e.g., of J. A. Montgomery, *A Critical . . . Commentary on the Book of Daniel*, 87, and of A. Lods, *Histoire de la littérature hébraïque et juive*, 846.

68. Ps. 149 is the only biblical text in which the Hebrew term *hasidim* appears in the absolute plural. It is the name borne by a group.

69. As. Mos. calls for nonresistance by force and for martyrdom (first third of the first century C.E., based on a Hebrew writing of the time of the Maccabees).

70. B. McGinn, *Visions of the End: Apocalyptic Traditions in the Middle Ages*, 35. McGinn writes: "Perhaps not since the days of Bar-Kochba's revolt in second-century Palestine has there been such revolutionary apocalypticism. Even in intertestamental and Jewish apocalyptic it was the exception rather than the rule—ancient apocalypticism, like its medieval successor, tended more toward a passive rather than an active role when it took a negative stance toward the establishment" (p. 148). This judgment is confirmed by Jonathan Z. Smith, "Wisdom and Apocalyptic," 154–155: "Apocalypticism is a Wisdom lacking a royal court and patron and therefore it surfaces during the period of Late Antiquity not in response to religious persecution but as an expression of the trauma of the cessation of the native kingship. Apocalypticism is a learned rather than a popular religious phenomenon."

71. J. de Menasce, "Daniel," 71, note e (concerning the parallel text, 1 Chr. 23:13).

72. Gerhard von Rad says: "The writer of Daniel sides with those who endure persecution rather than those who take up arms against it, and in so doing he is only being true to his own basic conviction that what must be will be. He is far removed from the Maccabees and their policy of active resistance" (*Old Testament Theology*, 2:283).

73. There are fragments from cave 1 and, written about fifty years later, 4QDan a. See *BA* 12, 2 (1949):33.

74. See D. Barthélemy and J. T. Milik, *Discoveries in the Judaean Desert*; fragments of Dan 1:10–17; 2:2–6; M. Baillet, J. T. Milik, and R. de Vaux, ibid., vol. 3, *Les petites grottes de Qumran*; fragments of Daniel 8.20–21 (?); 11.33–36, 38.

75. A. Dupont-Sommer, *Les écrits esséniens découverts près de la Mer Morte*, 336.

76. For further commentary on this text, see my Commentary on Daniel, 74–75.

77. See 1QMyst; 1, 2, 5 QJN; 4Q PrNab; 4QPsDan; 11QMelch.

78 J. A. Sanders, *Discoveries in the Judaean Desert of Jordan*, vol. 4: *The Psalms Scroll of Qumran Cave 11*, 85–89; cf. M. Delcor, "Le milieu d'origine et le développement de l'apocalyptique juive," 104–5.

79. As in Montgomery, *A Critical. . . Commentary*, 4 (based on the publication of the documents in S. Schechter, *Fragments of a Zadokite Work*).

80. Annie Jaubert, *La notion d'Alliance dans le judaïsme*, 83 n. 50.

81. See also Amos 5:13; Prov. 15:24; cf. Isa. 52:13. In the Rule of Qumran the term is applied to the Doctor of Justice (1.1; 3.13; 5.1 of MSS 2, 4, 7 of cave 4; 1QS 9.12, 21; cf. 1QSb 1.1; 3.22; 5.20).

82. Jaubert, *La notion d'Alliance*, 125.

83. Lou H. Silberman, "Unriddle the Riddle: A Study in the Structure and Language of the Habakkuk Pesher," 323–64.

84. In its Hebraic form *ptr* (*pitaron*, etc.), the term appears 14 times in Gen. 40–41 (not 9 times, as stated by Finkel in the article cited below). It means to discover the interpretation of a dream or of a vision (Gen. 41:25, 28, 39; cf. Dan. 2:28, 45; 7:16; 1QpHab 7.5). In traditional Jewish literature the interpretation of dreams found in the Bible is considered a key to all similar situations. See *Ber.* 56b and *y. Maasser Sheni* 55b: in Gen. 37:9 the sun stands for a Jew, the moon for his wife, and a star is a Jew; cf. Num. 24:17. Wine and olives symbolize women and children (Ps. 128:3). The ass is salvation (Zech. 9:9). In short, the dream is a sort of prophecy (*Ber.* 57b). We might compare this with Maimonides, *Guide for the Perplexed*, 2, 45, on the eleven degrees of prophecy, the lowest of which is the dream. See A. Finkel, "The Pesher of Dreams and Scriptures," 357–70. Guillaume remarks that in Akkadian, *pashir shunati* means "interpreter" (*Prophecy and Divination among the Hebrews and Other Semites*, 48).

85. Jaubert, *La notion d'Alliance*, 196.

86. Barthélemy and Milik, *Discoveries in the Judaean Desert* 1: appendix III, no. 72, "Second Exemplaire."

87. Martin McNamara, "Daniel," 651.

88. The religious convictions of the author of Daniel might also be compared (without confusing them, however) with those of the Zealots. It is clear that the Zealots were steeped in the apocalypses. Furthermore, as we shall see, concerning Dan. 7, e.g., the apocalyptists were attached to the temple of Jerusalem. The Zealots rose up against Roman domination, above all to prevent the profanation of the temple (Jos. *Ant.* 15, 8. 1–4).

89. Hengel, *Judaism and Hellenism*, 1:104, 231ff., et passim. The same opinion appears in G. H. Box, "IV Esdras."

90. Hengel, *Judaism and Hellenism*, 1:231.

91. Ibid., 251.

92. This is one of the reasons why Pharisaism and then Christianity appealed to the Hellenized masses.

93. M. Noth, *The Laws in the Pentateuch and Other Essays*, 18–19, et passim.

94. Thus the *Nomos* can be universal in its essence and still be applied by and to a given, particular population. This explains why Jewish thinkers interested in apologetics found it necessary to prove the universality of the Torah, which they found even more "universal" than any Greek philosophy of law.

95. In 161 Judas Maccabeus had to confront a royal Jewish army led by Nicanor. These men, according to 2 Macc. 15:1-2, were loyal to the king and to the Torah.

96. Bickerman, *The God of the Maccabees*, 88. F. M. Cornford, in *The Origin of Attic Comedy*, writes, "The reign of Zeus stood in the Greek mind for the existing moral and the social order; its overthrow, which is the theme of so many of the comedies, might be taken to symbolise . . . the breaking up of all ordinary restraints, or again . . . the restoration of the Golden Age of Justice and Loving-kindness, the Age of Kronos which lingered in the imagination of the poets, like the after-glow of a sun that had set below the horizon of the Age of Iron."

97. We can find even in Dan. 1, with all its apologetic character, an echo of this secularizing interpretation. After ten days of severely restricted diet, Daniel and his companions are in a good deal better physical shape than their counterparts, for the one reason that they have faithfully followed the dietary laws.

98. It is very probable that Bickerman is right when he states that underlying this intellectual opening out to non-Jews there was a broad philosophical consensus, according to which there was not at first any separation between Israel and the nations. He cites the theories of Posidonius (about 150 B.C.E.), for whom the views of the great legislators of antiquity were altered. This applies to the Jews as well, since the laws given by Moses were falsified in subsequent times and reduced to the state of superstitions (*The God of the Maccabees*, 86; see also Hengel, *Judaism and Hellenism*, 1:300).

99. Hengel, *Judaism and Hellenism*, 1:287.

100. From the Persian epoch on, there was a special word, *dath*, to designate this aspect of public life (see the books of Ezra and Esther).

101. Hengel, *Judaism and Hellenism*, 1:181.

102. Ellis Rivkin, *The Shaping of Jewish History*, 67–69.

103. Hengel, *Judaism and Hellenism*, 1:104.

104. The apocalyptic characteristics of Daniel will be further discussed in ch. 4.

105. Except in the prayer, borrowed from other sources, of ch. 9.

106. This is also the conclusion of Hengel (*Judaism and Hellenism*, 2:118 n. 462) and of E. P. Sanders (*Paul and Palestinian Judaism*, 423). Of the contrary opinion is S. B. Frost, *Old Testament Apocalyptic*, 125–26.

107. W. D. Davies, *Torah in the Messianic Age and/or the Age to Come*, 3 n. 4. Davies also cites A. N. Wilder, *Eschatology and Ethics in the Teaching of Jesus*, 30–31 and Rowley, *The Relevance of Apocalyptic*, 162. Also, Dietrich Rössler writes: "No party of Late Judaism had another theological center but the Torah. It guaranteed the unity of Judaism, so that to any outsider the Jews appeared as a homogenous people" (*Gesetz und Geschichte*, 13).

108. See my Commentary on Daniel (9:27).

109. G. Ricciotti, *Histoire d'Israël*, 2:296. Hengel, *Judaism and Hellenism*, 1:293, judges that the Hellenizing Jews were veritable "zealots against the Law." Not only was it necessary to abrogate the legislation of Moses as something that had become inapplicable, but it had to be replaced by an anti-Torah, for the ultimate consisted in destroying the theo-

cratic foundation of Jerusalem. Hengel's opinion is that the "orthodox" zeal for the Torah was aroused in response to the Hellenizers' rage for destruction.

110. Baron speculates that there was probably at the origin of this bizarre trait a popular etymology in which *Yao* (that is, YHWH) was derived from the Egyptian word for ass, *eio*. (*A Social and Religious History*, 1:534).

111. Jouguet, *L'impérialisme macédonien*, 437. We should add, however, that the Jewish resistance to Hellenism was not an isolated phenomenon. But no other opposition was comparable to it. See S. K. Eddy, *The King Is Dead*, 133–35.

112. See esp. 1QM 1.4–7; see A. Dupont-Sommer, *Les écrits esséniens découverts près de la Mer Morte*, 185 n. 2.

113. A. J. Sachs and D. J. Wiseman, "A Babylonian King-list of the Hellenistic Period," 202–12; Polybius 31.11; 1 Macc. 6:1–4; 2 Macc. 9:1–2.

114. This appendix was not part of the French edition. It has become necessary to discuss the arguments recently brought against the previous position held by scholars such as Emil Schürer, Martin Hengel, M. Delcor, F. M. Cross, and others, regarding the Hasidim.

115. J. A. Goldstein, *I Maccabees*, and *II Maccabees*.

116. Collins, *The Apocalyptic Imagination*, ch 2; "Daniel and His Social World."

117. This was already the view of E. Schürer, and he was followed by his modern editors in English G. Vermes, F. Millar, and M. Black (*The History of the Jewish People in the Age of Jesus Christ*, 1:157 n. 46. But, more recently, see Collins, *The Apocalyptic Imagination*.

118. For example, Daniel (esp. chs. 11–12) or As. Mos. (Taxo chooses martyrdom). Here, as Collins appropriately says, "The warfare is left to Michael and to God (*The Apocalyptic Vision of the Book of Daniel*, 208)."

119. E.g., the Animal Apocalypse or the Apocalypse of Weeks in 1 Enoch, two works that are correlated with the sect responsible for Jubilees and the Damascus Document. 2 Macc. is a combination of the two attitudes, for the individual martyrs expect their vindication through their bodily resurrection, while the sword of Judas will bring about the purification of their temple and the national restoration.

120. Goldstein has disavowed in *II Maccabees* some of his theories developed in the first volume because of their "dependence on improbable hypotheses" (p. 37; cf. p. 64 and note 462). This is a commendable sign of intellectual probity, but I for one do not see his new hypotheses as more probable.

121. Both had an apocalyptic origin. As far as Qumran is concerned, suffice it to refer to 1QH 3.12–19, or to the numerous mentions of mysteries and secrets revealed to the elect in 1QS 4.6, 18; 11.3–6; 1QpHab 7.3, 5; 1QH 4.23, etc.

122. *The Ancient Library of Qumran*, 98.

123. *The Apocalyptic Imagination*, 123

124. See Jos. *Jewish War* 2. 129: "They proceed to their dining room as to some holy precinct." As Cross says, "The common meal of the Essenes is hereby set forth as a liturgical anticipation of the Messianic banquet" (*The Ancient Library of Qumran*, 90).

125. *The Apocalyptic Imagination*, 133.

126. Frank Kermode, *The Sense of an Ending: Studies in the Theory of Fiction*, esp. 8–9, 16–17.

127. See M. Stone, *Scriptures, Sects and Visions*, 42.

128. It is also the same, I might add, when the secrets of the prophetic oracles are revealed by the Righteous Teacher (1QpHab 2.5–10; 7.4–5).

129. Collins, "Daniel and His Social World," 141: ". . . . another level of reality where things were different."

130. This does not mean that one cannot see in the passage from one set of interests (cosmological) to another (eschatological) an historical evolution (see Collins, "Daniel and His Social World," 137).

131. The synergism of the "saints" is not foreclosed, as 1QM shows. Besides, it was always the case in the wars of the "Divine Warrior" (Exod. 15; Judg. 5; e.g.).

132. *Enoch and the Growth of an Apocalyptic Tradition.*

133. Charles translates, "is accomplished," and E. Isaac, "is created." See *APOT* ad loc., and J. Charlesworth, ed., *The Pseudepigrapha of the Old Testament*, 1 ad loc.

134. See my article on 4 Ezra in *SBL 1981 Seminar Papers*, 237–58.

135. Cross, *The Ancient Library of Qumran*, 199; see also 92–94, 113, 198, 203.

136. Ibid., 72 n. 33. On the parallels between the two sects see C. Rabin, *Qumran Studies*.

137. Cross, *The Ancient Library of Qumran*, 141 n. 66.

138. Hengel, *Judaism and Hellenism*, 1:175–80; Delcor, "Le milieu d'origine et le développement de l'apocalyptique juive," *La littérature juive entre Tenach et Mischna*, 101–17.

139. Collins, *The Apocalyptic Vision*, 202.

140. *Pace*, J. J. Collins. See *The Apocalyptic Imagination*, 29.

141. Including my own Commentary on Daniel, I confess.

THREE

Daniel as a Work of Literature

LITERARY COMPOSITION

The question of the origin of the materials used by the author is a complex one because these materials differ greatly in nature. Once again a preliminary distinction must be made between chapters 1–6 (Daniel A) and chapters 7–12 (Daniel B). The early chapters contain edifying stories, parenetic and apologetic homilies. The later chapters contain eschatological visions that are hortatory in nature—in short, they are apocalypses. [1]

The discovery of the Dead Sea scrolls in the Judean desert has prompted renewed discussion of the problem posed by the first six chapters. A comparison of the language of Daniel and that of the Targum of Job (11QtgJob), for example, has led Johannes van der Ploeg[2] to the deduction that Daniel, because of its predilection for Iranian terms,[3] must have been written in Mesopotamia. Words of foreign origin are frequent in chapters 1–6; those chapters must be older than the succeeding ones.

For Yehezkel Kaufmann, Daniel 1–6 mirrors exilic Judaism.[4] The Jews lived in apparent peace among pagan and idolatrous nations. Some Jews even became princes of the royal court. At a deeper level, however, Judaism was incompatible with the idolatry of the pagan nations. As Daniel opens, the outcome of this collision course is foresee-

59

able: no adversary can successfully oppose God and his Anointed. Kaufmann points out that nowhere else in the Bible can we find an optimism regarding the pagan nations comparable to that of Daniel A. Its contrast with Daniel B is flagrant. In the latter, idolatry has gained the upper hand, and it has reached incredible heights. Times have changed, and the author of Daniel B lives among the persecutions of Antiochus Epiphanes. At that moment, Daniel A was reread and its text was reinterpreted to emphasize the triumph of Daniel and his companions over the idolatrous king and his men. Mattathias shares this point of view in his reference to the Daniel accounts in 1 Maccabees 2:59–60. It was at this point that Daniel himself was given dreams that reflected the irresistible victory of the good cause. In this manner, according to Kaufmann, two different books were brought together to make one.

Joseph Dheilly,[5] on the other hand, is in agreement with the opinion widespread among scholars that Daniel A was written in the third century.[6] H. H. Rowley recognizes the author's use of previous materials, but he places the composition of the work in the Maccabean era,[7] and, in a book that has become a classic in the field,[8] he discusses in detail all aspects of the problem. "Darius the Mede" never existed under that name, he asserts. The term is the sign of a joining of different traditions and of a total unawareness of the Persian epoch—a trait to be found throughout the book.[9] According to Rowley, in chapters 2 and 7 of Daniel the author presents the four world empires that succeed one another in an odd but uniform manner. Unless we choose to see these chapters, which belong to the two parts—A and B—of the book, as commentaries originating during the Maccabean era,[10] the entire book must be attributed to one writer. The fourth kingdom, Rowley states, is the Greek empire of Alexander the Great. As far as Daniel is concerned, this empire reached its apogee with Antiochus Epiphanes.[11] The same situation occurs in chapter 8, where the vision shows two animals instead of the four of the preceding chapters because the author turns his attention to the Median/Persian empire and to the Greek empire. Only one horn appears, representing the Seleucid dynasty, to replace the ten horns of chapter 7. The same is true from 11:21, which introduces Antiochus IV, through chapter 12.

Rowley's argument is convincing, particularly since the same historical error of crediting the Medes with the sway that in fact belonged to the Persians appears in the two halves of the book. By introducing a

DANIEL AS A WORK OF LITERATURE

Median kingdom between Belshazzar the Babylonian and Cyrus the Persian, the author introduces an overall chronological shift.[12]

Kaufmann rejects Rowley's conclusions, however. For Kaufmann, the same literary circle produced the final version of both parts of the book, but that does not prove their basic unity. In fact, the differences between them are of greater importance than their common elements, for persecutions and martyrdoms, found in both Daniel A and Daniel B, might belong to different periods in the history of Israel.[13]

In the first part of the book, Kaufmann continues, Nebuchadnezzar receives divine revelations with eschatological and messianic implications (4:10–14; 5:5). Daniel's only role seems to be that of revealing divine secrets (2:28, 29, 45). In the second part of the book, on the other hand, Daniel himself has visions but is unable to understand them, and he has to rely on the angels for an interpretation. Furthermore, the three kings of Daniel A—Nebuchadnezzar, Belshazzar, and Darius—no longer appear in person in Daniel B.

Antiochus IV has inspired a number of accounts in which the horror felt by the people found full expression (such as 2 Maccabees 6:18–7:41), but not stories like the one found in Daniel 4, where Nebuchadnezzar is compared to a great tree that shelters all living things (vv. 20–22) or in Daniel 6, where Darius is a great friend of Daniel's and is happy to throw Daniel's enemies into the lion pit. It should also be remarked that the early chapters make no mention of truly discriminatory measures against the Jews, who are not accused of being a people separate from the other peoples because they belong to the God of Israel; this contrasts with 7:21, 25; 8:10–14, 25; 9:26–27; 11:31–39.

Kaufmann arrives at what is probably his decisive argument by comparing chapters 2 and 7. If the four kingdoms are the same in both chapters and if they have the same chronological order, this would argue strongly in favor of one author and one date of composition for the entire book. In point of fact, most critics today believe that in both cases the four kingdoms involved are Babylonia, Media, Persia, and Greece.[14] It should be noted, Kaufmann points out, that in chapter 2 the four kingdoms have the same symbol (a statue), and that the ruin of the fourth brings about that of the other three.[15] Consequently, the book refers to only one empire, a "universal kingdom," considered at four different periods.

The term *malkhut*, in point of fact, has several meanings: power (as in Dan. 5:18); kingdom (7:27; 9:1); reign (1:1; 2:1; 5:26; 8:1); supremacy or empire (11:2).[16] There is no rivalry among the four "stages" of the statue, Kaufmann continues, because in fact they represent chronological divisions of the same entity. The first epoch (2:37–38) is characterized by the reign of Nebuchadnezzar, the "golden head" whose personal power is great in Chaldea. The second epoch, under the sign of the metal silver, is the reign of Evil-Merodach (561–559), Nebuchadnezzar's son. His name is not mentioned in the book, but Jeremiah 27:7 prophesies that after Nebuchadnezzar, Chaldea would be ruled by his son and his grandson.[17] The third reign is that of Belshazzar, so the fourth is that of the Median/Persian empire,[18] the last period of the world empire. At this point, there is a plurality of epochs and kings (2:43–44), and *malkhut* takes on a different meaning, that of national dynasty.

The decline in intrinsic value of the metal of which the statues are made symbolizes a sociocultural decline. The fourth reign is divided; it does not refer to the *diadochi*, but to the Medes and the Persians, who were to mix without ever becoming one homogeneous people.[19] The fatal stone is the explanation of the prophecy in Jeremiah 27:7 concerning the three successive kings of Babylon and the eventual enslavement of that empire. The fourth period is "messianic" in type, but the story's outcome is projected into an imprecise and quasi-mythic future.[20] The author and his generation live in an age without sensational expectations, and their gaze is fixed on "a distant or a fairly distant future" (Kaufmann, p. 431).

LITERARY LEVELS IN CHAPTERS 1–6

It would be a mistake to pit Rowley's and Kaufmann's theses against one another. They have a common denominator: chapters 1–6 were incorporated into a work of the second century. If they had an older origin (Kaufmann), their final composition was in any event during the Maccabean era.

From the point of view of biblical criticism it is important to distinguish between sources and literary levels. The accounts in Daniel A were certainly not invented by its author. We know now with certainty that there was a "Daniel cycle,"[21] the existence of which has been proven in recent years by the discovery at Qumran of the Prayer of Nabonidus (4QPrNab) and the apocalypse of pseudo-Daniel (4QpsDan). These texts have had provisional publication by J. T.

Milik under the title "Prayer of Nabonidus and Other Writings of a Daniel Cycle."[22] The Qumran text seems to date from the second half of the first century B.C.E. Other bits of evidence are added to these texts, such as Nabonidus' inscriptions at Harran[23] and the Wisdom of Ahikar,[24] an echo of which can be seen in Tobit and Sirach. In short, it seems legitimate to apply to all these texts Dupont-Sommer's judgment on the similarities and dissimilarities of Daniel and 4QPrNab: we are dealing with a "remote common source."[25]

Such a background explains why we have in Daniel A a cycle of scenes only loosely connected. In fact, the only tie between them is the name of Daniel (not even his presence, ch. 3). Were it not for the mention of Babylonian kings during whose reigns the stories are meant to have occurred, the scenes would be conceivably interspersed by considerable spans of time.

This is the situation regarding the question of sources. The studies of Alfred Jepsen come to our aid when we turn to the literary levels present in Daniel 1–6. Jepsen considers Daniel 2:41–43 to be complex additions to the text that distort or overburden the context.[26] When the text is reestablished, it should read:

(41b): The kingdom will be divided; it will partake of the strength of iron, as you have seen its feet, part iron, part clay.

(42b): In part the kingdom will be strong and in part weak, as you have seen iron mixed with clay.

(43a): And they will mix by the seed of man and will not hold together, as iron does not mix with clay.

The image of the feet, Jepsen continues, is explained in the current text in three different ways. Only the first of these is original, and it probably dates from the period following the division of Alexander's empire (fourth to third centuries). The fourth kingdom is divided, but it still has some of the strength of iron. The kingdom of God is nigh, but its coming is overdue, and the second explanation (v. 42b) puts it off somewhat longer. At this point the accent is on the weakness of the mixture of iron and clay. This may lead to a judgment concerning the future kingdom: verse 43a shows that there is no longer any connection between two such different entities—which refers to the rupture between Syria and Egypt (third century).[27]

Jepsen believes, with Ginsberg, that, with the exception of these inserted verses, the original text goes back to the fourth century and to the division of Alexander's kingdom among the *diadochi*. But what can we say of the reuse of older materials by the definitive compiler of what was to become the book of Daniel? Ginsberg writes, at the end of the first part of his study on the composition of the book of Daniel, "There would be nothing incredible about the view that the authors of Daniel B saw in Daniel A . . . a profounder message to them than the contemporaries of Daniel A (cf. Bentzen), and that that was why the authors of Daniel B made Daniel A their starting point."[28]

I cannot concur with all of Ginsberg's conclusions, but I would like to echo his insistence (and Kaufmann is in agreement on this point) on the absence in Daniel A of any "bitterness against any heathen monarchy." This fact, Ginsberg continues, "argues against dating him, without compelling reasons, during Epiphanes' attempt to eradicate Judaism."[29] After reviewing the salient features of Daniel A, Ginsberg remarks that in chapter 1 the element of dietary purity could, of course, be used again, giving it a hitherto unknown breadth, by an author of the second century, but that by itself it has too little chronological qualification to prove much.[30] Chapter 4, Ginsberg goes on to say, could hardly have been written about Antiochus IV,[31] because the *agadah* culminates in the king's repentance and, as a consequence, in his rehabilitation to the throne (Dan. 4:35). In chapter 5 no Jew is forced to participate in the orgy. Quite to the contrary; it is a wise Jew who is consulted, and in spite of his terrible prediction, he is richly rewarded. "All that happens is that another heathen dynasty is succeeded by another."[32] In chapter 6 it is hardly likely that the king who is so cleverly maneuvered by his courtiers could be Antiochus IV. The courtiers, moreover, are not—or at least not originally—Hellenized Jews, but non-Jews (and, Ginsberg adds, this would be true even if v. 6 were not part of the text).

Some of Ginsberg's arguments seem to me more solid than others.[33] In general, I concur as far as the original message of Daniel A is concerned. His discussion of chapters 2 and 3 seems to me weak, however: chapter 3 is dispatched with some haste, and his conclusions concerning chapter 2 are only partially correct. To my mind, although chapter 2 should not be seen as a list of Babylonian kings,[34] it is just as unlikely that it goes back to 246–245, as Ginsberg asserts.[35] Ginsberg argues this dating by citing the marriage mentioned in Daniel 2:43, which he sees as that of Antiochus II and Bernice in 252. The political imbalance mentioned, in this view, is the one that resulted from the "Laodicean war" of 246 (see Dan. 11:7). Ptolemy III won a lasting victory in this war, supposedly echoed in Daniel 2. This elicits several remarks:

1. With Jepsen, I believe verses 41–43 to be a gloss made up of elements of various origins. These verses interpret details that do not exist in verses 31–35, which describe the dream enigma. They are thus, to my mind, evidence of successive reinterpretations of the original text—that is, they are superimposed literary strata. If the earliest of these additions comes from the period of the division of Alexander's empire, surely we must go back at least that far for the origins of Daniel A.

2. With Kaufmann and Ginsberg, I am struck by the contemporaneity in the text of the four empires (or reigns) that are represented by the statue. Ginsberg's argument at this point seems weak. He states, "Right through the Greek age and well into the Roman, there existed residual Median and Persian kingdoms in the shape of the two more or less independent principalities of Atropatian Media (Strabo, *Geography* XI, 13:1; 5:6) and Persis (ibid. XV, 3:24; cf. 3:3)."[36] I believe, to the contrary, that the text should be seen in more fluid terms and that, paradoxically, a firmer conclusion should be drawn from it. As it happens, Alexander the Great dismantled Babylonia, Media, and Persia. But his premature death gave those kingdoms a chance to be "reborn," so to speak, in the form of *diadochi*. Seleucus I Nicator, the first of the Seleucid kings (306–281; see Dan. 11:5), adopted the title of "king of Babylonia" between 304 and 301, and the tribute he paid to the great city on the Euphrates could legitimately be interpreted as assuring the survival of that ancient kingdom, at least in the popular imagination, thus perhaps buttressed by Seleucus.[37]

3. The contemporaneity of the "four kingdoms" of Daniel 2 can thus be explained perfectly at the time of the struggles between Alexander's successors (Alexander died in Babylon in 323). Times were sufficiently troubled and uncertain at that moment to inspire the hope, in certain Jewish circles, that the entire structure of the unified world empire realized by that great pagan conqueror would collapse.

4. To summarize, the date of the composition of the text of chapter 2 could be brought back to the fourth century B.C.E. (or between 323 and 300). A first editing, found in verse 41b, dates from a period close to that time; a second, alluding to a marriage between representatives of Syria and Egypt that failed to accomplish its political aims, is to be placed in 252 (with Ginsberg)[38] or, preferably, in 193 (with Rowley). A third change in the text shows up in verse 43a after the rupture between

Syria and Egypt (third or second century). Finally, in a fourth and last reworking, chapter 2, along with all the rest of Daniel A, was inserted into an apocalypse that dates from 166 B.C.E., where it forms the first part of that work.[39]

In this new framework, all details are thrown into a new light. Thus, for example, a compositional parallel between Daniel A and Daniel B, rejected by Ginsberg, who is intent on defending his own thesis, merits consideration. Daniel 2:21 says, "He [God] changes times and seasons." In 7:25 we read, "He [Antiochus] shall think to change the times and the law [religion]." Comparison of these two passages is surely legitimate, as they are parts of the same work. Antiochus, in revolt against God, goes as far as to take his place. The difference in wording ("seasons" versus "the law") comes of the need for historical explanation in Antiochus' case.

This last detail, it should be noted, is part of a group of verses (16–23) in Daniel 2 whose originality has (rightly) been questioned.[40] They come from the same hand as Daniel 1, and the parallel I have suggested between 2:21 and 7:25 is thus all the more striking. In an important article Susan Niditch and Robert Doran write, "Vv 16–23 may be the work of the author of Dan 1. He assumes that Nebuchadnezzar has known Daniel for some time (1:18–20) and thus inserts v. 16." Verses 20–33 insert a passage from the literary genre of the hymn, Niditch and Doran continue, which "disturbs the folktale form of Dan 2, so that we now have a mixture of genres."[41] Hermann Gunkel and Sigmund Mowinckel, among others, have also studied this question.[42] More recently, W. Sibley Towner has shown the passage in question to be an individual psalm of praise, a genre also found in Daniel 4:1–3 [3:31–33]; 4:34–35 [4:31f.]; and 6:26–28. A comparison of these passages shows that:

a) they contain similar linguistic elements;

b) they imitate one of the stereotyped forms of prayer found in the Bible;

c) they fulfill the function of a theological summary of the narration;

d) they "appear to be composed *ad hoc*";

e) they "do not emanate directly from the cultus";

f) they "resemble . . . the learned psalms" (Pss. 51; 112).[43]

The sequence of narration and prayer also serves to underscore the theme of theodicy, and even—since the confession is put in the mouth of notorious enemies in a hostile land—of "universalist theodicy," the effect of which is "to denigrate the power of evil to prevail."[44]

Niditch and Doran show that in Daniel 1–6 the "tales of the courtier," as W. Lee Humphreys calls them,[45] fall into category 922 of the codification drawn up by the Finnish folklorists Antti Aarne and Stitch Thompson,[46] "Clever Acts and Words." Its characteristics are:

a) a person of humble extraction (e.g., a prisoner or a foreigner) is solicited by a noble to solve an enigma (often with threat of punishment if he fails to do so);

b) the problem is posed;

c) the solution is given;

d) the interpreter is rewarded (he receives half the kingdom, the hand of the king's daughter, sumptuous clothing, and so forth), as in Genesis 41 (Joseph) and Ahikar (in Syriac) 5–7.23.

The tale shows that wisdom leads to success; consequently, this type of story is not openly polemical. This point is important. It weakens the argument for a profound difference in atmosphere between Daniel A and Daniel B. The author could not transform the "tales of the courtier" into satires or polemic manifestos without betraying their generic nature.[47]

Chapter 3 is complicated. Daniel himself does not appear in this chapter, which has quite rightly been seen as proof that this legend originally existed apart. Furthermore, as Aage Bentzen has remarked,[48] the Septuagint version presents numerous additions to the Masoretic Text version, which is one indication, among others, that this *agadah* struck people's imaginations with particular force. In the course of a history studded with persecutions, verses 16–18 in particular were to become the martyr's declaration of faith par excellence.

Several aspects of the chapter need to be investigated in order to date the literary levels involved:

1. the statue erected by "Nebuchadnezzar";
2. the martyrdom for the faith;
3. the musical instruments mentioned;
4. the torture by fire inflicted on the three youths.

As we have seen, the date of chapter 3 has a terminus a quo, the Babylonian exile, and a terminus ad quem, the second century B.C.E. The very presence of chapter 3 within the book of Daniel militates for the latter date. In favor of the former, there is the Septuagint addition to verse 1, "the eighteenth year of Nebuchadnezzar"—i.e., 587. In this case the erection of the statue would be an official act to celebrate the ruin of Jerusalem.[49]

In point of fact, identifying the enormous statue presents a first chronological problem. H. H. Rowley is perhaps hasty when he speaks of statues (in the plural) placed by Antiochus IV in the temple of Jerusalem.[50] I concur with Ginsberg's judgment: "Chapter 3 is a tale in which Palestinian Jews in the years 167–4 could doubtless find a timely message for themselves . . . but it can not have been written by people in their situation."[51] Ginsberg goes on to point out the difference in historical setting with the second century: Idolatry is limited to a "colossus in the plain of Doura," and there is no question of any global antisemitism.[52] The mention in Ammianus Marcellinus (22. 13.1) of a colossal statue of Apollo at Daphne during the reign of Antiochus IV simply shows that second-century readers had one further opportunity to make the legend their own. Ancient authors attest to the presence of such statues: Herodotus, for example, mentions one in a temple in Babylon (1. 183).

In the first century B.C.E. Diodorus Siculus (2.9) speaks of three golden images surmounting the temple of Belus, portraying Zeus, Hera, and Rhea. Everyone has heard of the Colossus of Rhodes.[53] Of particular interest is the citation by J.A. Montgomery[54] of *Praep. Evang.* 9.39. There, Eusebius mentions a golden image by the name of Bel at the time of Jeremiah, and how Jeremiah prophesied the approaching calamity. As a consequence, "Jonachim [Jehoiakim] tried to burn him [Jeremiah] alive; but he said that with that fuel they should instead cook food for the Babylonians and as prisoners of war should dig the canals of the Tigris and the Euphrates." Finally, about 250 B.C.E. Berossus reported that the Persians introduced images of the human form at the time of Artaxerxes II.[55]

It is clear from all this that the element of the statue cannot in itself furnish a chronological indication of any precision for chapter 3 of Daniel.

With martyrdom for the faith, things become a good deal clearer. If the scene described by the author presents a persecution of the Jewish people *qua* Jews that applies to the religious as well as the political sphere, then the second century B.C.E. is the best candidate. Antiochus' pogrom is the first of its kind in history. Nevertheless, biblical criticism hesitates to draw firm conclusions concerning chronology, for the fact that Jews as individuals suffered for their religious beliefs under foreign political regimes is a phenomenon that was probably too frequent to permit us to pinpoint any one epoch in particular.

The third problem on our list is more promising. Musical instruments, mentioned several times in the chapter, are of either Iranian, Akkadian, or Greek origin. There are, for example, the *symphonia* (bagpipe, vv. 5, 10, 15) and the *psalterion* (psalterium, vv. 5, 7, 10). The latter has its earliest mention in Aristotle (384–322), and the former in Plato (427–347), but in its original meaning of harmony; as a musical instrument it first appears in Polybius (ca. 200–118), hence in the period of the Maccabees. This, therefore, is a first and an important chronological indication.[56] Bentzen is correct in concluding, "As the 'concrete' meaning [of *symphonia*] can be somewhat older than its first occurrence in Polybius, it follows that [Dan. 3] belongs to the Greek period, not to the Exile."[57]

The torture inflicted on the three youths, on the other hand, gives us little to go on for a precise dating. Punishment by fire is rare in Scripture (see Gen. 38:24; Lev. 21:9; Josh. 7:15, 25; also Jub. 20:4; 30:7; 41:19, 25). It was rare in Babylon (but see Jer. 29:22). Bentzen cites Hans von Soden, who, following Sidney Smith, sees in the narration of Daniel 3 traces of cult initiations involving sorcery resembling those practiced during the reign of Nabonidus in Babylon (555–539). Curt Kuhl sees the influence of the Croesus legend, and perhaps that of an Iranian tale.[58]

Of more help is Elias Bickerman's remark that trial by fire was applied in Persia to test the truth of a religion and its protagonists: Zoroaster was supposed to have walked through fire to prove the truth of his message.[59]

The third chapter of Daniel can thus find its remote origin during the Persian period and its point of departure in the figure of the Babylonian Nabonidus. The general nature of the definitive text is, however, more surely of the Greek period; and its final reworking, when it was inserted in the book of Daniel, is of the second century B.C.E.[60]

LITERARY LEVELS IN CHAPTERS 7–12

The atmosphere changes completely when we pass on to Daniel B. Here pagan kingdoms are clearly regarded with bitterness, and the allu-

sions to Antiochus IV Epiphanes and his persecutions are too numerous and too specific to permit any doubt concerning the origin of this
portion of the book. As in Daniel A, however, different literary levels
can be discerned. In *Studies in Daniel* Ginsberg has examined these levels
in detail, and his presentation provides the background for mine here.

In chapter 7, in contrast to chapter 2, the four kingdoms are
declared pernicious and doomed to disappear (the "beast" in 7:11
designates all the pagan nations, as discussed below). Ginsberg sees the
text as we have it as out of order. Using arguments taken in turn from
logic, philosophy, zoology, history, and even aesthetics, he reestablishes
the order as: verses 1, 2, 3, 4a, 5aγ-b, 4bα-β, 5aα-β, 4bγ-δ, 6ff. Certain
details attributed in the *textus receptus* to the second beast in fact apply to
the first, and vice versa. It is the lion who has three rib bones in his teeth
and who is commanded to devour much flesh. Furthermore, verse 4 is
translated significantly differently, because "it was lifted up from the
ground" (which is followed by the animal's upright position) becomes
"he disappeared from the earth"[61] (the upright position referring to the
bear, not the lion). Ginsberg makes much of this appearance of the first
and the fourth beasts (7:11), contrasting it to the fate of the second and
the third, which are not destroyed, but only have dominion taken away
from them. They barely last until the coming of the saints (7:12).[62]

Thus the Babylonian kingdom (the first animal) does not survive.
This corresponds historically to a period stretching from 260 to 63; consequently, it includes the Epiphanean period, 175–164.[63] The marked
hatred of Macedonia (the fourth kingdom) should also be noted. This
fourth monster is a more ferocious version of the first, and the author—
who has used all his hyperboles to speak of the lion and the eagle—is
obliged to fall back on saying that there is no animal in nature that
resembles the creature he has seen (7:7; cf. Judg. 14:18; 2 Sam. 1:23*b*).
This summit of monstrosity designates Alexander's empire, of course,
but beyond that, it stands for the epitome of all pagan empires.

The monster has ten horns—eleven, in fact. Whatever interpretation is given to these horns, it is clear that at times it is the tenth and at
other times the eleventh that designates Antiochus. From a critical
point of view, this is evidently intolerable. Ginsberg resolves the enigma
by considering all allusions to the eleventh horn to be secondary elements. This eleventh horn is first seen in verse 8, where an eleventh
horn uproots three of the preceding ones,[64] and it appears clearly in
verse 24*a*. Later in the book, modifications reappear in 8:9–14 and 23–

24, passages written after the profanation of the temple and the prohibition to practice the Jewish faith (toward the end of the year 167), but before the royal amnesty (winter, 164).

Thus the original literary level of chapter 7 goes back to the period preceding Antiochus Epiphanes' measures of 167. When these laws were promulgated, it was felt necessary to add specific allusions to the tyrant's indignities, which gives us the additions to chapter 7 and parts of chapters 8–12,[65] all of chapter 9 having been written by the same hand.[66]

Thus it is possible that an original version of Daniel 7 dates back to the post-Alexandrine *diadochi*, as Alfred Jepsen sustains. In this case it would not be impossible that the "saints" surrounding "one like a son of man" originally designated the angels of the Presence (as rabbinic tradition calls them). Their relation with the man in verse 13 leads to an interpretation of the latter as angelic as well as human, identifying him as the archangel Michael.[67] The notion evolves, however, and as early as the book of Jubilees (between 153 and 105) and the Testament of Levi (second century), the term "saint" becomes amphibolic (cf. Jub. 33:12; 9:15). The Testament of Levi 18:11 says that the Levitic Messiah "will ward off the sword menacing Adam and will give the saints to eat of the tree of life." In any event, the sectarians at Qumran called themselves "saints," as did the first Christians at a later date. According to W. D. Davies, "There are striking parallels to this association of angels with 'churchly' activity and with the communion of the saints in worship in the sectarian sources."[68] Davies cites CD 11.8–9; 1QSa 1.25–2.10; 11:8; 1QSb 4.25–26, where it is clear that the communion between men and angels actually occurs, for "the reference is not to the future but to the present experience of the community of worship." He cites Barthélemy and Milik on the phrase, "for the holy angels are [present] in their congregation," reporting their opinion that these texts should not be understood in the future, but in a mystical present, since the terrestrial liturgy is carried on *at the same time* in the "Temple of the Kingdom."[69]

This state of affairs is already that of Daniel B. We shall see later, in chapter 6, that the *Sitz im Leben* of Daniel 7 is liturgical and, more precisely, that of the Feast of the New Year (Succoth), the royal enthronement with its celebration of the covenant renewal. The "saints" (angels and men alike) are an integral part of these festivities, and they confirm their saintliness by this means.[70]

This survey of chapter 7 shows that the first level of chapter 8, in which mention is made of a small horn sprouting out of another and growing in an extraordinary manner, was written by the glossator of chapter 7. His additions date from 166–164, and he is responsible, as we have seen, for verses 9–14 and 23–24.

I should cite (to refute it, however) Ginsberg's opinion that verses 13–14 cut the development of the chapter and introduce elements irreconcilable with the remainder of the chapter. According to Ginsberg, the same foreign material can be seen in verses 26a and 27b, and again in verse 16, which should be treated separately.[71] The principal differences introduced by this second hand, Ginsberg says, lie in the fact that Daniel, who is presumed to comprehend the vision but who says nothing about it (vv. 16, 17b, 19, 26b), now confesses that he does not understand it at all (27b). Previously, the word *saints* represented the Jews (v. 24), as in chapter 7; now it designates the angels (see v. 13). In the text of this chapter *mare'èh* has the sense of revelation comprehensible to Daniel; in the sections that have been reworked, it means "incomprehensible mystery." As for verse 16, which is presupposed by 9:21, it was added even later, evidently by the author of chapter 9, who also wrote the final version of both chapter 7 and chapters 8–12.[72]

For several reasons, of both a technical and an exegetic nature, I cannot concur with Ginsberg's conclusions regarding chapter 8. First, there is an impressive amount of repetition: the word *hazôn* (vision) punctuates the entire chapter, appearing seven times,[73] the verb *ra'ah* (to see) is used ten times,[74] the two terms are used conjointly three times,[75] and the noun *mare'èh* is used four times[76] (as to its sense, one plus three).[77]

On the other hand, Ginsberg fails to note an important characteristic of this apocalyptical work. It is a mistake to oppose (as he does) the *order* of the comprehension given to Daniel and his *confession* of incomprehension. The root of the verb used in both instances is *bin* (to understand), which appears in verses 5, 15, 16, 17, and 27.[78] There is no logical impossibility—and above all, no "biblical" impossibility—in affirming the existential need to understand the mystery and Daniel's dismay at being unable to do so.[79] Nor is the further command, given in verse 26b, to "seal up the vision" unrelated to the global situation. Daniel does not understand the vision in its entirety, but he comprehends enough of it to be wary of bruiting about such awesome secrets.

DANIEL AS A WORK OF LITERATURE

As for the double meaning of the word *saints* in this chapter, it reflects a doctrine fundamental to the book.[80] It designates the Jews (v. 24, where the addition of the significant word "people" permits no ambiguity), and it refers to angels (v. 13; 4:10). Using here a syllogism, it can be said that as "man" is enthroned with the one who is like a son of man, so also the "people of the saints" achieve the angelic stature of saints through his triumph.

In conclusion, I see no compelling reason to divide chapter 8 into more than two literary levels. The first and original level comes from the post–Alexandrine era, when the empire was divided between the four *diadochi* (fourth–third centuries). The second level, represented by verses 9–14 and 23–24, alludes clearly to Antiochus Epiphanes and dates from 166–164.[81]

Chapter 9 has two distinct parts: verses 1–3 (or 1–4a) and 21–27 comprise the (a) section, and verses 4–20 the (b). Section (a) was first written in Aramaic, as Ginsberg has convincingly demonstrated;[82] we have the original Hebrew of section (b), which comes chronologically after (a).[83] It is a liturgical piece composed in Jerusalem during the Exile, and it is strongly influenced by Deuteronomist and Jeremian thought. There are several other versions of this prayer: in Ezra 9:6–15; Nehemiah 9:6–37; 1 Baruch 1:15–3:8; and 4QDibHam. The *Sitz im Leben* (setting in life) of this Qumran text is the synagogue liturgy for Friday, more specifically, the Yom ha-kippurim (cf. Dan. 9:24), a feast that Daniel 9 relates to the Jubilee year, as in Leviticus 25:9. Daniel makes full use of the eschatological overtones of this composite feast.

I have already noted that 9:21 presupposes 8:16. The author is evidently preoccupied by the calculation of the end of the period of Antiochus IV's persecutions. Thus, 9:27 parallels 7:25; 8:14; and 12:7.

Chapters 10 to 12 form one literary unit. The first part goes from 10:1 to 11.2a (this colon is a repetition of 10:21a). Ginsberg seems correct in inversing the order of 10:21a and 10:21b.[84] Verse 11:1 should read: "And I since the first year [*mi-šenath* instead of *bi-šenath*] of Darius the Mede,[85] have been standing . . . by him [Michael] as a helper and strengthener."[86] This explains the three-week delay mentioned in 10:3 (see v. 12). Verse 11:1 combines this motif with that of the three-year interval between 9:1 and 10:1. In this manner, the angel who speaks in chapter 10 is identified as Gabriel in 9.21.[87]

Therefore, Daniel 10:1 and 11:2 were written after Daniel 9. It is interesting to compare them with chapter 8. Ginsberg remarks that these passages make a notably different use of a common literary source: Habakkuk 2:2–3. In Daniel 8:17 and 26*b*, the *ḥazon* (vision), as in Habakkuk, is the point of departure for an eschatological revelation; in 10:14*b* (cf. 14*a*), 11:27*b*, and 35*b*, on the other hand, the key word is *mo'ed* (time)—or *yamim* (days) in 10:14. Ginsberg paraphrases these passages in the latter series as follows: "You know of course there is a *mo'ed*. Well, it still holds in store quite a lot of *ḥazon* . . . and a *qeṣ*." This means, Ginsberg continues, that *mo'ed* here has acquired the meaning "term of the present dispensation," and *ḥazon*, that of "events scheduled to take place during the said term." This misunderstanding was favored, according to Ginsberg, by the absence of an article before *ḥazon* in Habakkuk 2:2 and 3, and by the Masoretic reading *'od* (still) in place of the original *'ed* (witness). Between Daniel 8 and Daniel 10–11, we move from "relative freshness" to a "dry erudition and a maximum of artificiality."[88]

Ginsberg finds other proofs of the reworking of chapters 8 and 10, and he points out their many and varied points of contact. Thus, for example, the verbal expression *rdm 'al panim* (to fall into a lethargy) of 10:9 also appears in 8:18. As it happens, 8:17 contains another verbal expression (*n ph l 'al panim*) in which Ginsberg sees a synonym. Thus 8:17 and 18 represent two different literary levels.[89] Since a further comparison of 8.26*b* (keep secret the vision) and 12:4 (keep secret these words) proves, in Ginsberg's eyes, a similar duality of authorship, the conclusion is obvious: whoever wrote chapters 10–12 interjected his thoughts into chapter 8 (vv. 18, 26*b*). He draws a further argument from Daniel's falling on his face at the *sight* of the angel in 8:17; whereas in 8:18 and in chapter 10 Daniel faints on *hearing* the angel's words.

In my opinion there is progression rather than opposition between 8:17 and 8:18. Daniel falls prone at the sight of the angel—a trait typical of biblical texts found also in Numbers 24:4, 16; Ezekiel 1:28. Then, as he hears what the angel says to him, he falls into a faint or into lethargy. It is impossible to prove that an Aramaic verb *dmk* (to lie down; to sleep) has been translated correctly by the prone position represented in 8:17 and incorrectly in the similar position given in 8:18 and 10:9. To be sure, the use of *rdm 'al panim* in 8:18 and 10:9 takes liberties with the Hebrew that seem to be too great, but so many minor imperfections arose from the translation from the original Aramaic to the current Hebrew that it is difficult to pick out one particular thing as blameworthy. What seems more probable is that the translator simply rendered two different verbs indicating a progression in the action with two Hebrew verbs, one of which was an unhappy choice.

CONCLUSION

During the first half of the second century B.C.E., the person who wrote down the book of Daniel, and who was its true author, made use of tales that belonged to a popular cycle of stories concerning Daniel. His intention was to galvanize the spiritual resistance of the pious in face of the persecution of Antiochus IV and the Hellenizers. He therefore took over popular stories using Daniel's name that were in circulation, and he turned them to his own purposes. These are chapters 1–6, or Daniel A. Chapters 7–12, or Daniel B, are the more purely original work of this same author. Here the literary genre is the apocalypse, and its message is more directly fashioned for the martyrs of 167–164.

As the book stands, its dual composition poses a certain number of problems for the critic and for the exegete. It would be a mistake, however, to conclude that two originally independent works were more or less artificially juxtaposed. Taken in itself, to be sure, the *agadah* is not apocalyptical; nor is the apocalypse necessarily agadic. Nevertheless, as I wrote, in collaboration with Pierre Grelot in the introduction to the book of Daniel of the *Traduction Oecuménique de la Bible:*

The literary form of a text is always determined by two elements: the function it fulfills in the community for which it was written, and the conventions in practice in the cultural milieu surrounding it. Returned to the context of its times, the Book of Daniel presents an original combination of two of the favorite genres of Jewish literature of that epoch: the didactic narrative (the *agadah*) and the apocalypse.

NOTES

1. The harmony between the two parts of Daniel is not due to their proximity alone. J. Gammie, ("The Classification," 193 n. 15) calls attention to the "sub-genres" of apocalyptical literature: "vision report, *vaticinia ex eventu*, parenesis, liturgical genres (blessing, woes, hymns, and prayers), nature wisdom, stories, fable, allegory, dialogue, riddles, *mašal* or parable, interpretation of prophecy or *pešarim*, and eschatological predictions." There are, consequently, affinities between Daniel A and Daniel B. The same is true on the plane of ideas. Gammie (ibid., n. 16) speaks of "a cluster of ideational elements" in apocalyptic that have often been seen as including " 'cosmic dualism,' 'expectation of a new age,' 'pessimism,' 'determinism,' " and still other characteristics that he lists in the course of his article.

2. Johannes van der Ploeg, *Le Targum de Job de la grotte 11 de Qumrân*. See Paul Winter's review in *Revue de Qumrân*, 4:441.

3. J. A. Montgomery, *A Critical . . . Commentary*, 20ff., gives a list of borrowed foreign words in the book of Daniel. He first lists words of Akkadian origin: in 1:11, 20; 2:5, 26, 31, 41, 48; 3:15, 21; 5:5, 7, 16; 8:2; and probably in 3:10 and 5:2. He gives Persian words in 1:3, 5 (= 11:26); 2:5 (two words); 3:2 (four words); 3:5 (surrounded by three Greek terms, cf. 3:4); 3:16, 24. . . , and Greek words (cf. my Commentary on Daniel 3). Other useful studies include H. H. Rowley, *The Aramaic of the Old Testament*, 152–56; H. H. Schäder, *Iranische Beiträge* 1; R. D. Wilson, "The Aramaic of Daniel"; S. R. Driver, *An Introduction to the Literature of the Old Testament*; J. A. Fitzmyer, *The Genesis Apocryphon: A Commentary*; W. Baumgartner, "Das Aramäische im Buche Daniel"; G. R. Driver, "The Aramaic of the Book of Daniel."

On the Mesopotamian origin of the Aramaic portion of Daniel, see J. W. Doeve, "Le domaine du Temple de Jérusalem," 159–63.

4. Yehezkel Kaufmann, *Toldot haEmunah haYisraelit*," vol. 8.

5. Joseph Dheilly, "Daniel," in *Dictionnaire biblique*.

6. The same is true of J. Gammie, "The Classification," (see p. 201, where he places it under Ptolemy IV Philopator (203 B.C.E.).)

7. H. H. Rowley, *The Servant of the Lord and Other Essays*, 237–68. See H. L. Ginsberg, "The Composition of the Book of Daniel," for a pointed criticism of Rowley's position.

8. H. H. Rowley, *Darius the Mede and the Four World Empires in the Book of Daniel*.

9. Otto Eissfeldt, *The Old Testament*, 521, cites, among the many historical errors in Daniel, "the assumption of a deportation in the third year of Jehoiakim (605) in i, i; the view (v) that Belshazzar, as son and successor of Nebuchadnezzar, was the last king of Babylon; . . . the information in vi, i that, instead of the Persian Cyrus, it was the Mede Darius who was the successor of the last Babylonian king, and the further information that Darius was the son of Xerxes (ix, i) and that Cyrus was his successor (vi,29; x,1) . . . [and] that there were altogether only four kings of Persia . . . whereas in reality nine Persian kings reigned."

10. Rowley cites as holding this position: G. Hölscher, "Die Entstehung des Buches Daniel"; E. Sellin, *Einleitung in das Alte Testament*, 153–54; M. Haller, *Das Judentum Geschichtsschreibung, Prophetie und Gesetzgebung nach dem Exil*, 279–80, 295; M. Noth, "Zur Komposition des Buches Daniel," 143–63, cf. p. 155; J. A. Montgomery, *A Critical . . . Commentary*, 176–77.; R. B. Y. Scott, *AJSL* (1947): 294; G. Jahn, *Das Buch Daniel nach LXX*, 22–23. Cf. H. Junker, *Untersuchungen über Literarische und Exegetische Probleme des Buches Daniel*, for whom the entire book is of the Persian period, but glossed at the time of the Maccabees.

11. See Sib. Or. 3. 397; 4 Ezra 12:10–12. The Peshitto on Dan. 7:7 has the gloss "king of Greece," the terminus ad quem of which cannot be beyond 200–250 C.E., according to M. J. Wyngarden, *The Syriac Version of the Book of Daniel*. As we have seen above, this interpretation had already been offered by Porphyry, as by Ephraem, Polychronius, and others.

12. Rowley, *Darius the Mede*, 150–51; 176–78. Bickerman, *Four Strange Books*, explains the strange "Darius the Mede" thus: whoever edited the book of Daniel knew by Jer. 25:1 that the first year of Nebuchadnezzar coincided with the fourth

year of Jehoiakim, king of Judah. Therefore the "princes of Judah" (Daniel among them) were taken to Babylon "in the third year of the reign of Jehoiakim" (Dan. 1:1). On the other hand, according to 1:21, Daniel exercised his ministry "until the first year of King Cyrus," the date of the return to Zion from exile. The editor knew of a tale concerning Daniel in the lions' den, which took place under "Darius the king." As all the kings of Persia of the name of Darius ruled after Cyrus, the Darius of ch. 6 must have preceded Cyrus, and could not have been Persian. In agreement with Isaiah 13:17 and Jer. 51:11, 28, the author makes him into a Mede and places him between the last Babylonian king, Belshazzar, and the first "Persian" king, Cyrus (Dan. 6:1 and 2).

13. Kaufmann, *Toldot*. Kaufmann disagrees with E. Schürer (*Geschichte des jüdischen Volkes im Zeitalter Jesu Christi*, 3:264), for whom the "three kings" of chs. 2, 5, and 6 are none other than Antiochus Epiphanes. He also rejects the conclusions of R. H. Pfeiffer (*Introduction to the Old Testament*, 762) and of H. H. Rowley ("The Unity," 264–66). For Pfeiffer and Rowley, those who set the king against Daniel (ch. 6) were bad Jews exciting Antiochus against their brothers. Kaufmann does not see religious persecutions in the full sense of the term in 1–6, as contrasted to 7:25 or 11:33, but rather a conflict between the will of God and the will of the king. See my Commentary on Daniel, 8–9, 93n5.

14. In ch. 8, the contents of which follow ch. 7, the situation has changed slightly because the Babylonian empire no longer appears. The number of kingdoms is kept the same, however, by the addition of the regime of Antiochus Epiphanes after the empire of Alexander. (The first, "shorter," horn is the Mede empire; the second, "longer," is the Persian; the goat with one horn followed by four others is the Macedonian empire; the little horn taking the place of the four preceding ones is Antiochus Epiphanes.)

15. H. L. Ginsberg, *Studies in Daniel*, 7ff., refers to Daniel 2:47, where God is called "Master of Kings," which had been, he says, an Egyptian title for the pharaohs up to the time of the Ptolemies. This proves that the author knew of the regime of the Ptolemies, and that he might have had a global conception of successive kingdoms. To which Kaufmann answers that the title was known everywhere and that consequently the author of Dan. 2 did not necessarily need to have lived at the time of the Ptolemies (cf. Kaufmann, *Toldot*, 423).

16. As in the duality of the Latin terms *regnum, regula*.

17. As echoed in texts such as Dan. 5:2, 11, 13, 18, 22.

18. Kaufmann refuses to separate the Medes and the Persians in the book of Daniel. The historical error of the book is not, as is claimed, to have given Media preference over Persia, but to attribute to a Mede (Darius) power over Media and Persia (Dan. 5:28; 6:8 [9], 12 [13], 15 [16]; 8:3, 20; 6:25–26 [26–27]; 9:1). Daniel 6.28 says that Daniel served Darius ("the Mede") and then Cyrus the Persian: the two are associated and not sovereigns of two different kingdoms (9:1; 10:1). In the book of Esther as well, "Medes and Persians" form one kingdom. In Greek, "king of the Medes" designated the Persian king and the "Medean language" was Iranian. See n. 12 above, for Bickerman's explanation of the expression "Darius the Mede."

19. Kaufmann cites histories involving the personage of Cyrus (Herodotus 1. 55–56, 107ff.; Xenophon, *Cyropaedia* 1 ch. 2). The story circulated that Cyrus was of mixed blood and that his mother, the princess Amitis, was a prostitute and the daughter of the Medean king, Astyax—unless she was his wife, or perhaps both his wife and his mother.

20. Even if the narration takes a historical reminiscence as its point of departure, it is not historical.

21. Similarly, the book of Enoch is "what crystallized from the literature that circulated in the second and first centuries before Christ under the names of Enoch and of Noah" (F. Martin, *Le livre d'Hénoch*, lxviii).

22. J. T. Milik, "Prayer of Nabonidus . . .,": 407ff. See also D. N. Freedman, "The Prayer of Nabonide."

23. Published by C. J. Gadd in *Anatolian Studies* 8.

24. In part in the Aramaic papyri of Elephantine in the fifth century B.C.E.. The points of contact with the book of Daniel seem to be: a) Daniel, like Ahikar, explains enigmas, and this ability is viewed as the sign of true wisdom (Dan. 1:18–21; 5:10–12). b) Despite the evil intentions of their enemies, Daniel and Ahikar's lives are spared, and both are reinstated in their functions (Dan. 6). c) In both cases their adversaries suffer the fate devised for their victims. d) Dan. 4:36 (the reestablishment of the king Nebuchadnezzar in his kingship) seems to echo the reestablishment of Ahikar in his functions at the royal court. This parallel is all the more striking in Ahikar's description of his condition when he was in prison (long hair and beard, his body covered with dirt, and, above all, nails as long as an eagle's). e) From a formal point of view, on both sides there is a mixture of genres, narrative and wisdom.

The parallels suggested by Harris, Lewis and Conybeare (*APOT*) between Ah. 1.3 (Arabic) and Dan. 2:1, 27; 5:7; between Ah. 1.7 (Armenian) and Dan. 5:16; and between Ah. 5.4 (Arabic) and Dan. 2:11, on the other hand, seem details insufficiently significant for comparison.

25. A. Dupont-Sommer, *Les écrits esséniens découverts près de la Mer Morte*, 339.

26. Alfred Jepsen, "Bemerkungen zum Daniel-Buch." Jepsen's solution is a convincing response to Rowley's criticism, according to which the elimination of the expression "and toes" in 2:41a, 41b–43 is an "emasculation" ("The Unity," 252).

27. Jepsen follows Rowley's reading. If v. 43 refers to the marriage in 193 of Cleopatra, Antiochus III's daughter, and Ptolemy V, then v. 42 refers to the immediately preceding period—i.e., to the moment of the military superiority of Antiochus III, who in fact imposed the marriage in question on Ptolemy V. This union failed to achieve its aim (see Dan. 11:17), for Cleopatra, a Seleucid, worked for the interests of her country of adoption, Ptolemaic Egypt. H. L. Ginsberg deliberately ignores this fact ("The Composition of the Book of Daniel," 251).

28. Ginsberg, "The Composition," 259.

29. Ibid., 247 n. 2.

30. Cf. Tob. 1.:10–11 (*contra* Rowley). It is true that the book of Tobit is difficult to date, but it is anterior to Daniel (between the fourth and the second centuries).

31. Even if he was called by his subjects *Epimane* (madman), through a play on the word *Epiphanes*.

32. Ginsberg, "The Composition," 257.

33. Among the less solid arguments I would place the one on dietary purity put forth in Dan. 1. No epoch is better fitting for this sort of text than the second century B.C.E. Elias Bickerman writes (*The Maccabees*, 25): "In the days of the Maccabees, as in the period of Moses Mendelssohn, the law interposed a wall between Jews and non-Jews.

DANIEL AS A WORK OF LITERATURE

Nothing brings people closer together than a common table." This is why modernist Jews reversed this order and established a *polis* in Jerusalem.

34. So Kaufmann, *Toldot*, faithful to his thesis that Daniel A is a "mirror of exilic Judaism."

35. Ginsberg, "The Composition," 254.

36. Ibid., 249 n. 2. Ginsberg refers to the inscription of Antiochus I in F. H. Weissbach, *Die Keilinschriften der Achämeniden*, 132, and to E. Bickerman, "Notes on Hellenistic and Parthian Chronology," esp. p. 75 n. 16.

37. There is an ancient and famous parallel for this in the survival of the tribes of Israel (and of their names), united after the installation of the monarchy under Saul, David, and, in particular, Solomon—who nevertheless again divided his kingdom into provinces without respecting the traditional tribal geographical limits.

38. In this case the allusion was reinterpreted in the second century in light of the marriage of Cleopatra and Ptolemy V, and we add one more stratum to the final text.

39. Otto Plöger (*Theocracy and Eschatology*) argues this from the shift in Dan. 2 from the vision of Nebuchadnezzar to that of Daniel himself in vv. 19ff. Ch. 2 is thus a combination of Daniel A and Daniel B, which would give a valuable indication of the date of its last writing. In fact, Plöger sees in this chapter a thematic introduction on the model of Dan. 7, the purpose of which is to connect the two parts of the book from the very beginning (ch. 1 being a general introduction to the entire work). The discussion above on the bilingualism of Daniel reflects my agreement with Plöger's thesis.

We should note that Bickerman (*Four Strange Books*, 70) is also in agreement: "Composed under Nebuchadnezzar, revised under the successors of Alexander toward the end of the fourth century, the prophecy of Daniel was again adjusted some fifty years later to meet a new international crisis. In 252 Antiochus II of Syria married Bernice, daughter of Ptolemy II of Egypt" (vv. 41–43 are thus later additions). More recently, B. Childs points out the parallel between ch. 2 and 7 as well (e.g., the ten horns correspond to the ten toes; in 2:37 the kingdom is given to Nebuchadnezzar; in 7:27 this promise is transferred to the saints). In short, "7–12 extend the vision of chapter 2" (Childs, *Introduction to the Old Testament as Scripture*, "Daniel").

That the story reported in Dan. 2 was originally composed under Nebuchadnezzar (Bickerman's thesis) is highly improbable. The Babylonian king was seen by the Jews rather as an "archetype of evil," as J. J. Collins recalls in *The Apocalyptic Vision of the Book of Daniel*, 41. Collins adds, "However, there is evidence that during the Hellenistic period the Babylonians recalled the reign of Nebuchadnezzar as a golden age." (See Berossus and Megasthenes according to Jos., *C. Apion* 1.19).

40. Cf. my Commentary on Daniel, p. 44.

41. S. Niditch and R. Doran, "The Success Story of the Wise Courtier: A Formal Approach," 191.

42. Hermann Gunkel, *Einleitung in die Psalmen*, 32; Sigmund Mowinckel, "Psalms and Wisdom," 3 (1960).

43. W. Sibley Towner, "Poetic Passages of Daniel 1–6," 323, 324.

44. Ibid, 318, 325.

45. W. Lee Humphreys, "A Life-Style for Diaspora: A Study of the Tales of Esther and Daniel."

DANIEL IN HIS TIME

46. A. Aarne and S. Thompson, *The Types of the Folktale*; A. Lord, *The Singer of Tales;* V. Propp, *The Morphology of the Folktale*.

47. The categories of "tales of contest" for Dan. 2, 4, 5; and "tales of conflict" for Dan. 3 and 6 used by H.-P. Müller and J. J. Collins ought not to be pushed too far. See H.-P. Müller, "Märchen, Legende und Enderwartung"; Collins, *The Apocalyptic Vision*, 33ff.

48. Aage Bentzen, *Daniel*.

49. See F. Nötscher and J. Gottsberger, cited in Plöger, *Das Buch Daniel*, 59.

50. Rowley, *Darius the Mede*, 268–69.

51. H. L. Ginsberg, *Studies in Daniel*, 28.

52. Bentzen, *Daniel*, 35. The situation was one of professional jealousy rather than enmity toward the Jewish religion. G. Hölscher, "Die Entstehung," 113–38 presents the same argument.

53. One of the seven wonders of the world, it was the work of Chares, a pupil of Lysippus, who lived around 300 B.C.E.

54. Montgomery, *A Critical . . Commentary*, 194.

55. Bentzen adds to this already long list: Pliny 33.24; 34.9ff.; Letter Jer. 7.54ff.; Bel 7.

56. Polybius says that Antiochus IV shocked public opinion by dancing to the savage sounds of this instrument (31.4).

57. Bentzen, *Daniel*, 38.

58. C. Kuhl, *Altorientalische Texte zum Alten Testament*, 2nd ed., 273ff.

59. Bickerman, *Four Strange Books*, 99; cf., in a sense that is half literal, half figurative, the "fire" of the royal anger according to Ahikar 7. 95-110 (*ANET*, 428–29).

60. New strata were added after that date, as seen in two Greek versions and the secondary versions based on them. There is, e.g., a prayer of the three companions in the fiery furnace (vv. 24–90 of the enlarged text), which probably comes from a Semitic original.

61. Ginsberg cites, among other parallels, Sib. Or. 7. 39.

62. Ginsberg, *Studies in Daniel*, 6; cf. Dan. 7.27b. His thesis, discussed above, is that there were "residual Median and Persian kingdoms" during the entire Greek period.

63. Ibid., 9.

64. See E. Sellin, *Einleitung*, 153ff.

65. Ginsberg, *Studies in Daniel*, 21. There is a shift, as G. Hölscher ("Die Entstehung," 120) has shown, from the destruction of kingdoms in the first level to the destruction of kings in the second (vv. 20b, 24b).

66. Ginsberg cites seven precise linguistic comparisons, proposed by Hölscher, between the additions to ch. 7, on the one hand, and chs. 8–12, on the other (*Studies in Daniel*, 30).

67. See my Commentary on Daniel (intro. to ch. 7). Z. Zevit, "The Structure and Individual Elements of Daniel 7," thinks it is rather the angel Gabriel: see 9:21, which refers back to 7:13, with 8:16 as a transitional text. Some rabbinic sources precede Zevit in this reading.

68. W. D. Davies, *The Setting of the Sermon on the Mount*, 226.

69. Ibid., 227, citing D. Barthélemy and J.T. Milik, *Qumran Cave I*, 117.

70. See ch. 6 below on the son of man, under "From the Adamic to the Davidic."

71. Ginsberg, *Studies in Daniel*, 33.

72.   On Ginsberg's thesis that vv. 17 and 18 belong to two different literary levels, see my remarks on Dan. 10, below.

73.   Vv. 1, 2a, 2b, 13, 15, 17, 26.

74.   Vv. 1a, 1b, 2a, 2b, 3, 4, 6, 7, 15, 20.

75.   Vv.1, 2a, 2b.

76.   Vv. 15, 16, 26, 27.

77.   In v. 15 the word designates the human appearance of an angel; in the other verses the term keeps its traditional sense of vision.

78.   Of the five occurrences, the first and the last are similar and bracket the chapter. Daniel "tries" to understand (v. 5), but understanding is beyond human capabilities (v. 27). At the heart of the chapter (vv. 16–17) the order is peremptory and repeated in similar form: "Understand!" Daniel's attempts are pathetic: he searches for comprehension (v. 15 gives the only noun use of the notion). Once again, the literary structure seems to answer to a clearly established plan.

79.   Thus, Emil Fackenheim *(God's Presence in History*, 39) establishes the distinction between "revealed and hidden," on the one hand, and "explained and inexplicable," on the other. "There may . . . be revelation without explanation." Nevertheless, the "inexplicable" must be "understood." See Dan. 9:23; 12:8, 10; Job 37: 23; Prov. 20:24. Job, for example, knows that he *must* find the key to his mystery and he is tortured by his inability to do so. He finally cries: "I had heard of thee by the hearing of the ear, but now my eye sees thee" (42:5). See A. LaCocque, "Job and the Problem of Evil" and "Job or the Impotence of Religion and Philosophy." Similarly Jacob, at least before he is called Israel, knows that he does not know (Gen. 32:30–31).

80.   See my Commentary on Daniel (esp. Dan. 7). See also Ezek. 40:3 and Zech. 1:8–10; 2:4.

81.   This division into two literary levels affects the statistical situation discussed above thus: instead of 7 occurrences of the word *vision* there are 6 (two times three) in the first level. Consequently, even without the second level the text retains its structural majesty.

82.   Ginsberg, *Studies in Daniel*, 41ff.

83.   For a detailed critical study of section (b), see LaCocque, "The Liturgical Prayer in Daniel 9."

84.   Ginsberg, *Studies in Daniel*, 34.

85.   The anonymous angel? Gabriel? See below.

86.   An alternative translation can be found in my Commentary on Daniel *ad loc.*

87.   Particularly since the original Aramaic of the verb *lemahziq* of 11:1 would correspond to *limegabbér*, the root of which contains the name Gabriel (Ginsberg, *Studies in Daniel*, 46–47).

88.   Ibid., 35–36.

89.   Ibid., 36–37.

FOUR

Apocalyptic Characteristics in Daniel

THE APOCALYPTIC GENRE IN THE BOOK OF DANIEL

Daniel, especially in its second part, chapters 7–12, is an apocalyptical book. There are as many definitions of the term *apocalypse* as there are biblical critics. Today some long-standing judgments are being questioned. Two opinions in particular appear more to beg the question than to serve as proof. The first holds that apocalyptic was a new phenomenon in the second century B.C.E.; the second, that this literary genre, unprecedented in Israel, was born of foreign, particularly of Iranian, influences.

The term *apocalypse* (*apokalupsis*) originates in the Greek name for the last book of the New Testament (see Rev. 1:1). It has been extended to a particular literary genre, the existence of which begins, in its narrow sense, in the third or the second century B.C.E. It generally includes a collection of visions interpreted for the seer—who is often an antediluvian hero—by an angel. The vision often concerns the succession of historical epochs from a given beginning (coinciding, e.g., with the times of the legendary author of the book) up to a moment of crisis during which the real author lived.[1] When historical authenticity ceases in the text, it is an indication that the author is passing from retrospective chronology to mystical speculation.[2]

But, to return to the nomenclature of this literary genre, what does the word *apokalupsis* mean in this context? For the ancient translator Theodotion, God in Daniel 2:28, 29, 47 is *apokaluptôn mustèria*; he renders the Aramaic root *gl'* in Greek with the meaning of "the manifestation by God of secrets unknowable by natural means" (see Dan. 2:19, 28, 30, 47; 10:1). This concept is also found in the apocryphal writings. The Testaments of the Twelve Patriarchs, for example, show angels interpreting divine mysteries (T. Reub. 3:15; T. Jos. 6:6). Other examples can be found in Enoch 1:2; 72:1; 74:2; 75:3; 79:2–6; 81:1 (in Enoch 46:3 this role is taken by the son of man).[3]

These revelations are organized along two axes, according to J. J. Collins: a temporal axis (eschatological salvation) and a spatial axis (the world of the supernatural).[4] Although these two axes are not mutually exclusive, Daniel accentuates the temporal one. History is divided into periods, and it is envisaged in its entirety, from beginning to end. Thus divine revelations apply to all three of the larger divisions of history:

The past: major events are presented as yet to come, and their unfolding is predicted (see Jub. 2ff.; Apoc. Abraham 23–32; Enoch 85–90; 2 Enoch 23–25; 2 Bar. 53–59; Sib. Or. 3.819ff).

The present: visions concern supraterrestrial things (as in Enoch 14:8–36:4; 64–69; T. Levi 2:7–3.8; 2 Bar. 2–17).

The future (eschatology): there are messianic events, the ultimate victory of the righteous, the conversion of the surviving Gentiles, the new Jerusalem, resurrection, individual judgment, the ultimate fate of the righteous and of the wicked, and the fate of the world.[5]

What the apocalyptist attempts to sketch, then, is a veritable world history. He tries to show that all events from the "beginning" fit perfectly into a construction that is not only majestic but divine. Nothing is superfluous in this construction, and nothing is missing.[6] The "mystery" inherent in things is unsoundable only because men lack clairvoyance. In contrast, the fathers were great because they had the benefit of this prophetic spirit. They had a total vision of history from alpha to omega, while history was manifest in the events of their time. As the traditional teaching of the synagogue said, not only did God have the animals parade before Adam to see what name he would give to each of them; he also showed Adam *dôr, dôr, wedôrshayw*—all the generations to come, with their exegetes.

Daniel constitutes the apocalypse par excellence in the Hebrew Scriptures, but it would be a mistake to think it unique. Before Daniel other texts that were apocalyptical in the strict sense had been written and accepted into the canon of the Bible; for example, Ezekiel 38–39; Zechariah 1–8; 9–14; Joel 3; Isaiah 24–27. Furthermore, it is important to note that the apocalyptical genre is represented above all outside the canon, for it was regarded with suspicion by the Pharisees, who were responsible for establishing the canon in the first century of the Common Era. According to Rabbi Akiba, anyone who reads the apocalypses forfeits his place in the world to come. This is why some books written in Aramaic or even in Hebrew—certain of them even before 70 C.E.[7]—were rejected as "not soiling the hands."[8] This did not prevent other apocalyptic writings from appearing after 70 C.E., however.[9]

We can speak, then, of a prolific production of apocalyptical literature during the Hellenistic and intertestamental periods as an instrument of reaction against and resistance to Hellenistic culture during that period. We need to note the historical context of this literature. As we have seen in chapter 1, Judaism[10] was then undergoing one of the gravest threats to its existence. The *oikoumènè* instituted by Alexander the Great brooked no exceptions. As "the sound of the horn, flute, lyre, sambuca, psalterium, bagpipe, and every sort of musical instrument" was heard, men of all peoples, nations, and languages were to prostrate themselves and worship the golden statue set up by the universal sovereign (Dan. 3:4–5).[11] The central powers, which considered themselves charged with the noblest of humane and humanist missions, had no choice but to take anyone who refused to fall down and worship the statue and throw him into the fiery furnace with no further ado (Dan. 3:6). A spoilsport of this sort was intolerable: he refused to laugh with everyone else; he wept at all the most inconvenient moments. In the hour of the triumph of humanity, the *Kultur* had become irresistible—as irresistible as an instrument for torture that had been heated seven times hotter than usual (Dan. 3:19). This misfit, ignoring the triumphal chanting to celebrate an apparently universal harmony, wept for a profaned temple. All eyes shone, reflecting the light of the torches brandished by the followers of the New Order; he alone refused to see their light, but he felt the heat of their flames as they bit into his flesh.[12]

The gap widened ineluctably. On the one hand, there were the false promises of a world that refused to recognize its profound corruption and its approaching collapse; on the other, a Judaism disillusioned because the messianic age announced by the prophets of the Exile turned out to be so slow in coming. There was no one left who dared address the people and say, "Thus saith the Lord."There were no more prophets, and God no longer spoke; the Jews were undergoing the "eclipse of God," as Martin Buber put it (see Ps. 74:9; 1 Macc. 4:46; 9:27; 14:41).[13] The only possible way to confront the future was to dig into the past; the present remained resolutely mute. During this dramatic period the prophetic books were gathered and collected.[14] Thus Judaism opted decisively for its hopes, taking the current situation as deceiving.[15] The one and the other could not possibly both be true. Consequently, what was needed was to recover the prophets' ability to look deep into things and events in order to see, as they had, beyond appearances to the signs of the kingdom of God.

The apocalyptist arrives on the scene at this point. He is not a prophet but an heir. He is a man torn between his faith in God and history's disproof. To be sure, the prophet also knows this feeling of being torn, but his certitude that God acts in the present transcends his doubt. For Jeremiah, "midnight" (*saphôn*) announces the coming morning, rather than signaling the triumph of darkness. (Jer. 1:13ff.).[16] The apocalyptist, who is incapable of going beyond the crucial times in which he lives, is obliged to remain at "midnight"; he attempts to see, within the anguish of the present moment, the revelatory and salutary aspects— the "prophetic" aspects—of suffering and death at "midnight." The prophet was a man of history; a man of dynamic time. By appealing to the past and weaving present events into the fabric of becoming, he was able to set his sights on the future, thus putting contemporary events into their proper perspective. Master of his own contradictions, he would keep a cool head—for the Lord of history was God—when there were so many reasons for doubt and for terror.

The apocalyptist did not have the same stature. He followed the great prophets of the Exile; he was their successor (he is often called their *epigone*).[17] He found himself constrained to recognize the objective truth that the announcement of the coming of the messianic age seemed contradicted by a current situation that was becoming increasingly dramatic. The influence of apocalyptic is clear when as Jürgen Moltmann writes, "Hope's statements of promise . . . must stand in contradiction to the reality which can at present be experienced."[18] The extreme tension between the promises of a Second Isaiah or Jeremiah, on the one hand, and the persecution of the Hellenists, on the other, put enormous

pressure on the apocalyptist. According to "the books," the present
time should be blessed; human beings should have entered into a new
eon in which God was universally recognized as the Most High God,
master of heaven and earth. For if the Word of God had any meaning, it
was here and now that it should be manifest. If the promise of the Kingdom was to come true, it was today that this should come to pass. The
apocalypse, unlike prophetism and "official" Judaism, no longer
appealed to the past, for the epoch of sacred history was seen as over.
Nor did it evoke a true future, for it proclaimed the arrival of the "day of
the Lord," after which there would be no more days.[19] Time was telescoped into the current moment. For the first time in biblical literature
of a historical dimension we find no mention of the Exodus, of the covenant of Sinai, or of the promise to David. The present moment filled the
horizon. Hence, time seemed suspended in mid-air; it was to be interpreted cyclically, beginning and ending with the present moment.
Unlike the prophet, working attentively to see the *ṣemaḥ* (the germinating branch) ripening in events,[20] the apocalyptist used a mythopoeic
language and categories of cosmological thought that bordered on pure
mythology. The prophet—even an "emotive" prophet like Jeremiah—
seems calm and sure in comparison with these tortured apocalyptists.
They have reached a decisive turning point: the new world—the world
of God[21]—*must* come. We can see the full impatience of modern times
here in the second century B.C.E. When the world around them proclaimed, "God is dead," the apocalyptists replied with a cry from the
depths of their tortured hearts. In spite of the composite and even
hybrid nature of the apocalypses,[22] it is difficult to say that their authors
prove anything, or that they preach, or even that they bear witness. Nor
do they report a message they have received and feel compelled to pass
on. They cry "No!" against tyrants; counter to the evidence, and in
spite of themselves, they proclaim the impossibility of the death of God.
They "see" the Ancient of Days in triumph, judging the world, and
arriving at his aims at the precise moment at which humanity thinks he
is on his last breath. Faith takes on a new meaning. It is no longer simple fidelity, firm assurance, certitude, and hope; it is also a mystical
vision of God's truth *against* human lies. Hence faith is no longer a matter of historically "making the truth"[23] in concert with creation, but of
adherence to an uncreated Truth that is divine in spite of its human
aspects; transcendent in spite of the immanence of our perceptions. It is
hardly surprising that this led to a dualism regarding both the universe

86

and history. This tendency was to reach extremes at Qumran. As it appears in Daniel, it is still tolerable, for it has not yet become a system or a dogmatic affirmation, but is rather a largely unexpected and even unconscious consequence of a message that was to peak elsewhere.[24]

Apocalyptic is not an academic exercise.[25] The Hitlers of the time triumph and even manage to "cast down" "some of the host of the stars" (Dan. 8:10). The righteous "are slain all the day long" (Ps. 44:22). The impasse is total. This extraordinary situation called for drawing extraordinary conclusions. Since it was impossible to move in any direction, they felt, God must be harassing us in this way so that we will look up, as in the times of the *neḥuštan* (the bronze serpent) set up by Moses in the desert (Num. 21:8–9). In the sixth century B.C.E., in the days of Nebuchadnezzar, the Israelites believed it was all over for them, that they had been abandoned by God and men alike. It was precisely at that moment that the three greatest prophets of Israel arose: Jeremiah, Ezekiel, and Second Isaiah. They transformed distress into hope; catastrophe into victory; impasse into a way out (Isa. 40:3; 43:16). In the second century the book of Daniel returns the reader to the situation in Babylon because events in its own time were at least as threatening as those of the Exile. God intervened at that time in all his power; God today will intervene in glory. The lesson of the Exile was that the dereliction of the people was also, simultaneously, theophany: *galuth* meant both exile and revelation ("And to whom has the arm of the Lord been revealed?"—*galah*—Isa. 53:1). Like a hand that disappears from our sight when it is brought close to our eyes, when the Kingdom seems the farthest away, it is the nearest to hand.

This dramatic conception of history and of the relations between God and humanity was not new. It is only the apocalyptical formulation of it that was to some extent new. There is present all through the Scriptures an "apocalyptical" conception of the dialogue between God and man. God loves and, *in consequence*, he is the enemy of man.[26] He reveals himself, *therefore* he hides himself (1 Kgs. 8:12); he pardons, *therefore* he punishes (Amos 3:2); he is far, *therefore* he is near (Jer. 23:23); he is without repentance, *therefore* he repents (1 Sam. 15:29, 11); he promises a posterity like the sands of the sea, *therefore* he demands the sacrifice of Isaac.

This means that it is difficult indeed to trace the exact limits of apocalyptic. According to Gerhard von Rad, "In speaking of apocalyptic, it is necessary to remember that no satisfactory definition of it has yet been achieved."[27] Furthermore, he adds, "Neither esotericism, nor the periodic concept of history, nor the idea of the transcendence of the realities of salvation, nor the explanation of canonical texts, nor pseudo-nymity, nor the interpretation of dreams, nor accounts of celestial voyages, nor historical accounts in the style of predictions are traits specific to apocalyptic."[28]

In this negative manner von Rad gives a list of the characteristics of the apocalypse which, although they are not determinant when taken separately, are nevertheless impressive when they come together in one literary genre. Johannes Lindblom believes that the identity of apocalyptic resides in transcendentalism, mythology, a cosmological orientation, a pessimistic treatment of history, dualism, the division of time into periods, the doctrine of the two eons, number play, pseudo-ecstasy, artificial claims to inspiration, pseudonymity, mystery, and more.[29] H. H. Rowley considers these characteristics as more accidental than essential, and he later remarks that

> in all these works . . . coming from the second and third centuries B.C., we see the emergence of ideas which are found in the New Testament. All are concerned with the end of the age and the dawn of a new age and with the destiny of the righteous and the evil, but all manifest a certain fluidity in their thought. They build freely on the basis of ideas culled from the Old Testament or from one another, but the building of each rears a character of its own, and each contributes something to the stream of ideas that flowed into the New Testament.[30]

The validity of several of these traits of apocalyptic merits discussion—particularly that of dualism, determinism, and transcendentalism, which have become, in the opinion of many critics, the weaknesses of a minor literature.[31] Recently, Collins has given a more accurate and subtler definition: " 'Apocalypse' is a genre of revelatory literature with a narrative framework, in which a revelation is mediated by an otherworldly being to a human recipient, disclosing a transcendent reality which is both temporal, insofar as it envisages eschatological salvation, and spatial insofar as it involves another, supernatural world."[32]

As far as Daniel is concerned, the spatial axis is scarcely sketched in. Thus we need to turn instead to the question of salvation in history.

One of the most delicate problems is that of the position of the apocalyptic vis-à-vis history. We have already seen two aspects of this question: first, the apocalyptist attempts to elaborate a theology of universal history; second, he reduces past and future to an instant that is supposed to contain them both. What are the reasons for these contradictory tendencies?

I have insisted on the polemical character of Jewish apocalypse. It was an instrument of propaganda and of resistance in the hands of utopists in their struggle against Hellenism and its cultural and religious totalitarianism. Thus, for example, contrary to the philosophy that surrounded them and was oriented toward success and the "greater life," the pious in Judea asserted that God was at the origin of all historical events, even the most painful or the most mysterious ones. The very raison d'être of apocalypse is the conviction that God has a plan to unify human history, a plan that needs to be discovered, for it constitutes the secret of the universe. In this fashion history is both polarized by a final and historical coming, and suspended in the eternity of divine knowledge and wisdom. This is why the kingdom of God transcends history but is inserted into history in the reign of the saints (Dan. 7). This explains the synchronism of the apocalyptical vision. Mysteriously, there is a concordance between heaven and earth; between the phenomenon and the epiphenomenon. As M.-J. Lagrange writes, "Whereas in natural evolution things go from sprout to full bloom and then to death, here everything lives at the same time, and the future already exists."[33] Therefore, there is a "temporal" concomitance in defeat and ultimate victory that corresponds to the "spatial" concordance of heaven and earth.

Nothing could be more foreign to Hellenistic thought. But, as is often the case, the adversary imposes his set of problems and his categories, at least in the form of questions to be answered. By its "ecumenical" pretensions Hellenism forced Israel to enlarge its conception of history and of the universe. Also, "nations" such as Babylonia, Media, Persia, and Macedonia (the four kingdoms of Dan. 2 and 7) had become too powerful and their influence over the destiny of the Jews too great—if not even determinant—for Judaism to ignore them completely. Moreover, political and economic power was not all that was involved. Alexander had thrown something new onto the scales: a universal doctrine. It was inevitable that Judaism would have to confront this claim to total sovereignty and oppose it to the concept of the Most High God, creator of heaven and earth, Lord of the world, he who "removes kings and sets up kings" (Dan. 2:21; see, in Daniel A, 2:37; 4:31, 34; 5:18, 23; 6:27). A dynastic question set YHWH against the powerful of this world. From the second century B.C.E. to the second century C.E., Judaism affirmed that there is no other *kyrios* but the Living God. Because they judged that this cause was worth the sacrifice of their lives, Jews by the thousand died a martyr's death.

What was at stake was the very soul of Israel. For, faithful to its iconoclastic vocation (or, if you prefer, its "antireligious" vocation), the Jew refused to see the contingent enthroned as the absolute. In two different forms Daniel A and Daniel B raise the same protest against the divinization of man. One thing alone could save Nebuchadnezzar from the catastophe of his own making: humility (Dan. 4:24, 31, and esp. v. 34). All systems are rejected as enslaving and dehumanizing. All dictatorships are denounced, even—or especially—the ones that proceed from a humanistic idealism. Human liberty lies only in obedience to God.

The exclusive sovereignty of God over the universe found perfect expression in the complex theologico-ritual system of the royal cult of Zion. To be sure, the prophets had not completely accepted this system. They had shown its dangers, citing the sad example of most of the kings of Israel and of Judah. The cosmological basis of the feast gradually dominated its "Yahwist" historicization. But the myth of a warrior God (celebrated in epic hymns) had become after the Exile much less harmful for the good reason that there were no more kings in Israel. That there was a cause-and-effect relationship between the disappearance of royal power and the resurgence of this myth is proven by the exilic theologians' newly found freedom to use the image of kingship. Second Isaiah in particular uses (and without ambiguity) the model of the celebration of a royal enthronement (Isa. 42:10–16; 43:16–21; 51:9–11; 58:7–12).

I shall return in the following chapter to the devaluation of myth, which made it a tool useful to apocalyptic. The resurgence in apocalyptic of the royal cult of Zion, however—which in the past had been so open to the influence of cosmology—cannot be explained only by negative arguments, as does Paul Hanson.[34] The use of the pattern of a royal enthronement is more than a way to get around unfavorable political contingencies. It is also more than a simple means of expression adopted by a class oppressed by the *Realpolitik* of the socioreligious party in power. The ceremonial context of the royal enthronement of God is not just one language among others. The theme is central in the apocalypse. It is even, in my opinion, more primitive than that of eschatology. In the time of the apocalyptists, as in the preexilic and exilic periods, eschatology sprang from the cult. The opposition that Hanson establishes between a royal and priestly theology, on the one hand, and a prophetic theology, on the other, is too radical. For me, the proof of this is the exilic and preexilic use, by the prophets, of the royal feast of Zion (e.g. Isa. 6–11).[35]

It is particularly interesting to note that even in the absence of the temple and its liturgy, the cultic foundation remained solid. Thus the book of Daniel, in the midst of persecutions in a Jerusalem in which the temple had been profaned, takes the traditional feasts as its axes,[36] and its central chapter (chap. 7) presents the coming of the son of man as a royal and priestly enthronement. The apocalypse sees all of history as a dynastic quarrel between God and the false pretenders to the universal throne. There is thus much merit in presenting Jewish apocalyptic (as does Yehezkel Kaufmann[37]) as born from the awareness of this violent break between the kingdom of heaven, in which the true God reigns (albeit as yet invisibly), and the kingdom of the nations, where the Jews were prisoners and subject to a visible and idolatrous regime. The kingdom of nations had no reality; the other kingdom was the only truth there was. This explains the tendency, from the time of Ezekiel and of Zechariah, to represent God surrounded by his many servants. The setting is a royal and universal court, and what is emphasized is the cosmic dimension of Israel's struggle against idolatry.

URZEIT-ENDZEIT

The dialogue between God and Israel should be seen as an ellipse. One of its poles is God's covenant with the nation and the other his covenant with the dynasty of David. The first had its historical center at Shechem and it underlay the confederation of the tribes (Josh. 24; Judg. 9; 1 Kgs. 12).[38] Its view of history was open: successive events are kerygmatic, unheard of, charged with ever-new meanings, and they lend themselves to a cumulative count. An agreement of this sort needs to be renewed periodically, for there are moments when it is put to the test by events;[39] it has to be brought up to date.[40]

The second focal point of the ellipse is Jerusalem. It celebrates the kingship of YHWH over Zion with his anointed seated on a throne at his side.[41] By definition, this kingship must be lasting, a symbol of stability in the midst of the transitory. Here, history is considered as possessing an unconditional constant that underpins circumstantial variations. Whether it is considered at its beginning, in its unfolding, or at its end, the Omega moment is always present, waiting only to be manifest in all its glory. Thus a third level of correspondence, of *coincidentia oppositorum*, is added to the other two. Not only is there mutual exchange between heaven and earth and between defeat and victory, but also—and especially—between *already* and *not yet*.

Contrary to Hanson's view, the prophets were not totally opposed to this royal ideology. The prophet Nathan played a decisive role in the elaboration of the Davidic mystique. This mystique affirmed the durability of God's choice, the stability of his providence, and the continuity of history. Even when events seemed to contradict the validity of this concept, prophetic faith maintained the organic unity of this *Heilsgeschichte*. It discovered the message in what seemed mute, meaning in the absurd, and light in darkness. It adopted as its own the metaphor of the mythic—or rather, transhistoric—confrontation between creation and chaos, and it refused to separate the sacred from the profane, good from evil, or good fortune from adversity (see Isa. 45:7). God is in *creatio continua*; the divinity is experienced in an environment of death. "The morning is nigh."

The person of the king is at the heart of the myth and ritual that celebrates the victory of God the creator and sovereign. The "Anglo-Scandinavian" school saw clearly that in Israel the king was the pivot around which the combat of God and his saints against the forces of chaos ceaselessly turned.[42] In this context one of the "original" features of the apocalypse is pointing out that the victory of God supposes the presence of enemies to defeat. *There are* enemies, friends of chaos, who prevent creation from being completed. The more these evil powers are at work, the more God must also become involved in the battle. In other terms, the farther away he seems, the closer he is. Thus it is with his Kingdom.[43]

Before the rise of apocalyptic this idea had already existed in Israel in a liturgical form. It was above all when historical phenomena no longer permitted a simple affirmation of the victory of God over chaos that Israel continued to proclaim liturgically—hence, concretely—the king, conqueror of his enemies and of the entire universe.[44] The sovereign of Israel, the representative and the substitute for his people, already belongs, in a liturgical sense, to the world "on high." This is why he received ornaments, anointing, and appropriate foodstuffs during the ceremony; he is "son of God" and he sits on the divine throne.[45]

As it happened, the nations were to deprive Israel of more than the normal course of its history: they were to refuse it the refuge of liturgy as well. Nonetheless, even when the liturgy had been made impossible—by exile into a foreign land, by the destruction of the temple, by the vacancy of the royal throne, by the loss of national independence, followed, after a semblance of restoration, by the profanation of the Holy Place that Daniel calls "the abomination of desolation"—the feast of enthronement did not fall into disuse. It became clandestine and literary, arising here and there in preapocalyptical works,[46] then in works that were openly apocalyptical. Their authors said aloud and openly what was believed tacitly in the pious milieu of the people. It was at the level of history or of time that God would be the conqueror, as the prophets had asserted. The sovereignty of God the Creator must necessarily pass through the enthronement of man;[47] at that point, the world would come out of the darkness and pass into life.

It is impossible to pass over the background of this hope, which lies in the god of Sumer, Babylon, and Canaan, who dies and returns to life. The triumph of life over death in nature was celebrated by all the peoples of the ancient Near East. Israel stands apart from its neighbors in that, for it, this process was neither cyclical nor magic. The drama takes place *within* history, and will be resolved *be-aharit ha-yamim* (at the end of these days). Not that the end is indefinitely postponed, but the sense of the end of time should not be overly emphasized. We can, in fact, understand the prophetic expression as designating a historical event that will conclude the present period, each time, in a fashion that is decisive and conclusive, ultimate and eschatological—even if it is to be followed by a new era that in turn is fixed on its own omega point. The prophetic perspective is, in general, teleological. All events have a meaning, which will only be fully manifest in the "last" event. This will be the end point of a trajectory that we can discern only partially, in segments that make no sense, as our days pass. It is in light of the Exodus that the years in Egypt become meaningful; it is in light of the Conquest that the forty years in the desert are charged with meaning; it is in light of the return from Exile that the "seventy years" of the Babylonian captivity are interpreted as a punishment, but not a divine rejection. The Exodus, the Conquest, and the restoration are *aharit ha-yamim*. The prophets are convinced that they are en route to the definitive end of history (e.g.,

Isa. 2:2–5, 9–21; Zeph. 1:14–18; Jer. 25:30–38; 31:31–34; Ezek. 36:26; 37:1–14). In general, however, they do not speculate about it; and they take the announcement of the Day of the Lord, for example, not as an occasion for mystical flights, but to call to repentance here and now (Amos 5:18ff.; Isa. 2:11ff.; Zeph. 1:14ff.; Jer. 30:5–7; Joel 1:15).

In the temple of Jerusalem, however, there was less reserve concerning these matters. Around the royal ideology there developed—gradually, according to Sigmund Mowinckel[48]—a veritable cosmic eschatology that might even be called preapocalyptic. It was in fact taken up again by apocalypse, after it had permeated priestly sources such as P, Ezekiel, and proto-Zechariah. It is good to keep this important problem in mind; we will return to it in the last chapter to define it more clearly in connection with the figure of the son of man. Its contextual foundation is still that of the cult in Jerusalem. In this perspective, at the ultimate point in history, the eschatological king is crowned, and the kingdom of Israel becomes *tel qu'un lui-même enfin l'éternité le change*—the one into which at last it is changed by eternity (Mallarmé). In the meantime, all Israelite sovereigns are incarnations of the metaphysical qualities of the eschatological king. These transcendent attributes are described as demonstrated facts (although they are articles of faith) as follows:[49]

"The Lord's anointed" is "the *breath* of our nostrils, . . . under his shadow we shall *live*" (Lam. 4:20). He is "the *lamp* of Israel" (2 Sam. 21:17). Psalm 72:15–16 expresses the wish: "Long may he live. . . . May there be *abundance* of grain in the land . . . and may men blossom forth from the cities like the *grass* of the field!" The king has curative powers, and like God he is supposed to "kill and to make alive" (2 Kgs. 5:7). "My lord the king is like *the angel of God* to discern *good and evil*" (2 Sam. 14:17). He is "our shield" (Ps. 84), just as God himself is "a shield" (v. 11); cf. Pss. 89:19; 47:10.

The emphasized terms refer directly to the *Urzeit*. The inescapable conclusion is that the king of Israel is none other than the "son of Adam," the "son of man," the "image of God." It is as such that he receives the mandate and the power to dominate the universe (cf. Gen. 1:28). The ties between the royal ideology and the concept of primitive man are clearly expressed in the portrayal of the myth of primitive man found in Ezekiel 28:11–19. We might also note the universal wisdom of Adam according to Job 15:7–9, or that of the kings and the princes according to Proverbs 8:15–16, where the speaker is shown as "rejoicing

in his inhabited world and delighting in the sons of men" (Prov. 8:31).[50]
In Jewish literature after the second century B.C.E. the linking of the
king and Adam underwent a remarkable development, as in such texts
as Sirach 49:16: "Adam holds pre-eminence over all creation" (ca. 190–
180); Philo, *De Virtutibus* 203 (before 50 C.E.); Luke 3:38.[51]

Obviously, all this ought to be taken into consideration for a reading of Daniel 7:13ff. We should note an important element: the reconciliation of the two aspects of the covenant mentioned above. The figure
presented as like a son of man in Daniel 7:13ff. (the Davidic covenant) is
none other, in his collective dimension, than the people of the "saints of
the Most High" (Dan. 7:27; covenant with the nation).[52]

A fourth level of correspondence completes the list: the relationship
between the individual and the community—or what has come to be
called, after Wheeler Robinson popularized the expression in biblical
critical circles, the concept of "collective personality." The notion is
extremely old; it is simply reutilized by the apocalyptist. It takes on a
great importance here: following H. H. Rowley, D. S. Russell uses it to
explain the pseudonymity of most of the apocalypses.[53] Their authors,
he says, were conscious of belonging to a line that went back to Enoch,
Moses, Ezra, and Daniel. They were the heirs of these ancient heroes;
they represented these seers and their traditions.[54]

DUALISM AND DETERMINISM

It is in this perspective of *Urzeit-Endzeit* that dualism, one of the
most surprising characteristics of Jewish apocalyptic, should be examined. We can see traces here of an evident Hellenistic influence on the
Judaism of the second century B.C.E. As Claude Tresmontant has said,
"The Hellenic conception of the world was, it seems, haunted by a natural pessimism, warped by what one might call a Manichaeism before
the fact. Dualism appears as one of the congenital characteristics of
Greek philosophy: an opposition between the perceptible world and the
intelligible world, between matter and form; between the body and the
soul, action and contemplation, workers and the men of leisure."[55] To
Tresmontant, this should be contrasted with classical Hebraic thought
(as represented by the Torah and the prophets), which was monist as
well as monotheist. He writes elsewhere:

> Man is not, in biblical thought, *pars divinae essentiae*. He is created
> by God. Souls are not preexistent, since they are not of divine

95

essence. They are created. Man is not a soul fallen into a body. God created corporeal man. The body is nothing different from the man, nothing different from the soul. Man is a living soul, he *is* flesh, and these are one and the same. . . . Holiness is not a fact external to this material world, but a cooperation with the creative and redemptive work of God. . . . Biblical anthropology is a positive anthropology, delivered from the myth of preexistence, and of the fall, and of the transmigration of souls.[56]

In short, if an ontological dualism exists in Daniel, the book falls under its own condemnation of those who abandon their Jewish identity to become assimilated into other nations. But is it so?

It is true that the book of Daniel plays constantly on oppositions between polarized realities. It establishes a radical distinction between the power exercised by human monarchs and the true sovereignty of the On High; between the monstrous bestiality of the empires of this world and the rightful restorative humanity of the kingdom of God; between the barbarity of the persecutor and the patient fidelity of the persecuted; between this time of sorrow and tears and the coming felicity; between this life, destined for death (and often for violent death) and resurrection to a life that will know no end. This is hardly dualism. A simple recall of the historical circumstances in which apocalyptic arose invites the critic to a good measure of prudence, particularly since things are not simple on the level of the texts themselves. Dualism, transcendentalism, and determinism are more often than not immediately corrected by their antidotes.[57] We often have the impression that the author destroys with one hand what he has constructed with the other. We need, then, to pose the question of the author's intentions and of his ultimate aim.

The *Urzeit-Endzeit* complex permits one entry into the question. These extremes are not opposed in an implacable dualism; they are in correspondence with one another. There is a correspondence between heaven and earth, between the eternal and the transitory, the absolute and the contingent, the sublime and the quotidian, evident in such passages as Daniel 9:24ff.;10. The more one insists on one of these terms, the more the other is present. The Maharal of Prague said: The more the poles are pushed apart, the more they respond to one another.[58] This is the paradox of apocalyptic: the more history becomes catastrophic, the closer the kingdom of God becomes.[59] The book of Daniel takes us through a crescendo of horrors up to the coming of the son of man (Dan. 7) and to final resurrection (Dan. 12). Just as there is no resurrection without previous death, there can be no triumph of the son of man except after a provisory and deceptive victory of the forces of chaos. For the son of man is enthroned, precisely, in order to judge, condemn, and destroy the beast, and thus to make humanity emerge out of the cursed cadaver: the carcass of the lion gives honey (Judg. 14:9).

This schema of the transition from death to life was current even before Daniel, in particular in apocalyptical or preapocalyptical texts (Ezek. 38–39; Joel 3:9–11; Zech. 14:1–3). It is hardly surprising to find it after Daniel, fully developed in the Dead Sea Scrolls.[60]

We need to ask, then, whether this dialectical characteristic comes from foreign influences on Jewish apocalyptic. I shall turn to this question soon; in the meantime it should be noted that these influences are undeniable as far as formal aspects of the apocalyptical genre are concerned,[61] but that their influence on its contents should be weighed with great care.[62]

In this connection "dualism" receives a fatal blow from the fact that God is the first victim of the suffering that his people undergo. He is *with* the companions of Daniel in the fiery furnace; he is *with* Daniel in the lions' den; his honor is at stake in the fate of Israel (represented by the four exiled Jewish princes). Furthermore, we need to agree on the meaning of the term, for there are different sorts of dualism. John Gammie distinguishes at least ten.[63] According to Gammie there is a spatial dualism in Daniel (see 8:9–14; 10:10–21, and the Aramaic expression, "God of heaven" in Daniel A). Above all, dualism in Daniel is ethical (although this is more true in the spirit of the book than in its vocabulary). In Daniel 12:10 the dualism is counterbalanced in Daniel 9 by "a profound corrective to . . . [the danger] of self-righteousness" (Gammie, p. 378). There is not the least trace of ontological or cosmological dualism.

The same caveat can be found in authors as different as J. A. Montgomery, H. H. Rowley, and Svend Holm-Nielsen.[64] As early as 1927 Montgomery insisted on the Jewish character of Daniel, in contrast to other apocalypses. Its "dualism," he says, is moral, not ontological. Its "determinism" does not lead to fatalism. Repentance is not excluded (Dan. 4:25–27), and the prayers of chapters 2 and 9 show that dualism can be transcended. The author is concerned with human history; resurrection will take place on this earth, as will the coming of the eschatological kingdom.[65]

97

H. H. Rowley offers this warning—or, if you prefer, this appeal to good sense:

> We cannot think of light that is not the negation of darkness, or of a good that is without its logical opposite evil. When we say that God is good, we mean that in Him there is no evil; when we say that He is light, we mean that in Him is no darkness. In that sense the idea of evil is logically involved in the affirmation of the goodness of God. But this is far other than affirming that evil is co-eternal with the goodness of God, or that from all eternity to all eternity it must be embodied in a personal being standing over against God. In that sense neither the apocalyptists nor Christian theologians have been dualists.[66]

I might note, to continue Rowley's thought, that Satan and Belial are totally absent in the book of Daniel.

In short, it seems that the apocalypse uses a foreign mold into which to pour its strictly Hebraic message. In doing so, it follows the example established by a long tradition, particularly in a domain that we have seen before—the royal ideology and its corollary, the myth of the victory of God over chaos.[67] Perhaps foreign influences are even more evident in Jewish apocalyptical works, but this is purely a question of intensity. In any event, despite the framework he borrowed from Babylonian and Iranian religions, the author of Daniel to a large extent maintained the prophetic affirmation that God's victory would be manifest in history.

Nevertheless, history is, paradoxically, poorly designed for this revelation. It is even inadequate by its nature, for it arises out of a poor choice, which permeates it from one end to the other. Here is where apocalyptic eschatology differs from prophetic eschatology. The eschaton now has, so to speak, one foot in history and one foot in metahistory. Inaugurated in history, it marks the end of history and its accomplishment and also the advent of the transhistoric. Time and eternity, however, are consubstantial. One cannot affirm an unqualified "transcendentalism" (as does Lindblom, for example). As Russell has written, "In the apocalyptical writings, then, there is . . . a unity wider than that of a mere world history; it is a unity in which the temporal is taken up into the eternal by means of those moral and spiritual qualities which make up the purpose of God — a purpose which, whilst finding its actualization in history, must seek its justification beyond history."[68]

APOCALYPTIC CHARACTERISTICS

We might say that historical values are realized within temporal order, but that they require an eternal order for their interpretation and their justification. Indeed, the author of Daniel was so successful in maintaining the dynamism and the tension of this duality[69] that, as R. H. Charles affirms, "Daniel was the first to teach the unity of all human history, and that every fresh phase of this history was a further stage in the development of God's purposes."[70]

There are, however, certain statements in Daniel that come close to determinism (e.g., 4:14, 17, 22). Events are so far from being the effect of chance that they take place according to a plan predetermined by God, whose purposes are not our own (cf. Isa. 55:8). The apocalypse does not shrink from the scandalous statement — and it is painful to hear in an age after Auschwitz — that God is the author of the sufferings of innocent people. We have to admit that in apocalyptic, "history takes on a schematic, almost a mechanical, aspect."[71] How did the apocalyptist get to this point? He was led to it almost in spite of himself by a tradition that failed in two important ways. First, the framework of *Heilsgeschichte*, as we have seen, is here nearly nonexistent; the present moment was seen so strongly as the summit of the past that it to some extent swallowed up the past. Second, with the shift from prophetism to apocalyptic, there was a loss in the *pathos* that Abraham Heschel saw as one of the characteristics of prophetism.[72]

Once again, however, qualifications are decisively important. It is true that the apocalyptist disappears behind his work, but the *Sitz im Leben* of the genre itself offers a pathos that compensates for the objectivity of the author. It is true that the apocalypse is declarative, but it is also "performative."[73] Thus here "determinism" is not paralyzing. In point of fact, "apocalyptic determinism concerns only the external course of events. The fate of individuals is not predetermined."[74] The thought, once again, remains firmly Jewish. In the second century C.E. Rabbi Akiba, tradition says, stated: "All is foreseen, but free will is accorded" (*Pirke Aboth* 3.19).

When these necessary qualifications are respected, inquiry can continue within the biblical world. It is clear, however, that we are dealing with a process tending toward giving a cosmic dimension to sacred history. This process drags in its wake a more or less arbitrary division of time into periods (periodization), which also establishes a fixed framework into which contemporary events are forced (See, e.g., Jubilees; 1QS 10.3–8; Dan. 12:1, 4). But this rigidity is that of the liturgical

99

calendar itself (Jub. 6:32–38), and the resulting schematization of history is no odder and no more foreign in the apocalypse than it is in the cult. The telescoping of history into the instant is not a flight out of time any more than the liturgical *kairos*, which finds its natural place in the cultic eschatological present of the meeting with God. The instant is not a philosophical abstraction here, but the contemporaneity, the synchronism, of all events pertaining to salvation from alpha to omega. The covenant with the fathers, the Exodus, and Sinai are no longer evoked by the apocalypse, not because they were emptied of their substance, but because they are replaced by an event that concentrates all their meaning and that surpasses them. The eschaton is the omega of history toward which Abraham, the Exodus, Sinai, and the royal enthronement had been leading.[75] We shall return to this matter later.

It is true that the apocalyptists distance themselves from history in a way not encountered in the prophets, who were more politically involved and thus more distant from any sort of transcendent ideas. But the apocalypse, as we have seen, did not usurp the place of prophetism in Israel; it continued it, and it was conscious of going beyond it. The prophets had announced the birth of the Kingdom, but they failed to say, either out of ignorance or deliberately, that the Exile was a period of gestation that was to be followed by even more of the "pains of childbirth." This was the role apocalyptic took on. Apocalyptic stood as an interpretation of the prophecies and their dynamic vision of history. History was not to continue upward toward ultimate victory, as a superficial reading of the exilic oracles might have led one to think. To the contrary, it was to fall toward the final defeat, only beyond which — that is, beyond human history — would God accord a sudden, unexpected, and miraculous triumph. History had meaning only through this triumph, which, however, it was incapable of bringing about. The righteous had had an intuition of this from the beginning; the prophets had "seen" its pattern hidden in the fabric of history; the sages had already described the beatitude of the end. In the dramatic events they were living through, the apocalyptists recognized the last throes of a final struggle. They described what was to come in the following terms:

a) the arrival of bad times with corruption of all sorts;

b) God's intervention (in person, or through a Messiah);

c) the punishment of sinners (we have already arrived at the point at which it is too late for repentance);

d) the salvation of the righteous, who rejoice through all eternity.[76]

APOCALYPTIC CHARACTERISTICS

Time's clock reads midnight, that dead of night in which darkness is thickest and time vacillates between past and future, the accomplished and the unaccomplished, the already and the not yet. It is now too late to exhort people to convert and to resist the monster. This ambiguity is bearable only by its transitoriness and by its lack of duration, which already tears us out of history while history is still crucifying us. It permits the concomitance of contradictory affirmations:

a) all is written in the heavens (Jub. 2.1ff.; Dan. 4:15; 1QS 3.15, 16);

b) all depends on the faithfulness of Israel (Daniel *passim*); cf. Jub. 21:4.

The apocalyptist can go as far as the doctrine of double predestination (Jub. 10:5ff.) and still hold human beings responsible for their acts, for God's decree does not, paradoxically, prevent persons from acting freely and with full responsibility.[77] We are never very far from the more "orthodox" prophetic doctrine that states that men and women are the agents of history while God is its Lord, for he accomplishes his designs in history through his pious, his Hasidim.

To summarize: In the midst of the despair of the weak, the apocalyptists appealed to an "internal" view of events. Beyond appearances, we must look for signs of the kingdom of God. Thus, beyond the license proudly enjoyed by the powerful of this world, whose power seems unchecked and unlimited, there is the sovereignty of God, who alone "removes kings and sets up kings." It is also God's sovereignty that will "set up a kingdom which shall never be destroyed, nor shall its sovereignty be left to another people. It shall break in pieces all these kingdoms and bring them to an end, and it shall stand for ever" (Dan. 2:21, 44). The ultimate intention of the apocalypse is attained when the nations themselves, in the person of their most prestigious representatives, confess: "Truly, your God is God of gods and Lord of kings" (Dan. 2:47). There is therefore much truth in the thesis of Nils Messel, according to which there is a profound unity in Jewish eschatology: it all boils down to earthly hopes.[78] The world to come is not opposed geographically or spatially to the present world (seen in a dualistic perspective), but qualitatively (as a tension within a duality). The era of felicity will succeed the *time* of present suffering.

There is nothing in all this that is radically different from the rest of Scripture, unless it is that apocalyptic, for its own reasons, was led to employ frameworks and molds of contestable orthodoxy: dualism, predestination, determinism, ecstasy, calculations of the end of time,[79] individualism,[80] or even angelology.

ANGELOLOGY

The study of angelology in the book of Daniel calls, once again, for much prudence on the part of the critic. It is not really a novelty, for Scripture had often brought angels onto the scene.[81] They fill the space between God and men so that nothing truncates its continuity. Daniel gives them a personality, but they are never worshiped. They are not a hindrance to communication, nor are they indispensable and autonomous intermediaries (cf. Job 33:23).[82] Aside from Daniel, the only time an angel is sent on a clearly defined mission is in Joshua 5:13–15. Angelic apparitions cease after Elijah, for in classical prophecy it is the prophets who take the place of angels (see Hag. 1:13). Their reappearance in the books of Ezekiel and Zechariah announces the end of prophecy and the rise of apocalyptic: revelations are too profound to be grasped without divine explanation. In the period of the Second Temple angels fill the universe, in general keeping a low profile, however. Not so in Daniel, where the angel is a savior (3:25) and gives or transmits orders (4:14). For the first time entire chapters are devoted to an angelic message (11; 12). Here, also for the first time, tutelary angels are mentioned (e.g. 10.13; cf. the Septuagint of Deut. 32:8). This idea is taken up again in the apocryphal works, the Midrashim, and the Cabbala. As Edwyn R. Bevan notes in his commentary on Daniel 10:13, this belief is here presupposed and not defined; it is therefore already common at the time of Daniel. As it happens, in Parsiism, the *fravashis* are divine prototypes of all living beings; friends and protectors of men, they are created before the birth of men and they continue after their death. Sometimes they are stars (a trait that could be compared with Dan. 8:10–11; 12:3). Important rabbinic evidence indicates that this is a possible source of late Jewish angelology. Certain texts, in fact, speak to the Mesopotamian influence on Jewish angelology. In *Gen. Rab.* 48 and *Y. Rosh ha Shanah* 1.2, for example, we read, "The names of the angels were brought by the Jews from Babylon."[83]

In any event, there is a great sobriety in the use of notions of foreign origin. Furthermore, the development of angelology, like the "nonorthodox" categories discussed above, does not necessarily represent doctrinal verity in the eyes of the apocalyptist. These "curiosities" perhaps attract a disproportionate attention on the part of the modern reader. They belong in the literary genre used—i.e., in its formal texture.[84] As for the apocalyptical message itself, it is often superior to its expression.[85] It is form rather than content that constituted the greatest obstacle to the adoption of most of the apocalypses into the canon of Scripture.

FOREIGN INFLUENCES

The question of foreign influences on Jewish apocalyptic perhaps merits more systematic comment.

The presence of foreign influences has been remarked by the so-called "History of Religions" school (inaugurated by Hermann Gunkel, Wilhelm Bousset, Hugo Gressmann, and others). The phenomenon of borrowing is all the more probable, as far as Daniel is concerned, because the book was written at a moment in which Hellenism was at its height, both in Palestine and throughout the Mediterranean world from Rome to the borders of India. Greek ideas, but also Oriental ideas, circulated freely. Thus the division of history into specified periods (see Dan. 2; 7) had its origins in Babylon. Symbolizing succession in history by four kingdoms (Dan: 7; cf. T.Naph. 5:8) can also be found in Herodotus (1.95, cf. 130), Ctesias (688 F 1-8), and Polybius (38.22), speaking about Scipio, in 146 B.C.E. Even their being replaced by a fifth kingdom seems to have been a familiar theme. The symbol of the four metals of decreasing value (Dan. 2), can be found in Hesiod in the eighth century.

Daniel 2 is still based on the anthropomorphic symbol of the world seen as a microcosm. In Daniel 7 the same conception may underlie the notion of the son of man. The microcosm was an idea current in ancient astrology,[86] in Iran, and also in Orphism and in Hermetic speculation. Dualism, the resurrection of the dead,[87] the victory of the good god over the forces of evil, and angelology may also come from Iran. Even the cataclysmic type of eschatology found in the apocalypse is Iranian, according to some scholars.

The representation of the hereafter probably comes from Greek doctrines; divine inspiration and asceticism probably come from mystery religions. But, as Jean-Baptiste Frey says, "Many religious concepts were widespread in the ancient world in general, and were not the exclusive property of anyone. . . . As far as Parsiism is concerned, . . . one has to determine the age of the documents."[88] We should add, with

Martin Hengel, that Iranian eschatology was astrological, mythological, and dualist.[89]

Hengel points out the technique of the *vaticinium ex eventu* (foretelling after the fact) that frequently occurs in the apocalypse. Daniel offers excellent examples of this in chapters 7 and 11, and it can also be found in 1 Enoch 85–90, in the Assumption of Moses, and in the Sibylline Oracles, among other places. It is at the base of the Qumran peshers. The parallels with the Hellenistic period are impressive. They go from the "Demotic Chronicle" under the first Ptolemies of Egypt to the anti-Roman oracles of Asia Minor and Syria, examples of which can be found in certain of the Sibylline Oracles. Hengel traces the Israelite beginnings of this current in chronicle historiography under the Persian empire. But the genre as such had already existed in the Near East for a much longer time, as W. G. Lambert has shown, citing an Assyrian tablet of the seventh century that contains a refrain composed around the oracular phrase, "a prince will arise and rule for . . . years."[90]

The direction in which these borrowings took place appears beyond doubt. The movement is reversed, however, when we consider—again following Hengel—the Hellenistic parallels to the aretological genre represented in Daniel 2–6 (also 2 Macc. 3, the legend of Heliodorus, e.g.). As this literary type is already prefigured in 2 Kings 5; 20:1–11 (= Isa. 38), we must have an Oriental influence on spiritual and religious biography among the Greeks, rather than the reverse.

If questions of content have been left aside for ones of form, it is because inquiry fairly easily provides a positive solution to the latter, but is often inconclusive regarding the former. At the end of his examination of the extent of Persian influence on Old Testament thought, Peter R. Ackroyd concludes: "External influence may make itself felt, but internal developments are also of very great importance. In the event, there is likely to be a subtle inter-relationship between the two."[91]

Ackroyd is right. An example of this influence will also serve as an introduction to the next section of this chapter. The genre *vaticinium ex eventu* is ancient, as we have seen. As early as the Persian epoch the Chronicler's historiography imitates it in Israel. It reappears fully developed in Daniel. The chief characteristic of this genre is that the preoccupations to which it gives expression are organized as totally sequential events. Hence history completely fills space; it blocks the horizon. History is the scene in which all actions are played out, including judgment and its sequels, condemnation and salvation. In short, there is no room here for last things; eschatology is absent.

This is certainly not the case in the book of Daniel or in apocalyptic literature in general. The genre of the *vaticinium ex eventu* is thus not respected. It is transformed by the use the apocalyptists made of it. It is still recognizable in its form but no longer in its contents, since the human group and the religious tendency that the author of Daniel represents are totally different from those of the Chronicler and his party. They use the same tools, but in totally different ways. This is what we need to examine now. It was important, however, first to state clearly to what point literary forms had been adapted to other purposes and transformed by their borrowers.

BIFURCATION

No matter how one examines this question of borrowings from foreign cultures in the apocalypse of Daniel, the conclusion that I have suggested is inevitable. Whether we speak of "dualism," "determinism," or, as we have just seen, the eschatological vision of history, Iranian influences simply served as a ferment for a rediscovery of the parallel between the *Endzeit* and the *Urzeit*[92] In certain cases it led to a "dualist view of the world" that implied "a transcendental view of the coming kingdom."[93] In an attempt to show that apocalyptic is guilty of these charges, D. S. Russell insists that:

a) the transfiguration "thus wrought" is not evolutionary but cataclysmic;

b) supernatural powers, not historical process, bring about the resolution; the means are celestial and no longer human;

c) at this point, the outcome involves the individual's destiny rather than the community's. This includes the idea of resurrection and individual retribution.

All of this is true in part. But, first, the cataclysm of divine origin is not a notion foreign to the prophets (Amos 5:18; Zeph. 1:2-3, 18; Isa. 34; Jer. 25:15ff., Hag. 2:22; Joel 1-2). Second, in the book of Daniel final judgment is effected, not by God, an angel, or a pure spirit, but by "one like a son of man" who is identified with the historic people of the "saints of the Most High." Moreover, the scene takes place at least as much on earth and within history as in the heavens and in metahistory. We do not yet find here the distinction, apocalyptical or not—which

was to be made in certain books of the intertestamental period—
between the body and the spirit (or the soul).[94] The golden age to come
begins by being the final stage of human history on this earth. It
manifests the triumph of God *in* the triumph of Israel. (see Enoch 102:4-
11; 103–104; Wis. 2:1-5; 3:24). At that time, all that is good will be
established eternally, and all evil will be abolished forever. Inasmuch as
he represents this "finalist" comprehension of history, the apocalyptist
is the spokesman for a revolutionary conception in intellectual circles at
the time of the Second Temple. He takes a strictly eschatological theological position that contrasts with the priestly doctrine that has rightly
been called theocratic.[95] For the eschatological party, the most important event in the history of revelation remained in the future. This was a
path that some were to qualify as a wide breach in institutional walls.
For the idea of an "open" history of salvation, which implied an "open"
definition of the Holy Scriptures, ran headlong into the institutional
mentality for which *Heilsgeschichte* in its paradigmatic dimension had
already taken place. This was why they felt the time had come to fix the
canon of the sacred texts. No additional phenomenon of any decisive
influence on the relations between God and humanity was conceivable
during the current course of history.[96]

This last point of view is of course a reflection of Pharisaism (i.e.,
the Judaism that was to become "classic"). To be sure, history is not
considered static here either; all its evolution requires, however, is that
the rules of the Torah be adapted to new contingencies. Only one event
that could be qualified as new was still expected: the coming of the Messiah. But, on the one hand, it is difficult if not impossible to know what
the messianic era consists of; on the other hand, its originality in comparison with the rest of *Heilsgeschichte* was diversely interpreted by Talmudic scholars.[97]

This uncertainty is symptomatic. It betrays the truly difficult situation in which the rabbis found themselves, torn between the finality of
history and the decisive nature of Sinai. The only solution was to retain
the traditional expectation of the eschaton and at the same time to
reduce it to a relative status. At the time of Daniel, however, and even as
early as the time of the Chronicler, eschatology had almost disappeared
from the theocratic horizon. The restoration of the temple in 515 was
greeted as the only eschaton that was still to be expected. The kingdom
of God had descended on the sanctified and worshipful community of
Zion.

APOCALYPTIC CHARACTERISTICS

This was not the doctrinal position of everyone in Jerusalem. For centuries—from the fifth century to the coming of Christianity and of academic rabbinism—the triumphalist and theocratic proclamation was consistently rejected by Jews who were dead set against it. These "utopians" declared themselves incapable of distinguishing the signs of the presence of the kingdom of God in the Judea of their own days. Thus Judaism was torn by a profound crisis expressed, on the level of ideas, by radically different attitudes concerning the Hellenization of Palestine.

Some welcomed this philosophical, cultural, and social complex with enthusiasm. They saw in it a providential vehicle for the definitive triumph of the true law (*nomos*) of the humanized universe (*oikoumenè*)—that is, of the Torah of Moses.[98] Others rejected Hellenism as the most insidious and the most monstrous of Judaism's enemies. This group believed that no good would come of ideological commerce with the Greek and the Hellenized world. They preferred to wait with faith and courage for the final catastrophe that was to put an end to both this perversity and to history itself.

This so-called sectarian Judaism was "apocalyptic" in that it looked forward to the arrival of a decisive event in light of which history would finally reveal the meaning it had contained from the beginning. This Judaism was represented by a loosely defined party called the Hasidim in certain documents of the Second Temple.[99] Later, the torch would be picked up by the Qumran hermits and by the Christians of the primitive church. For them it was a mistake to confuse the current course of history with its normal course. Nothing could have been more abnormal; history had gone mad. Better, it was monstrous. Ferocious beasts imposed their law, and the law of Sinai was stalemated. Not that the law was relative or transitory; the theocrats' insistence on ritual observance was insufficient to establish the kingdom of God. What was needed was the arrival of another event, one that would—in accordance with the Torah, to be sure, but also transcending the Torah[100]—put an end to history by bringing it to its transfiguration. Apocalyptic was produced by the collision between the Torah as the presence of eternity and history as a caricature of God's governance.[101] The Torah was the charter of the Kingdom, but instead of sanctifying existence (as specified, e.g., in the Code of Holiness, Lev. 17–26), the Torah retreated before the progress of a more and more radical profanation. The point of no return had been reached. It was vain and self-deceptive to hope for a return of the preexilic "good old days" and a restoration of things as they had been. This world had chosen death, and apocalyptical hopes were pinned on the coming of another world; a new world.

The Torah is adapted to this transitory world. What it is to be in the world to come cannot be known and probably is not worth knowing. In any event, the apocalyptic texts do not speculate on this point, and they remain highly discreet concerning the real role of the Torah in this period of the end of time during which their authors believed they were living. Only primitive Christianity, convinced of being the bridge thrown between history and the kingdom of God,[102] was to draw conclusions of an extreme audacity from the impotence of both the Torah and human beings in a collapsing world. We need to emphasize, however, that far from mocking the ethics of the Torah, the apocalyptic "sectarians," both Jewish and Christian, were extremely demanding—to the point of demanding martyrdom for their communities. Moreover, these communities considered themselves as ultimate, charismatic, and prophetic[103]—in a word, messianic. They *were* the eschaton; an eschaton that was, paradoxically, both already realized and to come. It was inevitable, under these conditions, that the course of past history be seen as relative to the "absolute" of contemporary events. The shift from the collective to the individual goes hand in hand with this process. Even some representatives of paganism were challenged, on an individual basis, and brought to confession that the God of Israel was the one Lord. For Jeremiah, Nebuchadnezzar had received his reign from God, because that was God's will and his plan for the nations, especially for his people (Jer. 27). Daniel goes even further. Nebuchadnezzar is no longer an almost anonymous instrument: he must recognize the God of Israel and glorify him (Dan. 3:28-29). The universal password was: "Repent, for the kingdom of heaven is at hand" (Matt. 3:2).[104] It is addressed to the pagans as much as the Jews, but it also implies the rejection of the unfaithful Israelites as well as the unfaithful non-Jews.[105]

Is it possible to reach precise conclusions regarding the origins of apocalyptic in Israel? One of the most remarkable achievements of modern criticism concerning the apocalypse is to have shown its Israelite nature. Two fundamental principles serve as my point of departure in considering this question. The first, formulated by Russell, states that apocalypse is "a literature of the oppressed who saw no hope for the nation simply in terms of politics or on the plane of human history."[106]

APOCALYPTIC CHARACTERISTICS

This basic theme served to crystallize Hanson's thoughts in the work that he dedicated to the remote origins (the "dawn") of the biblical genre of apocalyptic. Hanson rightly sees the events of 587 as the precipitant that changed prophecy into apocalypse, for when Jerusalem fell into the hands of the Babylonians, "Israel's political identity as a nation comes to an end" and visionaries were gradually constrained to abdicate one of the principal dimensions of the prophetic role, "the translation [of prophecy] into historical events."[107]

The transition from prophecy to apocalypse occurred without a break, however. Furthermore, just as the prophetic vein in Israel was not reserved to a particular religious party, "Rabbinic texts and texts from pseudepigrapha alike can be cited to prove that no party within Judaism was bereft of the vision we associate with apocalyptic, nor did any sect or party fail to feel the tug of responsibility to the mundane world."[108] This important conclusion constitutes my second fundamental principle. To summarize, apocalyptical literature emanated from milieus that had been profoundly affected by the catastrophe of 587, and from men who were forced by circumstances to rethink their conception of history—in particular, what was contained in a hope for a final accomplishment of *Heilsgeschichte*. This wrenching theological revision was judged all the more necessary because those who undertook it saw themselves harassed by conservatives dreaming of a return to the situation that had prevailed before 587. As positions hardened, a particular sociological group gradually formed, the members of which were recruited from all levels of society. As the adepts of this group grew more and more isolated, their eschatological vision of history created the Hasidic party. Their organization into a party sui generis was the consequence of an increasing polarization of opinion in Judea at the time of the Second Temple.

Thus the problem of the birth of the phenomenon of apocalyptic is cast in totally new terms. In order to find its source we must look, not to enthusiasts who had lost the prophetic sense of history, but to the disciples of the great prophets; for example, to those who were responsible for the third part of the book of Isaiah and the second part of Zechariah. The apocalypse was born of men who had a vision of authentically prophetic inspiration. It was only the circumstances in which they lived that led them to detach their hope from all political applications and reorient it toward events of transcendent origin and cosmic significance.

In the eyes of the conservatives of the time this vision was subversive. On the level of ideas it threw into question established dogmatic positions; on the practical level it questioned the modus vivendi established between the Jewish community and the foreigners who held power. On a theological level, moreover, what was contested was no less than the validity of the revived cult and of the proclamation that the prophecies of restoration had been accomplished at the predicted time.

Some among the Israelites, in fact, adapted very well to foreign occupation. They even elaborated theological justifications of the status quo. To be sure, the Jewish community on its return to Zion was only a drop in the ocean of the various peoples; the nations held it to be insignificant. Some members of the community lost courage and developed an inferiority complex; others dreamed of the coming of catastrophic events that would overturn history and change the face of the earth. The conservative opinion was that in the purity of the temple and in its liturgy Israel was the incarnation on earth of the perfect theocracy. The rest did not matter. Political and social events in "this world" were powerless to change the fact that Israel was now and forever the kingdom of God inaugurated within the universe, for only within Israel was God worshiped and served with purity.

The Chronicler, for example, illustrates a "quasi total disappearance of the eschatological expectation,"[109] because for him Israel, in opposition to the renegade brothers in Samaria, constituted theocracy in this world. In short, "a provincial cultic community tolerated by the Persian Empire ... portrays history from Adam onwards as taking place all for her own sake!"[110]

Here we can arrive at the essential difference of interpretation separating the partisans of Israel as theocracy in action, on the one hand, and the utopians of an apocalyptical eschatology, on the other, if we compare their respective readings of Jeremiah's famous prophecy of the seventy years (Jer. 25:11-12; 29:10). For the Chronicler, the promise had been accomplished by Cyrus' edict putting an end to the Jews' forced exile in Babylon. This political act "made eschatological hope pointless."[111]. At the opposite end of the scale from this conception, Daniel 9 had the revelation—which "can only be understood as a protest"[112]—that this must be understood, not as seventy years, but as seventy weeks of years, which had the effect of shifting the moment of restoration into a near future (near from the point of view of the Jews of the second century) and of making Cyrus' edict of 538 meaningless.

APOCALYPTIC CHARACTERISTICS

It would be a mistake, however, to see the theocratic ideal of the Chronicler as an antiprophetic reaction. Ezekiel was the first to state this notion in chapters 40–48 of his book, and Haggai and Zechariah were his faithful disciples. For them, the restoration had taken place around Zerubbabel, the entitled descendant of the Davidic dynasty, and Joshua/Jason, the Zadokite high priest. Historical continuity with preexilic times was thus emphasized. The Exile was hence an accident, incapable of deeply modifying *Heilsgeschichte*. "In contrast to the view of many visionaries," Hanson writes, "the catastrophe of 587 was not interpreted by Ezekiel as a judgment upon the Zadokite temple theology; only as a result of the defilement of the temple through idolatrous rites was YHWH forced to withdraw from Zion. What Ezekiel therefore called for was the restoration of the proper cult and the reorganization of legitimate priesthood to safeguard the sanctity of that cult."[113]

Hanson has well described the "leftist" opposition as it is expressed in Third Isaiah or Deutero-Zechariah. For theological reasons, but also perhaps for economic and political reasons, the have-nots and the noninfluential (by choice or by accident) could not subscribe to the proclamation of the accomplished restoration. It was for other people than themselves. They had no part of it; they were unable to see themselves as its beneficiaries in any way. The truth was that the real restoration announced by the prophets had not yet arrived. Those who claimed the contrary were only seeking to justify on a theological basis their own social injustice and their political compromises with the foreigners. They called restoration the exaltation of an exclusive priestly class and a liturgical service from which the people were not excluded, to be sure, but in which the people were barely tolerated. (The Chronicler's insistence on priesthood and on the hierarchization of priestly families was tending in that direction.) This is why the coming of the true restoration was constantly deferred. The priestly caste of the temple was what was preventing the realization of the promise, which would, however, come to pass, but preceded by *apocalyptical* events. The judgment of God separating the just and the unjust would come in good time, "at the time of the end," not only to chastize the idolatrous nations, but also to purify Israel of its alienated elements. "These cosmic events will go beyond the human realm to effect even the world of nature so as to establish a suitable natural setting for the restoration people."[114]

To conclude, the apocalyptic phenomenon in Israel must not be seen as having an absolute beginning in the second century B.C.E. Because they have misconstrued the long period of gestation of the Jewish apocalypse, scholars have often been stopped by false problems, such as that of totally foreign sources from which it is supposed to have originated. Without denying what Iranian or Greek sources brought to the spirit and the thought of apocalyptic, what must be emphasized is that the phenomenon began by being a spiritual and literary tendency in certain Israelite prophetic circles, and that this was true as early as the sixth century. It was only with time that the subterranean and relatively timid current—timid above all because of the repression to which it was subjected—emerged above ground as a torrent of extraordinary force. It reached its definitive stature with parts of the Enochian literature and the book of Daniel. After Daniel, the genre becomes less pure. It becomes contaminated by elements of an increasingly suspect orthodoxy, such as ontological dualism. Daniel was accepted into the canon, whereas other later apocalyptical works were not, largely for that reason.

We should note, finally, that the evolution of the apocalypse continued, after it emerged into public view, and was followed by a return to underground existence and then by sporadic reappearances up to our own day.[115]

NOTES

1. Thus Daniel describes the profanation of the temple by Antiochus IV in 168, but the text does not take us as far as its rededication by Judas Maccabeus in 165. This gives us a terminus a quo and a terminus ad quem by which to date the book (or at least to date Daniel B).

2. See G. F. Moore, *Judaism in the First Centuries of the Christian Era*, 2:279ff.

3. See J. B. Frey, "Apocalyptique."

4. J. J. Collins, "Apocalypse: Toward the Morphology of a Genre."

5. "An apocalypse is a pseudonymous collection of allegorical visions representing the fate of the world in the form of a struggle among the powers of evil, a struggle resolved brusquely by the unexpected triumph of God in a catastrophe that puts an end to the world. The inauguration of this divine reign is accompanied by a universal judgment of men and by the resurrection of the righteous" (J. Steinmann, *Daniel*, 24).

6. "The chief characteristic of the form is that not only predictions of the future, but also historical narrations take on a prophetic character. The author succeeds in doing this by means of a fiction: he places his words in the mouth of some ancient patriarch or prophet—Enoch or Moses . . . as if, from the remotest times, they had revealed history

and the last things concerning the world and, in particular, concerning Israel" (L. Dennefeld, in *La Sainte Bible*, 7:636).

7. E.g., Enoch (written in Aramaic at the beginning of the second century B.C.E.); T. Levi (Aramaic, third century B.C.E.); Jub. (third century B.C.E.). See M. Stone, *Scriptures, Sects and Visions*.

8. A rabbinic expression that indicates that the nature of the book is not sacred, hence there is no need for a ritual washing of hands to read it.

9. E.g., 4 Ezra, 2 Bar., and, last but not least, the Apocalypse of John (Rev.) in the New Testament (originally a Jewish work revised by John or by a Judeo-Christian?).

10. One can speak of "Judaism" from Ezekiel on.

11. E. Bickerman writes: "From its beginning Greek culture was supranational, because the Greeks never constituted a unified state. . . . Their culture was Panhellenic, and was the same on the Nile as on the Euphrates. . . . Greek culture, like modern European culture, was based upon education. A man became a "Hellene" without at the same time forsaking his gods and his people, but merely by adopting Hellenic culture" (*The Maccabees*, 22-23).

12. Historical circumstances are enough to explain the pessimism of the apocalypses and their tendency toward dualism. I shall return to the question in this chapter.

13. A. Guillaume, *Prophecy and Divination Among the Hebrews and Other Semites*, 162-63, advances the most interesting theory that the shift from prophecy to the apocalypse was due to a fierce opposition to the magic and the divination of the Babylonians. Aside from its obvious importance for dating the birth of Jewish apocalyptic, Guillaume's opinion also throws light on the pseudonymity of this literature. He notes that Zech. 13:3 is in a context of condemnation of idolatry. Apocalyptic literature is anonymous because its authors feared the malediction that weighed on the heads of the prophets.

14. So that Dan. 9:2, e.g., could refer to the book of Jeremiah as a book that was known and of incontestable authority.

15. According to Emil Fackenheim, the Jews after Auschwitz choose life over death, hope over despair, and sanity over madness (lecture at Chicago, 24 Jan. 1971).

16. A. Neher, *Jérémie*, esp. 191ff.

17. The term expresses a misconstruction, however, since apocalypse did not come to remedy an absence with the first means at hand. It *replaced* prophecy with a new temporality. See ch. 5 below.

18. Jürgen Moltmann, *Theology of Hope*; 18.

19. The future of the apocalyptists is in reality our present, since they project themselves into a distant past under borrowed names in order to speak of contemporary events.

20. Isa. 4:2; Jer. 23:3-5; 33:14-26; Zech. 3:8; 6:9-15; see J. G. Baldwin, "Ṣemah as a Technical Term in the Prophets."

21. See 1 Enoch 72:1; 91:16; Jub. 1:29; 2 Bar. 32-36; 4 Ezra 7:75; 2 Pet. 3:13; Rev. 21:1. Preceded by a cataclysm: 1 Enoch 99:4ff.; 100:1ff.; 4 Ezra 4:51ff.; 6:11ff.; 9:1ff.; Rev. 6ff.

22. One can find histories and testaments among apocalyptical texts, parenetic, apologetic, and hagiographic characteristics, oracles and decrees, proverbs and topographical portrayals of heaven and earth, and more. All these aspects of the apocalypse

offer connections with traditional literary genres such as narration, wisdom literature, prophecy, apologetics, etc.

23. See, e.g., Ezek. 18:9; 1QS 1.5, 6; John 3:21; 1 John 1:6.

24. Partial resurrection reflects the same duality. Humanity is divided into two groups: one lives "for nothing," the other for eternal life.

25. It would be false, however, to try to see it as a popular genre. "It appears increasingly clear that all the apocalyptic literature of the Second Commonwealth was not, as once assumed, the literature of the man on the street, but rather the esoteric Midrash of the intellectual élite" (S. W. Baron, *A Social and Religious History of the Jews*, 2:314).

26. E.g., Abraham receives the order to sacrifice his only son (Gen. 22); Jacob wrestles with the angel until morning (Gen. 32); Moses is attacked by God, who "sought to kill him" (Exod. 4:24); David falls "into the hand of the Lord" (2 Sam. 24:14).

27. Gerhard von Rad, *The Message of the Prophets*, 271. W. Baumgartner: "Ein Vierteljahrhundert Daniel Forschung," writes: "Pseudonymity, eschatological impatience and exact reckoning up of the time to the end, comprehensive and fantastic visions, a horizon which takes in universal history and is even cosmic, numerical symbolism and cryptic language, the doctrine of angels and the hope for the life beyond."

28. Von Rad, *Old Testament Theology*, introduction to Daniel. The same idea appears in C. Westermann's *The Old Testament and Christian Faith*, 208-9: the *Heilsschilderung* (portrayal of salvation) that is found in apocalypse is already present in prophecy (e.g., Isa. 2:1–4; 11:1–10). Its roots are in ancient blessings (e.g., Gen. 49:11–12; Num. 24:5–7a).

29. J. Lindblom, *Die Jesaja-Apokalypse*, 102.

30. H. H. Rowley, *The Relevance of Apocalyptic*, 25 n. 2, p. 92. Rowley is thinking in particular of the hope of the afterworld and the expectation of resurrection as individual retribution (see Isa. 24–27; Dan. 12).

31. One might ask to what extent these modern judgments, in particular those that discover traces of determinism and transcendentalism in the apocalypse, are simply anachronisms.

32. Collins, "Apocalypse," 9.

33. M.-J. Lagrange, *Le Judaïsme avant Jésus-Christ*, 77.

34. Paul Hanson, *The Dawn of Apocalyptic: The Historical and Sociological Roots of Jewish Apocalyptic Eschatology*.

35. To be sure, Ahaz the Davidite is replaced by Emmanuel, the child of the miracle, but it is Ahaz who has disqualified himself (Isa. 7).

36. See ch. 6 below, under the heading "From the Davidite to the Adamic."

37. Yehezkel Kaufmann, *Toldot*, 8:434. (*The Religion of Israel, from its Beginnings to the Babylonian Exile*).

38. The covenant of Sinai is organically involved in this, since all the tribes of the confederation "recognized" that they had left slavery in Egypt and had found God in the desert.

39. E.g., the sin of Israel is so great that it requires the renewal of the covenant, for the malediction invoked at the time of its ratification for recreants would annihilate Israel; see K. Baltzer, *Das Bundesformular*.

40. See Josh. 24; 2 Kgs. 23; Neh. 10; 2 Sam. 23; Ps. 89. Similarly, Sir. 45:24–25 distinguishes between "a covenant of peace," which involved the priests and the people,

APOCALYPTIC CHARACTERISTICS

and the "covenant . . . with David" in direct succession from father to son ("the inheritance of the king is his son's alone"; cf. 2 Sam. 7:12; 1 Kgs. 8:20; Jer. 33:17–26). Sir. calls the latter "the decree of kingdom" (47:11).

41. As in the description in Dan. 7:13ff. The covenant with Abraham is of the same nature, a "covenant of grant." See M. Weinberg, "The Covenant of Grant in the Old Testament and in the Ancient Near East"; R. Clements, *Abraham and David: Genesis 15 and Its Meaning for Israelite Tradition.*

42. Once again, Dan. 7 can serve as a late example of this theme. Edmond Jacob summarizes the essential points in this cultic drama as follows: a) struggle of the god represented and incarnated by the king, ending in the victory of the king over mythical adversary forces; b) proclamation of the king's victory throughout the world; c) the king swears to reign with justice; d) he is royally garbed and adorned; e) the king receives sacramental food, baptism by water, and unction with oil; f) the king is proclaimed the son of God; g) installation of the king on the throne of God; h) sacred marriage of the king. *(Les thèmes essentiels d'une théologie de l'Ancien Testament,* 189).

43. "The Maharal forcefully affirms that the coexistence of extremes in one object is always possible, at the price of an indefinitely renewable effort, an effort that is the very expression of the continuation of creation. The human being, as soon as he knows himself to be—and wants to be—God's associate in the work of creation, attempts ceaselessly to bring back to the Creator the truth that He had deliberately thrown onto men's earth, charging men with making it germinate" (T. Dreyfus, "Comprendre le Maharal de Prague," p. 29). On the truth thrown to the earth, see *Gen. Rab.* 8. 5 (cf. Dan. 8.12).

44. Israel believed that the enemy will prevail only when all hope is abolished. As long as there is hope, the enemy, in spite of all appearances, is vanquished. Certain of the events behind the Iron Curtain in recent years are a modern illustration of this principle.

45. See 2 Sam. 7:14; Pss. 2:7; 89:26. See also Pss. 45; 47:10; 84:12; 89:19. See n. 42 above for Jacob's summary of the royal cultic drama.

46. See Hanson, *The Dawn of Apocalyptic,* for a study of Third Isaiah and Second Zechariah.

47. In the *Urzeit,* God had already delegated his powers to man (see Gen. 1:28). I shall return to this point.

48. Sigmund Mowinckel, *He That Cometh.* Israelite eschatology cannot be reduced to the postexilic period, however, as he believes.

49. See Jacob, *Les thèmes essentiels,* 191.

50. Cf. Isa. 9; 11:6–9; 65:17–25; Pss. 2:6; 45:4–7; 48:2; 89:27; 110:1, 3.

51. Cf. Barn. 6.13: "Behold I shall make the last things like the first."

52. There are, what is more, important precedents for this "reconciliation." David installs the ark of the covenant in the temple/royal chapel, the center of Israelite amphictyony (I am using the term at face value without necessarily concurring with it). The secession of the northern kingdom implies the survival of the amphictyonic principle, combined with a kingship of the charismatic sort. King Josiah proclaims the Torah of Moses as the official constitution of the state, but he identifies the state with "Israel." On this question, see the studies of Martin Noth.

53. D. S. Russell, *The Method and Message of Jewish Apocalyptic, 200 BC–AD 100,* 127–39.

54.   See ch. 1 above on the question of pseudepigraphy; also A. Guillaume's opinion in note 13, above. The problems discussed in this section will return in ch. 6.
55.   Claude Tresmontant, *Etudes de métaphysique biblique*, 14.
56.   Tresmontant, *La doctrine morale des prophètes d'Israël*, 30.
57.   See von Rad's overly rigid judgment: "In the panorama of history given in
Daniel's two great night-visions, the picture of the empires and the vision of the four
beasts, there is absolutely no mention of Israel's history; here God deals only with the
empires, and even the son of man does not come from Israel, but 'with the clouds of
heaven.' " One might ask, von Rad continues, to what extent the thought here is not fundamentally ahistorical, since the experience of historical contingencies scarcely appears
any longer. For von Rad, the apocalyptical vision of history is extremely pessimistic: the
full measure of crime must be reached (Dan. 2; 8:23). The apocalyptist recognizes the
providential hand of God in history, working through a strict historical determinism. The
presence of the great human empires leads Dan. 2 and 7 to the extreme limit where history
rejoins transcendence (*Old Testament Theology* 2:303, 309).
58.   See A. Neher, *Le puits de l'exil*.
59.   The apostle Paul speaks of the same notion, using the metaphor of childbirth;
see Rom. 8:22 and the entire context.
60.   "In the Dead Sea writings the end of the world is depicted as a great turning
point at which the present order and all its standards will be turned upside down. For the
form of this world is anti-God: the devil is in command and the mass of mankind is know-
ingly or unknowingly subject to him. The righteous man suffers. Only the consciousness
that everything will soon be radically different makes it possible for him to bear injustice
and oppression. More, his lot fills him with joy and pride. The man who suffers now will
soon triumph; he whose worldly fate seems without hope will participate as accuser and
avenger at the last judgment." O. H. Betz, *What Do We Know About Jesus?* 48.
61.   Similarly, the Septugint, Philo, and Saul of Tarsus speak in Greek, but their
thought remains Jewish.
62.   I am happy to find the same warning in Hanson, *The Dawn of Apocalyptic* (see p.
8).
63.   J. Gammie, "Spatial and Ethical Dualism in Jewish Wisdom and Apocalyptic
Literature"; this study includes an extensive bibliography.
64.   S. Holm-Nielsen, *Hodayot; Psalms from Qumran*, 281 n. 16: "Both [dualism and
predestination] are theological attempts to create order in an old-fashioned dogmatism of
the good governing by God of His world, which no longer seems to fit the actual
circumstances."
65.   J. A. Montgomery, *A Critical . . . Commentary*, 84.
66.   Rowley, *The Relevance of Apocalyptic*, 175.
67.   H. Gunkel, *Einleitung in die Psalmen*. For Gunkel, the apocalypse is merely the
projection into the future of the most remote past. Similarly, C. Westermann, (*Genesis 1–
11:A Commentary*, 51): "Apocalyptic, both in content and in intention, is subordinated not
to salvation history but to primeval history, especially to the history of creation and of the
flood." According to S. H. Hooke, *Middle Eastern Mythology*, the book of Daniel inaugu-
rates an original use of the myth. "It is being used as propaganda in a Gentile environment. YHWH is displayed as Pantocrator, as having universal dominion, raising up and
putting down kingdoms at his pleasure, and able to protect his servants under every kind

of danger, so long as they remain faithful to him" (p. 163). Hooke also emphasizes the use of the myths of creation and chaos in the apocalyptic (a theme closely connected to that of the sovereignty of YHWH). He sees the literary source of this in passages such as Isa. 27:1 and 51:9–11.

68. Russell, *The Method and Message*, 224.

69. Using the term *dualism* would be a contradiction in terms, for in true dualism the opposed terms are mutually exclusive. For a more extensive development of this question, see ch. 6 below, under "The Resurrection."

70. R. H. Charles, *A Critical and Exegetical Commentary on the Book of Daniel*, cxiv–cxv.

71. J. B. Frey, "Apocalyptic," cols. 326ff. Cf. Add. Esth. 7:7,8; Jub. 5:13; 10.5ff.

72. Abraham Heschel, *The Prophets*, 2:1–11.

73. At least in spirit. See J. J. Collins, "The Jewish Apocalypses," 26: " All apocalypses . . . are concerned with human conduct on earth . . . [and] are therefore hortatory in purpose, whether this purpose is expressed explicity or not." G. W. E. Nickelsburg, "The Apocalyptic Message in 1 En. 92–105," 326: "The revelation of God's unseen world and future paradoxically calls the oppressed community to faith, courage, and joy in the present." See also W. Schmithals, *The Apocalyptic Movement*, 36.

74. J. J. Collins, "Pseudonymity, Historical Reviews and the Genre of the Revelation of John," 336.

75. "Something greater than Jonah is here" (Matt. 12:41; cf. John 8:56, 58).

76. L. Hartman (*Prophecy Interpreted: The Formation of Some Jewish Apocalyptic Texts and of the Eschatological Discourse in Mark*, 55ff.) has brought together more than twenty apocalyptic texts in which this sequence can be found: Jub. 23:11–13; 1 Enoch 10:16–11:2; 80:2–8; 91:6–11; 99:1–16; 100:1–9; 102:1–11; 103:1–15; 104:1–105:2; T. Levi 4:1–4; 14:1–16:5; T. Judah 21:6–22:3; T. Zeb. 9:5–9.

77. "For when God uses men and nations to perform His will He does not compel them to their course of action, or destroy their freedom. He but uses their action, freely chosen for themselves, to perform His purposes. The divine activity in history does not override human freedom" (Rowley, *The Relevance of Apocalyptic*, 169–70). See Enoch 98:4; Sir. 2:27–28; Pss. Sol. 5:6, but cf. 9:7; Jub. 5:13, 15, and 41:24ff.; 21:25; 22:10. In Daniel see 4:17, 25, but also v. 27. L. Robberechts writes, "A cause and a motive have nothing in common; nor do a compact determinism and this same determinism integrated into the becoming of a conscience. It is not prediction that makes us less free" (*Husserl*, 100).

78. Nils Messel, *Die Einheitlichkeit der jüdischen Eschatologie* and *Der Menschensohn in den Bilderreden des Henoch*. See also the section "Resurrection" in ch. 6 below.

79. We should not forget that their faith led the apocalyptists to practice this exercise of imagination in perfect contradiction to their situation. While the Hellenists were acclaiming the new order that was to inaugurate the golden age, they announced the imminent end of a world in decomposition because it had become cut off from the Source of life.

80. In Daniel the son of man leads the "people of the saints," but the entire book focuses on Daniel as an individual. After Daniel individualism continued to develop, and it finds a privileged place in the Qumran texts (e.g. 1QpHab 7.4; 1QS 8.11–12; 1QH 1.21; 12.11–13.

81. Angels can be found beginning with the traditions concerning the origins of the world, in the history of the Deuteronomist and then of the Chronicler, in the Psalms, in Qoheleth, etc.

82. This was not so in Babylon or in Ugarit, where the gods of the heavenly court surrounding the major divinities had their own autonomy. Angelology in Israel was the result of the demythologization of foreign pantheons. Thus a human can be equal to an angel (see Enoch 6; 14; 1QH 3.19–23).

83. In addition to the sources cited, some other useful works are: S. E. Loewenstamm, "Mal'ach"; Y. Kaufmann, *Todlot* 2:422–42; P. van Imschoot, *Théologie de l'Ancien Testament*, 114–30; N. Snaith, *The Jews from Cyrus to Herod*, 132–38; E. Jacob, *Theology of the Old Testament*; M. Testuz, *Les idées religieuses du Livre des Jubilés* , 75–80, 85–87; L. Askenazi, *Anges, démons et êtres intermédiaires*. Askenazi states, "Between the Creator and myself, there is the will of God. The will of God in some manner traverses all these hierarchies of the angels. But, in the other direction, in the face to face [confrontation] between myself and God, there is nothing other than God" (p. 210). Other points concerning the question can be found in my Commentary on Daniel, esp. 10:13.

84. As we have seen, many critics have made this point. Rudolf Otto writes: "The new motives which are active in the eschatology of late Jewish apocalyptic are far from being absolutely and radically alien to ancient Israelite religious feeling, for in that case we should have to do with a syncretism in the sense of mechanical addition, and the eschatology of late Judaism would then be simply and solely an alien phenomenon, which is not the case. Rather they work upon germinal ideas found even in ancient Israel." (*The Kingdom of God and the Son of Man*, 39).

85. The same reproach could be made to many other prestigious authors: to John the Evangelist, e.g., when he speaks of "the Jews," or to the apostle Paul in his attacks on "the Law."

86. Dan. 8:2–8 demonstrates a real knowledge of ancient astral geography: the ram was the star of Persia; the goat, that of Seleucid Syria.

87. Dan 12. "The ethical and eschatological dualism taught by Zoroaster and Mazdaism found a welcome in this late Jewish community of Palestine [Qumran], and there they combined with the Old Testament bases of this community, whereas Gnosticism represents a *later* stage of the infiltration of Parsi dualism. At that point, it was revised under an entirely different influence—that of Greek thought—and it became a physical dualism of the two substances. This is how, for the first time, there appeared the notion decisive for Gnosticism that *matter*—that is, the world in its physical substance— is the enemy of God" (K. G. Kuhn, "Die Sektenschrift und die Iranische Religion," 315). On resurrection, see ch. 6 below.

88. Frey, "Apocalyptique," col. 341. On all this development, see M. Nicolas, *Les doctrines religieuses des Juifs pendant les deux siècles antérieurs à l'ère chrétienne*, 49–55, 294–310; H. Gunkel, *Schöpfung und Chaos*, 286–93, 323–35. Gunkel's position, to summarize briefly, is that the origin of the materials used by apocalyptic (fantastic form, cosmological contents, eschatology, visions, and speculations concerning angels) is not Judaic but mythic (the Babylonian myth of chaos). Judaism, usually so touchy about such matters, might have absorbed elements so foreign to its thought, omitting the names of pagan gods. The source is not Greek, for Zechariah and other texts that predate Hellenism are already apocalyptical. Two possibilities remain as sources: Babylonia and Persia, either separately or in

combination. Other works to be consulted include N. Soederblom, *La vie future d'après le mazdéisme*; H. Gressmann, *Der Ursprung der israelitisch-jüdischen Eschatologie*; W. Bousset, *Die Religion des Judentums*, 540–94.

89. Martin Hengel, *Judaism and Hellenism*, 1:190–93.

90. W. G. Lambert, *The Background of Jewish Apocalyptic*, 10.

91. P. R. Ackroyd, "Israel Under Babylon and Persia," 344.

92. This parallel was, to be sure, of Babylonian origin, but it had long been adopted into the spiritual treasury of Israel.

93. Russell, *The Method and Message*, 269, citing Mowinckel, *He That Cometh*, 125ff., 270ff. As I have said, I do not believe that this judgment should be applied without qualification to the book of Daniel.

94. See the Song of the Three Young Men; Parables of Enoch 62:16 and Ascension of Isaiah (first century B.C.E.); Apoc. Ezra 7:88; Secrets of Enoch 23:5; Wis. 8:19–20; 9:15; 15:8, 11; 16:14. Echos of this concept can be found in the Talmud: *Hagigah* 12b (the souls are in the seventh heaven before they enter into human bodies; cf., later, the Zohar); in the Midrash, *Sifré* 143b (the souls are in a special chamber before their incarnation). Contradictory affirmations can be found, however: Adam and Eve 48.1ff.; Apoc. Moses 37:4–40:7; 1QM 12:1–5; 2 Bar. 49:2–51:6; Matt. 27:52–53 (the resurrection of the body); Enoch 61:12; Apoc. Abraham 21. See Snaith, *The Jews from Cyrus to Herod*, 115–31.

95. O. Plöger, *Theocracy and Eschatology*; Hanson, *The Dawn of Apocalyptic*.

96. "Since the law was the ultimate and complete expression of absolute truth, there was no room for any further revelation" (*APOT* 2:9).

97. Those who saw no essential changes:

Mar Samuel said: "There is no difference between the present and the days of the Messiah, except that we are subject to the dominion of the empires" (*Sanh.* 99a).

Rabbi Hillel said: "Israel must not wait for the coming of the Messiah, for the prophecy of Isaiah on this subject was accomplished in Hezekiah the king" (*Sanh.* 98b).

"Rabbi Akiba was severely reproached by Rabbi Josi the Galilean for 'having profanated the divine presence' by teaching that the Messiah occupies the throne next to that of God." If miracles are to occur, God himself will accomplish them. The coming of the Messiah will change nothing in the course of nature (*Hag.* 14a).

Those who saw essential changes:

Rab said: "The coming age is not like the present age. In the age to come there is neither eating nor drinking, nor engendering, nor commerce, nor jealousy, nor hate, nor rivalry" (*Ber.* 17a).

"In the age to come, there is no death, no sorrow, no tears" (*m. Mo'ed Qat.* 3, 9).

Rabban Gamaliel II said: "Women will bring children into the world daily, and the trees will give ripe fruit every day" (*Šabb.* 30b).

98. I am speaking here only of the most honorable intellectual position. Facts show that many, even—and especially—among the high priests and the upper clergy of Jerusalem, lowered themselves to consent to the most unthinkable compromises with the foreign powers.

99. See ch. 2 above, esp. the section "Daniel in His Time."

100. Jewish mysticism also hesitates between the provisory and the definitive nature of the Torah as it was revealed at Sinai. See G. Scholem, *The Messianic Idea in Judaism and Other Essays on Jewish Spirituality*.

101. Our own times are apocalyptical in that the believer must necessarily "reconcile" creation and chaos, Scripture and Auschwitz, revelation and Hiroshima, the Torah and the Gulag.

102. Here we are, in my opinion, at the heart of the debate between Jesus and the "Pharisees." The message of the New Testament is that the kingdom of God is present here and now in the person of Christ and in the community assembled around him. The same concept of the eschaton can be found in the *Hôdāyôt* of the Dead Sea studied by H. K. Kuhn, *Enderwartung und gegenwärtiges Heil, Untersuchungen zu den Gemeindeliedern von Qumran.*

103. It is not by chance that classical Judaism saw in Haggai, Zechariah, and Malachi the last prophets, with whom prophecy disappeared. Sectarian Judaism, for its part, gives a tendentious definition of prophecy. For Sir. 48:22*b*–25, e.g., Isaiah was the prophet par excellence, for "unto eternity he declared the things that shall be, and hidden things before they came to pass." Mention of the expectation of a new prophet can be found in: e.g., 1 Macc. 4:46; 14:41; 1QS 9:11; Mark 9:11; John 1:21.

104. This is still the conception of Daniel A, but it no longer appears in Daniel B.

105. Another trait characteristic of Jewish sectarianism. The virulence of the Qumran attacks on the clergy of the temple and on their adversaries in general belongs to a different conception of "Israel" than the one that was to prevail in "classical" Judaism. This goes so far that, according to Jub. 38:2ff., apostates are sons of Esau: they can be killed without committing a crime; they have become heathen (Jub. 6:32–38). One of the clearest passages in this regard is 3 Macc. 7:10ff.

106. Russell, *The Method and Message*, 17.

107. Hanson, *The Dawn of Apocalyptic*, 16.

108. Ibid., 20.

109. W. Rudolph, *Chronikbücher*, xxiii.

110. Von Rad, *Old Testament Theology*, 1:347.

111. Plöger, *Theocracy and Eschatology*, 43.

112. Ibid.

113. Hanson, *The Dawn of Apocalyptic*, 238. Unless the final chapters of Ezekiel should be understood as describing a restoration of the temple so idealized that it already no longer belongs to this world. In this case the rebuilding of the sanctuary in Jerusalem (520–515) indicated a false interpretation of the prophet and a banalization of his spiritual program. The problem has remarkable parallels today, "after Auschwitz." Similarly, after Golgotha the Jewish community was profoundly divided in its interpretation of what had happened.

114. Ibid., 152.

115. There is a clearly apocalyptic element in Jewish movements such as Franckism, Sabbatianism, and Hasidism. Apocalyptic resurgences in Christian sects are too numerous and too well known to be cited here. Works to consult include B. McGinn, *Visions of the End: Apocalyptic Traditions in the Middle Ages* and *Apocalyptic Spirituality.*

FIVE

Symbolic Language, Dream, and Vision

THE CONFLICT OF WISDOMS

The written Torah does not exhaust revelation. There is also a parallel esoteric teaching reserved to the pious (Moses wrote only two tables, but on Sinai seventy other secret books were revealed to him; 4 Ezra 14:1-50). Now that the time of the end was at hand, it was necessary that this all-inclusive, universal, totalizing wisdom be known and that contemporary happenings be considered in light of a complete revelation that, even though it surpassed all the world's wisdom, nevertheless included it. Now and then it had been possible, in Israel, to think that the message of the nations was false, or in any event was overly occupied with things that lacked real importance. Hellenism, however, was too compelling a force to be ignored or treated lightly. "Daniel," the ancient and venerable sage, was transplanted to the impure land of the pagans and exposed to a world view that was all the more pernicious for containing elements of an undeniable intrinsic value, but that called in question the traditional bases of the thought of Israel. A half truth, we are told, is more dangerous than a pure lie. The only response lay in working methodically at the interpretation of reality to restore what adversaries had twisted.

For the apocalyptist all argument began with the idea that the revelation of the Living God to his people leaves no secret (Aram. *raz*; Heb.

121

sod) concealed. There was no need for supplementary teachings drawn from a foreign philosophy for knowledge of all truth and the understanding of all secrets. The conclusion was evident: There was no good and no truth in what pagan culture had to offer that did not already exist in plenitude in sacred revelation.

It is interesting to note this apocalyptical deviation of prophecy in the direction of wisdom; all of revelation had drawn closer to wisdom in the struggle against Hellenistic propaganda, since on the intellectual level that propaganda took the form of philosophical demonstration. This needed to be shown as narrowly contingent in comparison to the absolute character of the Torah, but, at the same time, the contribution of the best that paganism contained is recognized and even approved in the book of Daniel. Here we are far from the consciously unjust sarcasms that prophecy had directed at the wood and iron supposed to have been worshiped by benighted nations (Isa. 40:19-20; Jer. 2:27; 10:3ff.). The fact remains, however, that all of this worldly wisdom continues to be mysterious writing on the wall until someone, inspired by the Spirit, comes along to interpret its meaning. The role of Israel was precisely to reveal the direction of history to the nations. Israel is a revealer, a developer.[1] Heathens live as in a dream, without comprehension, which is why their despair can turn into a destructive madness. If only there were a "Daniel" at his side at the opportune moment, Nebuchadnezzar's dream would torment him no longer (Dan. 2:1,3). False ideas invented by evil minds to distort the meaning of existence would be unmasked (Dan. 2:2, 8–9,27). The gods of the pagan religions, ideologies and philosophies that claim to be universal, have no control over events. The God of Israel, to the contrary, "changes times and seasons; he removes kings and sets up kings; he gives wisdom to the wise and knowledge to those who have understanding; he reveals deep and mysterious things; he knows what is in the darkness, and the light dwells with him" (Dan. 2:21–22; cf. 2:28).

When Nebuchadnezzar is faced with the incontestable truth about himself, there is no way that he can resist it. He falls upon his face and although it costs him dear, he acknowledges the truth and admits that Daniel has been able "to reveal this mystery" (Dan. 2:46–47). Revelation may be hard to listen to, but it is a liberation. Daniel/Israel is the catalyst that brings about the revelation of history to the nations. He is thus their liberator. This is also the role, awesome but imperative, that the apocalyptist plays among his people,[2] for the evil forces that defeat history and throw it back into 'the unformed and the void' of the *Urzeit* are found within the people as well as without. Daniel is a model of fidelity, perseverance, and piety, but not everyone can be a Daniel. Many of his compatriots doubted that God was the one and only salvation. Their attitude, what is more, is comprehensible: they had objective evidence, political logic, and the forces of evolution on their side. Daniel himself needs no less than interpreting angels to penetrate appearances.[3]. In the unequal combat between historical determinism and "mysticism" it was nonetheless mysticism that had the last word. The author of the book of Daniel was right and the theorists of *Realpolitik* were wrong: the tomb of Judaism was in reality its cradle. Two thousand years of existence after the disappearance of Alexander's empire stand as proof.

Nothing could have seemed less sure at the time of Daniel and, perhaps, throughout the history of Israel. The "signs of the times" were always so obscure, so ambiguous, and so open to question that their interpretation profoundly divided the people. Modern historians are more and more struck by the evident fact that although the texts give the impression of consensus in Israel, in reality they conceal a perennial struggle between two irreducible parties. Daniel is the product of a polemical movement that was directed not only against the external, Hellenistic enemy but also, internally, against the party of compromise. This confrontation was the worm in the apple, perhaps, but the phenomenon was far from new. Our next task is to examine this struggle, seemingly present throughout the whole of Israel's history, at the level of language.

As early as 1857 the German Jewish scholar Abraham Geiger published his *Urschrift und Übersetzungen der Bibel*. His thesis was that in the final form of the texts as they have come down to us, the Bible reflects the conflict between Pharisees and Sadducees at the time of the Second Temple. Morton Smith went further in his *Palestinian Parties and Politics That Shaped the Old Testament*: all of the religious history of Israel is under the sign of the rivalry between "the syncretistic cult of Yahweh" and the "Yahweh-alone" party. Begun under the First Temple, the struggle reached its peak during the Exile, and the intransigent minority triumphed under the Maccabees (ca. 168).

It is not necessary to espouse Smith's hypercritical position to appreciate the validity of his general thesis. The Anglo-Scandinavian school had already demonstrated the persistent traces of an internal struggle between a pure Yahwism and a popular religion in Israel. However that may be, it is clear that with the apocalypse, the last dikes of the syncretist tendency (and, we might say, the humanist tendency), were swept away. Daniel, with its decisive persuasiveness, falls into the last phase of the struggle for the triumph of "pure" Yahwism in Israel.

This makes it all the stranger that the apocalyptists put myth to the service of the purist victory. I shall return to this soon. One point is important to note: With the period of the Second Temple, the age-old struggle within Israel to "historicize" the myths of the Middle East finally ends. The disappearance of the national monarchy decided the issue; the end of the last representative of the House of David, Zerubbabel, is veiled like some shameful event. Until then, the monarchy in Jerusalem (or in Samaria before 722) had provided Israel with the perfect mythical catalyst. The royal ideology of the Middle East was adopted by the Davidic complex, probably with some extensive adjustments. What was needed in Jerusalem was to transcend a regime that was by nature autocratic and give it the dimensions of a cosmic and eternal kingdom through the king's participation in the lordship of YHWH. By proclaiming God king (*Yhwh malakh*), the Davidic domination of the universe could be realized liturgically—that is, proleptically. The Davidic complex was a mystique of holy war. Not only did worshipers at all levels, from the king to the humblest commoner, participate in this mystery, but nature, the cosmos, the stars, the angels, and God himself.

In short, the royal rite of the temple of Jerusalem was a dramatization of a cosmic myth. What was at stake was the submission of the cosmos to divine law, so that within it human life would be harmonious and peaceable. This was already true, on another plane, in the Mesopotamian ideologies. According to them the cosmos follows the repetitive rhythm of the eternal return. Israel put its stamp on this system in that in Jerusalem temporal cycles were subjected to a historical process marked by eschatological expectations.[4]

THE REDISCOVERY OF MYTH

Form does not bend to the imperatives of a new content without resistance, however. It is a commonplace that nothing is slower to die than myth. Mircea Eliade finds traces of it in folklore and in the uses and customs of supposedly developed, modern, and Christianized nations.⁵ To the precise degree that myth dominates eschatology, it arouses the vehement protest of the prophets. When the national royalty of Zion disappeared, however, the prod of myth became so blunted that mythopoeic language, even in its cosmological form, was opened to use by as difficult to please Yahwist circles as apocalyptic Hasidism.

The prophet Ezekiel (in many regards the father of Jewish apocalyptic) had shown the way. E. W. Heaton points out, in this connection, that the decisive factor was perhaps that Ezekiel combined priesthood and prophecy in his person, which led him to "subordinate the complexities of history to the over-simplified assertions characteristic of liturgy."⁶ Be that as it may, Ezekiel distanced himself from his preexilic colleagues. He no longer says, "I saw," or "Yahweh showed me"; he creates expressions for the translocation of his person when gripped by his vision, and he has revelations of the celestial spheres, including the throne on which God in person sits. This phenomenon may have come of extraordinary visionary experiences. In any event, the language of Ezekiel remained, and was considered by its successors as particularly appropriate to the communication of apocalyptic visions. From that moment on it was possible to avoid the condemnation of the orthodox for having remythologized the thought of Israel, to people the sidereal spaces with angels, to make use of the myth of primordial man, and to evoke the mythology of the *Urzeit* in describing the bestiality of human empires and the creative triumph of God over these empires.

It became logical—though it was paradoxical in a polemical, anti-Hellenistic literature—to express from a universal point of view (as in Daniel A) the hope that the nations would relent, receive the Living God, and convert to his worship. Thus, one after another, the kings of Babylon, Media, and Persia confess there is no Lord but the God of Daniel (2:46–47; 4:1–3 [3:31–33]; 4:34; 6:26–27 [27–28]). This trait is one indication among others that the transfer to myth was not complete "in any composition within Jewish apocalyptic. Something of the experiment of the prophets adhered stubbornly to the visionary tradition, . . . even the events of the eschaton followed an historical sequence. One must wait for Gnosticism for the completion of the return to the mythic worldview, for only in that last phenomenon was the historical experiment overcome."⁷

In short, the Jewish apocalyptic of the second century rediscovered the use of myth on two planes.

On the one hand, the events that it expected in the near future were both *in* history (in their "incarnation") and *beyond* history (in their unlimited significance). The monsters of the old cosmogony were now historicized to represent the empires of the world. Their destiny, however, was of a cosmic dimension, and their fate was to be judged in the heavenly tribunal. Their condemnation to death inaugurated a new heaven and another earth.

On the other hand, since its polemic was directed at forced Hellenization, apocalyptic felt obliged to use the language of its adversary. By the same logic it rediscovered the use of myth. The immediate danger, for the second-century Jews of Jerusalem, came not so much from the rationalist demythifying of the Greek philosophers as from Hellenistic myths and from Oriental popular religion with a veneer of Hellenism. Indeed, each people was organized according to its own customs and its own laws. The local religion was kept, but its forms underwent Greek influence, and it was opened up to the world that Alexander's conquests had put within reach.

Religious language, wherever it is found, is mythical language. Myth is congenital to religion. This is why the upsurge of the cosmological dimension in apocalyptic thought so evidently brought with it the rediscovery of myth—if indeed it had ever been lost. It was thanks to this mythopoeic language that dialogue took place with Hellenism on the outside and with the Hellenized Jews within Jewish society.

Language had taken on a new importance. This was an age of cultural exchange, of the translation of texts, of compared thought. It is this context of effervescent humanism that both Palestinian Judaism and the Judaism of the Diaspora adopted designations of God more general than YHWH: the "Most High," for example (Dan. 4:24[21]; 7:25, etc.) or "the God of heaven" (2:18f, 28, 37, 44, etc.), "the Ancient of Days" (7:13, 22), and so forth. This phenomenon of mimesis of the then prevailing philosophy—particularly of Stoicism, from the third century on—was cause for grave misunderstandings. Thus in 166 the Samaritans accused the Jews, before Antiochus IV, of having a nameless God (Jos. *Ant.* 12.5.5). "When this characterization appeared in the works of Graeco-Roman writers hostile to the Jews, the Jews made a virtue of necessity and argued that the true God had to be nameless."[8]

Paul Ricoeur teaches us that myth is symbol integrated into a narrative. That is, narration gives the symbol its multiple meanings on different levels. There are three characteristics of myth, Ricoeur says: the expression of human experience in universal terms; the tension of an ideal history between a beginning and an end; and the transition from the alienated history of men to the ideal life of the gods.[9]

In light of this triple definition, it would be difficult to exaggerate the role of myth in Jewish apocalypse. To be sure, the aim of someone like Daniel is at first parenetic. He is not content with a description of an ideal *Endzeit*; he wants to console the victims of pagan persecution and arouse the resistance of the people to the "empires," catalytic agents for the powers of evil. But it is precisely the representative nature of historical kingdoms—Babylonia, Media, Persia, Greece—that reintroduces myth. Empires are political entities, but they are also the instruments of a panhistorical and universal satanic reign (although there are no satanological terms in Daniel) that can be represented by horrifying monsters, on the model of the mythical monsters of chaos. Thus the question is to understand how the insertion of myth into the apocalypse changed the nature of myth to serve the aims of apocalyptic.

The remarkably substantial discussion between J. J. Collins and Norman Perrin can be of help at this point.[10] According to Perrin, the apocalypse understands myth as allegory (what he calls a "steno-symbol").[11] That is, the relation of the signifyer to the signified is an exclusive relation, just as direct as $pi = 3.1416+$ in mathematics. The "tensive symbol" stands opposed to the "steno-symbol"; its meaning is not exclusive.[12] However, it takes us to a domain different from that of the apocalypse.

Collins readily convinces me that Perrin's thesis is inexact as far as apocalypse is concerned. Allegory has the aim of deciphering—that is, of effecting the passage from the mysterious and the difficult to the revealed and the simple. Can we recognize apocalypse here, with its deliberately obscure language? Following Collins, let us consider the example of the four monsters of Daniel 7, "allegorically" identified in the text itself as designating the uncomplicated realities of empires that succeeded one another in history: Babylonia, Media, Persia, and Greece. However, "even a reader who is ignorant of, or chooses to ignore, the echoes of Canaanite mythology and of the biblical Leviathan in the beasts which rise from the sea, must concede that the vision has an evocative power which is lacking in the interpretation."[13]

Allegory is Greek. It proceeds from a dualist conception that opposes the ideal to the contingent. The terms of the allegory belong to the contingent and serve as a springboard for reaching the world of ideas. We pass from one level to a totally different level. The apocalypse, on the other hand, remains Jewish. Just as much as allegory is, even by definition, ahistorical, apocalyptical symbolism is rooted in history. For example, the monsters of chaos "reinvented" by the apocalyptists are not, on any level of interpretation, symbols of aesthetic or moral failings. The son of man does not represent a given virtue, and "He-who-lasts" (the "Ancient of Days") is not an impersonal criterion of the good or evil actions of man. The terrible beasts are well-known historical empires, the son of man is the representative of the people of the saints, and He-who-lasts is the Living God, bound in a relation of alliance by his covenant with Israel. In short, in employing myth the apocalyptist, like his predecessor the prophet, took care to assure its insertion in history. In reality, the apocalyptist makes a demythologized use of myth.

Furthermore, can we speak of allegory when the visionary takes such great pains to express the reality he seeks to describe through linguistic approximations such as "one like a son of man," thus considerably reducing the thrust of his image? Similarly, Ezekiel speaks of having seen "the likeness of four living creatures. And this was their appearance: they had the form of men" (1:5). Likewise Revelation 19:1 specifies that the voice heard by the visionary presents only a vague resemblance to the sounds perceived in human experience.[14]

Moreover, we might seriously ask ourselves whether such a thing as a "steno-symbolic" allegory exists in literature. Even in the case of the most "uni-referential" apocalyptic symbols, Collins is certainly right in saying that it is more accurate to describe them as symbols that exhibit an ancestral vitality.

As Paul Ricoeur has written:

> The establishment of an analogical relation between one situation and the other thus underlies the very operation of apocalyptic discourse. The symbolization of the intended events contributes to this process. The statue which the three young men of chapter three refuse to worship is just as much the golden calf as it is any other idol. . . .[15]

MYTH AND DREAM

We have spoken of a demythified use of myth. Just how far this paradox can go becomes clear when we analyze the ways in which apoca-

128

lypse makes use of the world of dreams to express its message. There is a direct relationship between dream and myth. Dream is the individual expression of the psyche, whereas myth is its collective expression.[16] Indeed, when the apocalyptist uses materials furnished by dream, he is attempting to raise his personal emotion as a visionary to the level of collective myth. In this aim he quite naturally has recourse to symbolic language—that is, to a mythopoeic language. As D. S. Russell has shown, divine inspiration by means of nocturnal dream establishes a link between the original inspiration of the prophets and the poetic or literary inspiration that modern writers speak of.[17] Whatever origin a modern might assign to this poetic trance, it is clear that for the apocalyptist, dream does not emerge from the imagination but is an objective reality that comes from God himself. The beneficiary undergoes a true psychic experience, and it is most unlikely that the visionaries' narrations of such second states are merely a literary device.

Non-Jews were also granted premonitory dreams, for in the Bible dream is a device by which God reveals his will that belongs to the category of divination.[18] Thus it is logical in the ancient East that the king demand of his "seers" that they dream for him—that is, that they put themselves in a state of receptivity (for other biblical examples see Gen. 41:8; Jer. 27:9). "Occasionally," Marguerite Rutten writes, "the king (or a subject) might be favored with a vision, as was the case with the king of Babylon, Nabonidus, who saw in a dream the gods Marduk and Sinn, announcing to him the defeat of Astyages and the coming of Cyrus."[19]

Given that Middle Eastern thought linked events of interest to men and women with causes on a "universal" level, it was admitted that life's vicissitudes had a relationship with changes that occurred in the heavens.[20]

A certain broadmindedness toward magic fitted with the spirit of the times. Nabonidus has just been mentioned; in the Prayer of Nabonidus from Qumran there is a Jewish "miracle-worker" who cures the king of Babylon. Also from Qumran, the Genesis Apocryphon shows Abraham curing the pharaoh by a laying on of hands (20.25-30). Moreover, in the book that bears his name, Daniel becomes chief of the magicians (2:48; see also Jos. J. Wars 2. 159 and the skeptical attitude portrayed in Sir. 34[31]:1–8).

The art of divination was held in high esteem among the Essenes. On this level Daniel again shows evident signs of its relationship with

the Hasidic milieu.[21] The parallel with the only other biblical oneiro-
mantist, Joseph, has often been traced. Both men found themselves at
the court of a pagan ruler, and both transformed their "science" into
prophecy (Gen. 40:8; 41:16, 38–39; Dan. 2:17ff.; 5:11–14; 7:16; 8:16).
The *hartumim* of Genesis 41:8 and the *ḥakimim* of Daniel 2:27 or the *kas-
dayya* of Daniel 4:3–4 take on the task of interpreting "secrets" (*raz*).
This parallel with the age of the patriarchs, to whom God had so often
communicated his presence in dreams (especially according to E; see
Gen. 15:12–21; 20:3–6; 28:11–22; 37:5–11; 46:2–4) is an indication that
with "Daniel" we are in the last generation before the End. Total revelation is accorded at the end point of history as it was, previously, to
those who began prophecy. According to *Sifré* on Numbers 12:6: "God
spoke to all the prophets but Moses, *be-ḥalom u-be-ḥezyōn*"[22] (cf. Hab.
2:1–2; 1QpHab 7.1–5).

Dream is an enigma in narrative form. Its ciphered language is
perfectly adapted to ancient thought, which was first and foremost analogical. It can be found above all in the *mashal*, one of the basic functions
of which is to establish comparisons (Prov. 26:11), analogies (Prov.
6:27–29; Amos 3:3–6), and similarities in the form of parables (Isa. 5:1–
7). In all its various forms the enigma is based on more or less strict correspondences between the signifier and the signified. It is the task of the
sage to make these correspondences explicit.

Israel shared this analogical mode of thought with the rest of the
Middle East. But, unlike other nations, Israel took it on itself to show
the infinite transcendence of the signified over the signifier and, consequently, the lack of essential analogy between the two. At this point,
although the Hasid could use a common language with other peoples,
this language became different in its use, at least as far as one of its
dimensions was concerned.

As to other aspects, however, ties with Hellenistic culture do exist.
Most relevant for our discussion are the reflections of E. R. Dodds in his
epoch-making distinction between "dream-pattern and culture-pattern."[23] Dodds calls "culture-pattern" those oneiric themes that are due
to a given culture, as is precisely the case with Greeks and Jews alike.
So, he says, the *chematismos* or "divine dream" belongs to the religious
experience of the people. The poets, for instance, feel free to use it as a
literary motif (Homer, e.g.), and this certainly applies to Daniel and
other apocalyptic literature. Such "divine dreams" emanate from a

dead father or from any figure that is a "father-substitute discharging the parental functions of admonition and guidance."[24]

On the one hand, to be sure, dream, in Israel as elsewhere, revealed a particular truth, the privileged vehicle of which was a specifically oneiric language. "As a variant of this principle," H. P. Müller writes, "Daniel 2 and 4 offer a mythic dimension of depths revealing the numinous aspect of a universally verifiable truth: the statue is the divine-demoniacal dimension of present humanity; the cosmic tree is that same dimension of the monarchy of those times."[25]

On the other hand, dream is thrown from its magic pedestal; it is "historicized" or "psychologized." Nebuchadnezzar is the spectator of a nocturnal scenario that merely projects onto the screen of "his spirit" (Dan. 2:1, 3) what he has in "the heart" (2:30). Psychoanalysis, that "Jewish science," has already begun! Daniel A is punctuated with these "Freudian" dreams. Explained by Daniel, they become liberating for the dreamers.[26]

These are still only preparatory skirmishes for the apocalyptist, however. He himself remains nearly imperturbable before the dream, even when its interpretation has to be communicated to him by God or an angel (cf. 2:17). This is precisely because the "mystery" is not ultimate here—that is, in the apocalyptic perspective, eschatological. It is a secret for which the dreamer himself is responsible in that it resides in the depths of his soul and is really the key to his being. In short, this secret is not lodged in the deepest corner of heaven, but at the bottom of his heart. As Henry S. Gehman correctly notes, "In producing [dreams], God works according to the laws of the mind."[27] Jewish tradition goes further: Rav Shmuel Eliezer ben Yehuda Halevi (1555–1631), abbreviated Maharsha, wrote in his *Hidushei aggadoth*, "Only what someone has already thought will be shown to him."[28] Rashi comments, speaking of Daniel 2:29: "During the day, you wondered what would happen to your empire after you. When you retired for the night, this care had not left you." Literally, "your thoughts went up to bed [with you]."

This is why, for example in Daniel 2, when King Nebuchadnezzar says he does not remember his dream, we should see a psychological block against a revealed truth, the fatal import of which he senses. Moreover, Daniel says to the king in verses 29–30: "He who reveals mysteries made known to you what is to be [and which Daniel is about to expound to him] . . . that you may know the thoughts of your mind."

That this is a divine communication is verified by the fact that the dream is a direct expression of reality—a reality that is historical, not magical or allegorical. Although the conception of dreams in Daniel comes close to what psychology would discover twenty centuries later, it is remarkable that what occupies the center stage in the apocalypse is not what Nebuchadnezzar feels, but his history; his historical destiny. What Nebuchadnezzar is feeling is marginal and serves only to underline the seriousness of what is happening. Daniel is not charged with helping the king to integrate—as the psychologists say—external factors to produce a more balanced personality. He has the task of preparing the king to assume his historical role, even to modify history by his repentance.

The seer's interpretation is all prospective; that of psychoanalysis is retrospective, "archaeological," as Paul Ricoeur says. True, the two methods are not mutually exclusive. Quite the contrary, for that matter. But one of the two must take the lead and point the way to the other. If our archaic depths belong to the unconscious, the conscious mind must take total charge and orient it. This is the passage from dream to vision in Daniel.[29] Once again, Ricoeur sheds light on the question: "The argument will be that the dream looks backward toward childhood and the past, while the art work is an advance on the artist himself. It is a prospective symbol of personal synthesis and of the future of man . . ."[30] However, "Re-immersion in *our* archaism is no doubt the roundabout way by which we immerse ourselves in the archaism of humanity, and this double 'regression' is possibly, in its turn, the way to a discovery, to a prospection, and a prophecy concerning ourselves."[31] This is because "man has a responsibility to grow out of his childhood and shatter the process of repetition by constituting ahead of himself a contrasting history of hitherside forms through eschatology. The unconscious is the origin or genesis, while consciousness is the end of time or apocalypse. . . . We must therefore understand that, although opposed, the system of hitherside figures and that of figures which always refer to a previously given symbolism are *the same*."[32]

DREAM AND VISION

We need to be alert to a change in vocabulary that occurs in the transition from Daniel A to Daniel B. In the latter we no longer have dreams that serve to bring on the revelation of mysteries, but visions. In fact, dream is inadequate to the true transmission of a transcendent reality. Dream (*ḥalôm*) in Daniel A becomes vision (*mareʾèh*) in Daniel B. Daniel 7:1, which still uses the term *ḥalôm*, does so only as a supplementary link with what precedes, as confirmed by the use of the explicative "visions of the head," as in 2:28 and 4:5 [4:2]. Beginning with the next verse Daniel speaks of his visions. To be sure, dreams and visions need interpretation. This is the common denominator that unites them. There is one pesher for the dream (ch. 2), one for the inscription on the wall (ch. 5), one for the vision (ch. 7). But their resemblance stops there.

We might ask, first, whether Daniel did not perhaps want to avoid severe criticism of dreams of the sort found in Deuteronomy and the prophets (Deut. 13:1ff.; 18:10–11; 2 Kgs. 21:6; Isa. 8:20; Jer. 23:25–28, 32; 27:9–10; Zech. 10:2). But that is not a sufficient explanation. As during the age of the patriarchs, vision returns in full force in Daniel, taking the place of prophetic inspiration. In general, the critics have seen in this phenomenon a sign of literary degeneracy. The apocalyptists, according to them, were merely *epigoni* of the prophets. Since they could no longer boast of such high inspiration, they had to be content with imitating their masters through the use of literary devices. They were no longer prophets; they were "visionaries."

This is certainly not the way the apocalyptists themselves felt. Quite to the contrary, they considered their mode of inspiration to be above that of their predecessors. Moreover, as we have already seen, it is difficult to reduce the mystical experience that the visionary relates to a simple case of poetic license. We must look elsewhere to see why vision replaced prophecy.

First of all, we need to take into account that we are at the time of the Second Temple, during the aftermath of the Deuteronomic reform, which considerably weakened prophetic authority in Israel by insisting that Moses was the one true prophet (see Deut. 34:10–12, which to some extent modifies Deut. 18:15ff.).[33]

To be sure, Daniel is not the direct heir of D (nor P). Their line continues in the Chronicler, not in the apocalypse, which, to the contrary, is attached to the prophetic tradition. Nevertheless, there was certainly an advantage for the "utopians," in the polemic between the two currents of postexilic thought, in not insisting on a prophetic inspiration that had become suspect. A text like Zechariah 13:3ff. (from the fifth century B.C.E.)[34] is an important milestone in this evolution. We should also keep in mind that prophecy had fallen into disrepute among skeptical circles in Jerusalem (which probably included many others than just the party of the "ideologists") since its literal fulfillment had failed to come to pass after the Exile. On this level as well, the apocalyptist had every reason to set himself off from his predecessors, the prophets, and to claim the benefits of a more certain and definitive inspiration than theirs in *vision*, with all the apparatus of images and symbols that it implies.

This choice turned out to be on the whole fortunate, if we can judge by the attraction that the new genre held for the people. We must admit that symbolic language contributes a good deal to the power of apocalyptic writing. It uses the very images of our unconscious, awakening in us a deep natural sympathy and what we might call a profound assent. "Mystery" is such only for the conscious mind; not for the unconscious, accustomed to oneiric images of the sort, the exotic quality of which is both troubling and familiar. The "key" to their interpretation also opens the unconscious for the conscious mind.

Thus, apocalypse accomplished more than a simple semantic transfer from dream to vision. Between the dreamer and the visionary there is a world of difference. The dreamer is from beginning to end passive, a simple terrain for numinous revelation. The visionary, to the contrary, can be hyperactive at the start: he goes into a trance, he is frenetically agitated, all of his senses are tensed (Dan. 8:15–17: "When I, Daniel, had seen the vision, I sought to understand it. . . . I heard a man's voice . . . . I was frightened and fell upon my face"). But at the "finish line" he is paralyzed; he falls into a cataleptic fit (cf. 10:8-9); he is prostrate (8:17), so that he seems to return to the dreamer's state of sleep. Now, however, sleep is a "second state," a condition indispensable to receiving visionary experiences. Thus and only thus could one receive the secret of unsoundable mysteries.

As a universal religious intuition testifies, this process is an initiatory death.[35] The visionary has the appearance of a corpse: εικων του θανατου (T. Reub. 3:1; also Rev. 1:17). This clarifies the second part of Daniel 8:18, where the angel touches Daniel and sets him back on his feet: he brings him back to life. The miraculous touch is also found in Daniel 9:21; 10:10, 16, 18. Its model can be found in, for example, Isaiah 6:7, Jeremiah 19, or Ezra 1:5, but the theme was to be exploited much more thoroughly in later writings (1 Enoch 60:3; 4 Ezra 5:14, 15; Rev. 1:17).[36]

SYMBOLIC LANGUAGE, DREAM, AND VISION

Dream is the writing on the "plaster" of the unconscious. Vision is the writing on the hidden face of history. The secret of history—the object of the apocalyptic quest, the goal of true wisdom and of true prophecy—is the "unconscious" of history. It presents no dichotomy with human reality; it does not sweep us toward the levels of the ideal of the abstract. There are no Platonic Ideas involved; these are abstract, whereas the pleromatic objects of apocalyptic revelation are concrete. Only their comprehension by the unfulfilled Adam remains clouded. The secret of history is the very meaning of history. All human beings are, in a certain sense, Nebuchadnezzars and Belshazzars walking through life as in a dream, the meaning of which escapes them. The meaning is there, however, asking only to be grasped. History appears to us, Kafkaesque personages that we are, like a labyrinthine castle, yet the terrible dungeon that offers no escape is always about to reveal its authentic reality as a Garden of Eden.

This, it seems to me, is the explanation for the alternating sympathy and antipathy that has greeted apocalyptic writings from one age to another. The very ambiguity of dream and the symbolism of vision—which the apocalyptist sees as corresponding to the ambiguity of history and of existence—arouse in the reader feelings of both comfort and discomfort, as do the images produced by the unconscious. It often happens that one rejects one's nocturnal vision and relegates it to oblivion. The "secret" is too difficult to discover, and perhaps its revelation would be too much to bear. When the interpretation is given and accepted, however, the dreamer is liberated, even if the vision was unflattering to him, for the explication makes what was absurd pass to the level of sign and of signification. The myth is demythologized without being either sterilized or annihilated. To the contrary, for the first time, it now becomes a message received, an informative message—kerygma that is not only grasped but also capable of generating history.

This kerygma remains remarkably Jewish. As we reach the end of this study of apocalyptic symbolic language, we find confirmation once again that the Jewish character was jealously preserved in this literature of a new genre. It is for good reasons that Daniel found a place in the canon of Scripture. Under its unusual external trappings, it contributes effectively and legitimately to the authentic biblical message.

We need to keep this in mind as we study the "son of man" of Daniel 7. There is no notion of an abstract man, a mythical man, or the ideal man here,[37] and even less of the idea of "Man." As Collins writes, "the literal man can also be symbolic."[38] Similarly, as far as eschatological expectation is concerned, it would be false to see its formulation in Daniel as the symbol of a flight to escape time.

NOTES

1. In the sense of the term in photography (see Dan. 2:29). A similar point of view can be found in Sirach, the writing of which was nearly contemporary with that of Daniel. God's wisdom is at work in all peoples (Sir. 24:6), but it is condensed and summed up in Israel. Wisdom, in fact, is identified with the Torah (24:23), and it is priestly (50).

2. This was true of the priest of Israel, according to D and P in particular, who carried out "internally" the priestly function that the people fulfilled "externally" (Exod. 19:6).

3. Dan. 7–12 (and already present in Ezek. 40–42 and First Zechariah).

4. On the ideology of the monarchy in Jerusalem and its apocalyptic reinterpretation, see ch. 4 above, under *"Urzeit-Endzeit"* and ch. 6, under "From the Davidic to the Adamic."

5. See esp. Mircea Eliade, *Myth and Reality*.

6. E. W. Heaton, *The Old Testament Prophets*, 119.

7. Paul Hanson, *The Dawn of Apocalyptic*, 28.

8. Martin Hengel, *Judaism and Hellenism*, 1:267.

9. Paul Ricoeur, *The Symbolism of Evil*, 10ff.

10. J. J. Collins, "The Symbolism of Transcendence in Jewish Apocalyptic," 5ff. Norman Perrin "Wisdom and Apocalyptic in the Message of Jesus."

11. Actually the term comes from P. Wheelwright, *The Burning Fountain*.

12. Jesus, according to Perrin, rejected the "steno-symbol" of apocalyptic and adopted the "tensive symbol," as in the "kingdom of God," e.g.

13. Collins, "The Symbolism," 15.

14. As M.-J. Lagrange writes, "The author cannot always untangle all of the springs and the agents of this divine mechanism; all he can do is to note how it works: 'the books were opened,' 'his name was named,' 'cords were provided' (1 En. 47.3; 48.3; 61.1)" (*Le Judaïsme avant Jésus-Christ*, 76).

15. Foreword to LaCocque, *The Book of Daniel*, xxii. Mircea Eliade writes, "To be sure, the 'success' of any such vision depended on the already existing schemas: a vision in basic contradiction to the traditional images and scenarios was not likely to win easy acceptance" (*Myth and Reality*, 146). We are by definition dealing with a polyvalent symbolism, which is altered as the signification changes.

16. Carl Jung writes: "Just as the body has an anatomical prehistory of millions of years, so also does the psychic system. And just as the human body today represents in each of its parts the result of this evolution, and everywhere still shows traces of its earlier stages—the same may be said of the psyche" (*Memories, Dreams, Reflections*, 348). See Mircea Eliade (*The Sacred and the Profane*, 209: "The contents and structures of the unconscious exhibit astonishing similarities to mythological images and figures."

17. D. S. Russell, *The Method and Message of Jewish Apocalyptic*, 161ff.

18. See 4 Ezra 10:59; 1 Enoch 14:2; 83:7; 85:1; Shepherd of Hermas 2.4, 1.

19. Marguerite Rutten, *"La Science des Chaldéens"*, Que sais-je? 56.

SYMBOLIC LANGUAGE, DREAM, AND VISION

20. "Meaningless . . . is our contrast between reality and appearance. Whatever is capable of affecting mind, feeling, or will has thereby established its undoubted reality" (Henri Frankfort, *Before Philosophy*, 20). This was already true at Ugarit: e.g., Baal III, col. 3; Keret I, col. 1.26–39, 46–51.

21. The Pharisees inherited the cultivation of mantics: see Matt. 12:27 (= Luke 11:19).

22. "In dream and in vision." Thus we find confirmation that the apocalyptist was conscious of being the representative of final prophecy. Prophecy, as we have seen, was awaited as an eschatological sign, after it had been agreed that Haggai, Zechariah, and Malachi signaled the end of ancient prophecy.

23. E. R. Dodds, *The Greeks and the Irrational*, chp. 4.

24. Ibid., 109. It is not surprising, on the other hand, to find that for Aristotle ("On Dreams" and "On Divination in Sleep") no dream is godsent, but may be called daemonic, "for Nature is daemonic" ("On Divination . . .," 463 b 14).

25. H.-P. Müller, "Der Begriff 'Rätsel' im Alten Testament," 476.

26. See my Commentary on Daniel 5:26–28. Freud's "secondary elaboration" means telling the dream in giving it coherence and intelligibility; i.e., in Dodds' categories, bringing the dream closer to traditional culture patterns (Freud, *The Interpretation of Dreams*, 391).

27. H. S. Gehman, "Dream."

28. The Talmudic text in *Ber.* 55b says: "R. Shmuel bar Nahmani says in the name of R. Yonathan: The dreamer has only the vision of the very thoughts of his heart." Martin Buber says, "Everything on our way involves decision, purposive, dimly seen, wholly mysterious" (*I and Thou*, 86).

29. If J. C. VanderKam is right that in the Book of the Watchers of Enoch (third century B.C.E.) dream and vision are interchangeable, then there is evolution from Enoch to Daniel (*Enoch and the Growth of an Apocalyptic Tradition*, 110ff). VanderKam refers to 1 Enoch 13:8, 10; 14:2. 4QEn^c 6.10 reads "dream" in 14:1.

30. Paul Ricoeur, *The Conflict of Interpretations*, 140.

31. Ricoeur, *The Symbolism of Evil*, 13.

32. Ricoeur, *Conflict*, 118.

33. See Joseph Blenkinsopp, *Prophecy and Canon*. Blenkinsopp sees in Deut. 34:10–12 "the last touch, later than either D or P but using language borrowed from the former" (p. 83).

34. Cf. my commentary on this text in Amsler, Lacocque, and Vuilleumier, *Aggée, Zacharie, Malachie*, 194ff.

35. See Eliade, *Myth and Reality*, 79ff.: "Traditional techniques for Going Back" or *regressus ad uterum, ad originem*; cf. 126ff.

36. Note that people have always seen a similarity between sleep and death. Dream is to the sleeper what vision is for the initiate whose trials are ritually a return to non-existence. "In Greek mythology Sleep and Death, Hypnos and Thanatos, are two twin brothers. We may note that, for the Jews too, at least from post-exilic times on, death was comparable to sleep. Sleep in the grave (Job 3:13–15; 3:17), in Shéol (Eccl. 9:3; 9:10) or in both at once (Ps. 88)" (Eliade, *Myth and Reality*, 126).

37. *Pace* Mowinckel, *He That Cometh*, 346ff.

38. Collins, "The Symbolism of Transcendence," 19.

SIX

The Major Theological Lessons of the Book of Daniel

THE APOCALYPTIC MYTHOS

The structure of Daniel B is of the type that Northrop Frye calls a "single archetypal structure."[1] It is single because all of it is cast in the apocalyptic mold. It is archetypal in that it presents a typological unity. Its language is in keeping with its generic character: it is significative, metaphorical, mythopoeic—which means that it is not descriptive and not literal. Even on the formal level we need to beware the traps of the literal as we review such great passages in Daniel as the one on the son of man (chs. 7ff.) or on the resurrection of the dead (ch. 12).

Its ideological level is even more remarkable. As we have seen on several occasions, the apocalyptical message—above all, that of the period of the Second Temple—was based on the message of the pre-exilic or exilic prophets. As it happens, these were for the most part prophets of woes. Jeremiah even makes a rule of it as far as his predecessors are concerned: "The prophets who preceded you and me from ancient times prophesied war, famine, and pestilence against many countries and great kingdoms" (Jer. 28:8; the prophet referred to is Hananiah). Prophecy had become nearly synonymous with catastrophe. A catastrophe of a resolutely historical nature, moreover; for, according to the conception generally shared by the prophets before the restoration, prophecy centered on the destruction of Jerusalem at the

138

hands of an enemy who was used as an instrument of divine wrath. This future disaster is so central in prophecy that it was all that could be seen on the horizon, but it was not impossible that the sky turn blue again after the storm. This is what Second Isaiah (40–55) announces, to pick one example. The exile to Babylon was not—or at least, not necessarily—the last event in history (see Jer. 24:5-6; 25:12; 29:10, e.g.).

This mythos of disaster followed by restoration obviously had excellent letters of credit in Israel. The prophets recalled the Egyptian captivity and the liberation from slavery by the Exodus. Second Isaiah combines this theme with that of God the creator of being from nonbeing (see also Ezek. 37, e.g.), to which we will soon return. It was also this mythos that provided raw material for the apocalypse. Where it had been repetitive and typological, however, in the apocalypse it became absolutist (i.e., unique) and hieratical. Where it had been historical, it became cosmic and eschatological. It had other secondary characteristics that will be discussed in due time, but we need to pause first over this theme of the final cataclysm, for it provides the background against which all other problems must be seen.

If misfortune is synonymous with "classic" prophecy,[2] catastrophe has become associated with the apocalypse. Still, it is not the only, nor even the first, time that we can see cosmic revolution in the tradition of Israel. Noah's flood (Gen. 6–9) presents all the signs of an apocalyptic calamity. The parallel is hardly new.[3] Hermann Gunkel speaks in his *Schöpfung und Chaos* of the apocalyptic as a projection into the future of a distant past. More recently Claus Westermann writes, in his magnum opus on Genesis: "Apocalyptic, both in content and in intention, is subordinated not to salvation history but to primeval history, especially to the history of creation and of the flood."[4] In a related tradition the absolute and universal divine punishment by water is changed into an annihilation by fire. The microcosm of Sodom and Gomorrah disappears in a cosmic conflagration (Gen. 19). This variation on a theme is worth noting, for the apocalypse opted for the latter mode for the destruction of the world (or of the final enemy; Dan. 7:11), probably under the influence of Iranian thought. "In Persian eschatology," Carl Kraeling states, "the mountains, which are made of metal, melt at the end of the world, and the molten metal pours over the earth like a river. All men pass into this river of molten metal and in so doing are either purified or destroyed."[5] Kraeling believes that this gives us the origin of so many "realistic interpretations of the function of fire in the final judgment."

To my mind, what we see here (and elsewhere) is the extent to which Iranian influence reinvigorated elements in Israelite tradition.[6]

What ideological connection is there between the flood, the fire consuming the world entirely, and the cataclysm of the end of time? The flood marked the end of a natural cycle on the cosmic plane; the apocalyptic catastrophe marks, once more on the cosmic level, an end on the temporal plane. In the two cases, however, the end of the cycle is transcended; in the first instance by a nature redeemed, in the second by the redemption of time. From this point of view the apocalypses that introduce the element of the messianic millennium between the End and the coming of the kingdom of God[7] establish a more distinct parallel, since the reign of the Messiah represents the triumph of time redeemed.[8] Where that element is absent—and especially in Daniel—it is because of the transitoriness of this stage of the voyage toward "eternity." Apocalypse uses the latter term without defining it, leaving us at the mercy of translations, but one thing is clear: Eternity immediately follows the end of time in Daniel.

We need to summarize before we go on: Israel considered the question of nature to be settled with the flood. Nature follows a generic rhythm, and that it does so is a sign of divine grace. God put his seal of approval on nature with his rainbow. But it was a barely sufficient, minimal sort of grace. The fact that nature was redeemed did not mean that it was not transitory. The rules imposed on nature once and for all by the Creator—causality, for example—can only be justified in relation to a higher aim, a purpose on a different level. They permit the history of the relationship between God and humanity to unfold in a preestablished framework that presents no problems. One and one will make two, and "while the earth remains, seedtime and harvest, cold and heat, summer and winter, day and night, shall not cease" (Gen. 8:22).[9] I shall return to this question soon.

Next, the question of time. Time, after the deluge—as, to a certain extent, before it[10]—was in process of redemption. It was the time of history, or, if you like, of *Heilsgeschichte*. As long as time lasts, the last bet is not down. There is at every moment the possibility that time will arrive at its own transfiguration. This *kairos*, the pleromatic point of arrival in time that will redeem history, is saluted by the king-centered ideology of Zion as the messianic coming.

We can now return to the cataclysmic paradigm. The *Endzeit* corresponds to the *Urzeit* (the final catastrophe corresponds to the flood), but is not a simple repetition of it. The fall—and with it, all of *Heilsge-schichte*—was only possible in a universe that was from its postcata-strophic origin, suspended between life and death, good and evil, hot and cold, light and shadow, the cosmos and the chaos, according to the laws stipulated in the covenant with Noah.[11] These laws are adapted to the postlapsarian existence of man. Human life finds its place in them in a tension between chaos and cosmos that is itself negative and posi-tive—that is, painful and creative, just like the labor of men and women described in Genesis 3:16-19. But at the end of time these laws will be suspended: "And there shall be continuous day (it is known to the Lord), not day and not night, for at evening time there shall be light. On that day living waters shall flow out from Jerusalem, half of them to the eastern sea and half of them to the western sea; it shall continue in sum-mer as in winter. And the Lord will become king over all the earth; on that day the Lord will be one and his name one" (Zech. 14:7-9).

This apocalyptical vision, in a prophet of the fifth century,[12] shows once again to what extent the apocalyptic model can truly be under-stood only against the background of prophetism. But comparison also shows the full measure of their differences. As long as the prophetic notion of the *aharit ha-yamim* (the end of days; Isa. 2:2; Jer. 23:20; 30:24; Hos. 3:5, etc., and still in use in Dan. 10:14) prevailed, with the sense of a conclusive event that gives validity and meaning to what preceded it but does not itself necessarily constitute the end of history as such, the appropriate typology was the slavery in Egypt and the Exodus, the trek through the desert and the theophany of Sinai or even, in a minor key, the battle of Midian and the glory of the set of concepts centering on David and Jerusalem. This typology no longer works, however, when the *Endzeit*, the ultimate eschaton, is involved. The typology that takes over then is that of the *Urzeit*—mythical and cosmological typology.

This means that the apocalypse does not substitute a foreign (Ira-nian?) typology for a traditional and biblical typology. In the spiritual patrimony of Israel, there was already a cosmological typology at hand, ready to be used. In overlooking this, modern scholars have proven unjust toward apocalyptic. Guilty of historicism themselves, they con-clude from the absence of *Heilsgeschichte* that apocalyptic was a minor literary genre that never should have entered the canon.[13] However, making *Heilsgechichte* the fundamental criterion for the canonization of authoritative documents in Israel (and subsequently in the church) is a principle, as has often been said, that is severely limited by the presence of ahistorical biblical literary genres such as wisdom literature or hymns. The apocalyptic phenomenon is more important than these two categories, however; for, unlike the aphorism or the hymn, it is primarily concerned with the problems of time and history—like the saga, like prophecy or historiography in Israel, but in a totally different fashion. From a structural point of view the presence of apocalyptic at the end of biblical revelation and, from a semantic point of view, its eschatological preoccupation are both highly significant. For the apocalypse—*beyond* the classic definition of *Heilsgeschichte*—attains the universal and the cosmic qualities of the "history of origins" in Genesis 1–11. This means that *Heilsgeschichte* is flanked, as it begins and as it comes to fruition, by a temporal and a spatial transcendence that make its import only relative. The particular is transcended by the universal.[14]

This last point has an evident relevance to what follows on the "one like a son of man" (Dan. 7:13). In any event, we now have the proper tools for dealing with apocalypse: we have a typology of destruction and restoration; we have a general set of problems regarding the *Urzeit* and the *Endzeit*; and we have their specific resolution in the framework of a cosmological model. Within this mythical setting the particular has meaning only in relation to the general; the event is absorbed into the great design and the historical into the "eternal."[15]

This paradigmatic idea, as I have emphasized, itself develops from another (and prophetic) model that precedes it. In prophecy a central figure plays a determinant role—the Messiah. Obviously this model required just as much reinterpretation toward the universal as the other elements that apocalypse had borrowed and adapted. The Messiah was, traditionally, the key figure who opened the transition from the chaos of history to the eternal bliss of a redeemed Israel. This was what the apocalypse was all about, provided that the prophetic nationalism be replaced by cosmic interests. As Northrop Frye writes, "Symbols of humiliation, betrayal, and martyrdom, the so-called suffering servant complex . . . in their turn are succeeded by symbols of the Messiah as bridegroom, as conqueror of a monster, and as the leader of his people into their rightful home."[16] But the apocalypse accentuates the polarization of the two symbols. The negative symbols of humiliation and betrayal are used to portray evil incarnate, the monster straight from chaos, Antiochus IV. The positive symbols of martyrdom—soon to change to triumph—characterize the pious Jews. In strong contrast to the language of darkness from which their enemy emerges, they were, in the terminology of Qumran and of the New Testament, the children of light.

This was how the forces of evil and the forces of good lined up to face one another. But the mythos demanded the individual personification of these powers. Antiochus IV is the dragon, that obstacle omnipresent in legend and myth, thanks to whom—or rather, at whose expense—there were both story and history, both redemption and salvation. But if Antiochus played the dragon, someone had to play Saint George: in Israelite terminology, the Messiah. Something essential to the structural equilibrium apocalypse held dear is pushed off balance with this term, however. The Messiah comes as a "repairer of the breach" (Isa. 58:12). He comes second; he comes *after*. This is how things are in *Heilsgeschichte*, which is not embarrassed by this imbalance. In order to avoid it, the apocalypse, as we have seen, adopted the *Urgeschichte* as a typological model. From that point on, the balance was restored. In the beginning there was Man: Adam. At the end there would be Man: the second Adam, in Paul's felicitous formula.[17] As a first result of our inquiry we can thus say that as *Heilsgeschichte* is inserted beautifully into the universal and the cosmic, so the Messiah is bracketed by what comes before and after him: Man. From the Davidic, we pass to the Adamic.

FROM THE DAVIDIC TO THE ADAMIC

There is a messianic residue in the term "son of man."[18] The son of man is anointed and chosen; he is just, wise, light of the peoples,[19] judge, leader, and so on. He has kingly traits and royal power (Dan. 7:14; cf. 2:37; 5:18). But this "king" is celestial (if not by nature, at least by situation), and it is evident that the political dimension of the king-Messiah has been transcended.

As it happens, this relegation of the political (a dimension perfectly appropriate to *Heilsgeschichte*) allows the apocalypse to return to the true ideological foundation of kingship in the ancient Near East and the eastern Mediterranean. To be sure, the military dimension is not absent. But it is secondary to the sacral nature of kingship. From Egypt and the Sudan to the Aegean Sea, from India and Iran to Canaan, the king (or, in Egypt, the pharaoh) was on earth the one gifted, by birth or by divine delegation, with generative forces. He was the source of life, a reservoir of fertility and fecundity. He was the divine presence on earth, and that presence alone kept the world in life.[20] He was antichaos.

No community could survive the absence of the king. The dikes that held off the forces of chaos were swept away if this occurred. For Babylon of the sixth century, the "heterodox" reign of someone like Nabonidus, who neglected the rites of fecundity of the Akitu festival (the New Year), was a traumatic experience. The Babylonian Chronicle states it simply: "The king is mad" (*ANET* 314). The madness of a king had incalculable consequences for the destiny of Babylon (Herodotus *History* 1. 191). What happened, then, when the royal line disappeared in Judah after the Exile?

It is remarkable that such an enormous loss was to so great an extent compensated by the birth of postexilic Judaism, thus by the survival of Yahwism itself.[21] This does not mean, retrospectively, that the historical royal house necessarily constituted a handicap for classic Yahwism,[22] but that Israel had an incredible capacity for conserving spiritually what it lost from a material point of view. "One day," *Aboth of Rabbi Nathan* states (A 4.5),

> Rabbi Yohanan ben Zaccai went out of Jerusalem, and Rabbi Joshua followed him. He saw the Temple in ruins and he exclaimed, "Woe unto us, the place in which the sins of Israel were atoned for is in ruins." Rabbi Yohanan said to him, "My son, do not be dismayed, for we have an atonement that is as good as the first, which is the practice of love. As it is written, "I desire steadfast love and not sacrifice" (Hos. 6:6). Indeed, we find in Daniel a greatly beloved man who busied himself with the practice of love. . . He provided well for the bride, and he contributed to her joy. He accompanied the dead [to the cemetery]. He gave alms to the poor. He prayed three times daily (6:11)."

When circumstances made one practice impossible, another replaced it; but this did not happen by chance. This substitution was the fruit of reflection that focused on rediscovering the profound meaning of rite: the ritual gesture may be lost but its significance remains.[23]

Not only is rite reinterpreted in this manner, but with it all the elements that belong to *Heilsgeschichte*, messianism included. The apocalyptist saw the revision of this principle as all the more urgent because for him the history of salvation ended in catastrophe and not in apotheosis, whatever the theocrats of Jerusalem might think. If it was vain at this point to continue to expect a *Heilsgeschichtlich* Messiah—who was no more apparent on the horizon than restoration of the monarchy—he nevertheless continued to furnish to the visionaries a deeply rooted spiritual and existential model. Moreover, the loss of such principles on the phenomenological plane was not really regrettable, for it did not affect their noumenal "presence"—to use a Kantian term—and it served to recognize a defeat within history that had been well deserved. In point of fact, kingship had had an ambiguous status from its start in Israel (1 Sam. 8), and it had become, everywhere and always, the expression of an insupportable arrogance (Daniel A). It was clear that it never had been more than "only a shadow of what is to come" (Col. 2:17) or, what amounts to the same thing, a feeble echo of the authentic kingship of the earliest ages as represented in the *Urgeschichte*. Then Man was king of creation. According to P, Adam is the image and the resemblance of God. In Psalm 8:6, this resemblance to the divine is signified by Adam's sovereign sway over the whole of creation. Ezekiel, on the other hand, describes on the heavenly throne "a likeness as it were of a human form"—of an "Adamic" form. Thus from the point of view of *Urzeit*, the monarchic function in history is to some degree sacramental. It is, in any event, paradigmatic. It signifies the Adamic kingship over the created universe. This was, however, exactly what was obliterated by monarchic power, which had become everywhere its own reason for being and its own justification. The return to a veritable and Adamic king would restore the crown to its authentic dimension of reflecting divine kingship. The signifier would once again be one with the signified.

The apocalypse of Daniel 7 accomplishes this by the use of the highly polysemic symbol of the son of man, which introduces us into a world of an extraordinarily rich set of meanings. The stroke of genius was, as has been pointed out, to combine eschatological vision with the mythical time (*"in illo tempore"*) of the beginnings, when all was possible and asked only to be. Thus all that had indeed been during *Heilsgeschichte* would be reconstituted—along with what had not been and could have been. This is why, on the one hand, the expression "one like a son of man" immediately became one of the most powerful ferments in theological thought. On the other hand, it is why sounding out the full implications of this formula poses an enormous challenge to the exegete.[24]

In taking up this task as it applies to Daniel 7, it is important to remain within the context of the second century and to avoid extrapolation based on the later development of the notion of the Son of man. Nonetheless, we need to keep in mind that these are just the beginning stages of a hermeneutical current of thought concerning the Messiah in a sectarian Judaism of the Maccabean epoch. The breach was opened, and a flood of innovative ideas was to rush through it. The heart-wrenching revision of "ancient things" that Daniel inaugurated was to go in the direction of an increasing radicalization. Not only would the individual figure of the Messiah be redefined on the basis of the new theological needs of the community as its political and even religious liberty was gradually taken away;[25] the process of reinterpretation was even to go as far as "democratizing" what had initially been conceived as the privilege of select, if not unique, individuals. Thus the Judean community was to appropriate kingly, prophetic, and priestly functions and titles. It would end up viewing itself as the Holy of Holies of the profaned or the destroyed temple,[26] because during its trials it had become aware that it could proclaim: "Before institutions, I am"; "The sabbath was made for man, and not man for the sabbath." Never before, in fact, had events so implacably relativized institutional structures, to the point of destroying them completely. The day was coming in which Israel was to find itself without a king, without prophets, with no active priests, with no temple, with no state—and eventually with no homeland.

This forced "disincarnation" had a great deal to do with apocalypse's recourse to the mythopoeic model—that is, to cultic language.[27] As Benedikt Otzen has written: "It is . . . characteristic of myth that it is, in one way or another, bound to the cult."[28] We will have occasion to return to this question. We need first to ask what had become of the process of "demythologization" that was so evident in nearly all biblical literature, and in particular in the Genesis accounts of protohistory. As it happens, in Daniel 7 the process continues. Here, as before, myth serves as raw material uniquely because of the symbolism attached to it. That symbolism remains, thanks to a rigorous filtering process (but one that was obviously imperfect, for otherwise there would be little chance of discovering the mythic origins of these materials today).

Two main criteria guided the filtering out of myth. First, God is unique, and he transcends his creation. Second, cosmological and anthropological phenomena[29] are not accidental, nor do they result

146

from divine whim. They spring from an existential choice on the part of mankind of what Israel calls sin.

There is perhaps no one who, upon reading the first verses of Daniel 7, fails to think immediately of the mythical background of this sort of vision—particularly when the fourth beast arrives on the scene. It is described on the model of the primordial dragon, symbol of the cosmic waters, of the shadows, of the night, and of death—in a word, of the amorphous and the virtual, of all that does not yet have "form."[30] Daniel 7 continues the process of "historicization" from where Jeremiah had left it, when, for example, he described Nebuchadnezzar as a monster (*tannin*) who was swallowing up Jerusalem. Although in Daniel 7 the beast is not specifically called a monster, its devastation is nonetheless clearly parallel to that of Nebuchadnezzar as described by Jeremiah (Dan. 7:7). Another comparison can be seen in Isaiah 27:1, where YHWH destroys Leviathan, the dragon of the seas.

This defeat of the "ancient serpent" is equivalent to a renewal of the act of creation (which is the profound meaning of judgment by the son of man).[31] Central in the "festival of Jerusalem"[32] that this scene reflects, this theme in the first part Daniel 7 of the chaotic monsters emerging out of the primordial waters orients the meaning of the entire chapter (even if vv. 13ff. are to be taken as secondary, as many, and recently Ulrich Müller,[33] have held).

As with the festival of Jerusalem, it should be noted that the myth in its apocalyptic form omits—as do the Israelite accounts of *Urgeschichte*—the two motifs that preceded the enthronement of Baal in Canaan: the death and resurrection of the god of fertility, and his *hieros gamos*. We ought not to exaggerate the mythologic dimension of what seems to be a transfer of powers from God to the son of man, following the model of Baal as successor to El. It is a mistake to undertake an exegesis of these passages in Daniel solely from the point of view of the history of religions. The Israelite kerygma may have come of a general fund of religious experience, but it left that common ground to take its own route. Its dominant note is that "the world and man are located in *a field of tension between chaos and cosmos.*"[34]

The Davidic substratum that is evident in Daniel 7:13ff., to which I shall return, reminds us that it is YHWH himself who crowns David's heir and who gives him the gift of power, source of blessing and of eternal life (Ps. 21:1-7; cf. Pss. 72:5; 89:29, 36). In short, the king operates like a divine being,[35] which is why he is called son of God (Pss. 2:7;

89:27-28) or even simply "God" (Ps. 45:6). He delivers judgment, which promises death for the enemies (Pss. 2; 72:4*c*) and life for the oppressed among his people (Ps. 72:2, 4, 12-13).

Adam is not far away in all this. He is present as delegated king over all creation. All historical kings resemble him (or ought to), for all kingship is founded in God, whose *imago* on earth is Adam (Gen. 1:26).[36] In point of fact, the apocalypse is an admission that this ideal has failed. Kings are not "Adamic" but bestial; they are not forces for order (cosmos) but for anarchy (chaos). What is necessary is a return, somehow, to the beginnings—*Endzeit wird Urzeit*—and to enthrone an Adam/judge/king so that he can facilitate the emergence of a new world.

The Chronicler combined the characters of Moses and David to obtain a founder and organizer of the cult of Zion for the veritable redemption of the people and of the world. Daniel also combines two figures: Adam and David, with the accent on the kingly bringer of peace.[37] The scene of the thrones in Daniel 7 inevitably recalls the throne of David, promised "for ever" to his posterity (e.g., Pss. 89: 4, 29, 37; 110:1ff; 132:11-12.). The same is true concerning the universal and eternal nature of this pleromatic kingdom (Dan. 7:14). It is clearly the fulfillment of the promises made to David (e.g. Pss. 2:8; 72:8; 89:25, 28-30, 37-38).

David is a complex figure, however.[38] The Chronicler saw in him the organizer of the cult. In a nearly similar vein Daniel emphasizes the priestly function of "one like a son of man" in many passages, in particular in chapters 7–12.[39] Leaving chapter 7 aside for the moment, the expression "Prince of the host" in 8:11 is to be understood in the combined sense of high priest and angel, for it is speaking of the same personage as in chapter 7.[40] In 9:24 the expression "the most holy place," which usually refers to a specific place in the temple, here signifies the faithful priesthood (cf. 1 Chr. 23:13). We see confirmation of this in the very structure of this passage and in the parallel that is constantly drawn by Daniel between the temple and the people. It is in fact clear, especially in verses 24-26, that the "messianic" expectation (note the frequency of the notion of anointment) is here centered on the person of the high priest.[41] The mysterious personage in 10:5ff. is often (mistakenly) taken for the angel Gabriel. It is really the same son of man as in chapter 7. Again, he is characterized by his clothing and his priestly attributes. In 12:1 the archangel Michael (one of the aspects of the son of man) combines the functions of priest, judge, and king. Here in chapter 12 as in chapter 7, the scene described is the enthronement of YHWH within the liturgical framework of the feast of Succoth. Finally, the epilogue of the book begins with 12:5. Here we see the angel Gabriel and the son of man dressed in linen like the high priest (12:6) and as in 10:5 (cf. 8:15ff.; 10:16). At verse 7 the man/priest raises his two hands to heaven to appeal to God himself, who becomes a witness, along with the other angel and with Daniel, to his oath regarding the End.

We can now return to chapter 7 of Daniel to remark, in preamble, that there is an evident reason why "one like a son of man" combines the kingly and priestly functions. The historical process of transfer of royal powers to the high priest had begun as early as the sixth century. In Zechariah 4:14 and 6:13 Joshua evidently is associated with Zerubbabel;[42] and soon the Hasmoneans, who were nearly contemporary with the author of Daniel, were to combine the two sources of power.[43]

But although Daniel reflects the normal evolution of a process that had begun during the sixth-century Exile, it nevertheless gives an original twist to this evolution. The same "return to basics" that we have signaled in connection with other aspects of the son of man in this vision occurs on the level of the priestly interpretation of this figure. What I propose to show is that the sovereign pontificate of the son of man was the result of a fourfold *épokhè* (phenomenological reduction) that took place through successive reinterpretations of the function (priesthood), the setting (the sanctuary), the temporal aspect (now and every time), and, finally, the central character (the high priest).

1. The function: To be sure, the sole function of the priesthood was not sacrifice; but, as Gerhard von Rad has pointed out, "The most important aspect of this particular function which the Priests had to manage was the ritual eating of the sin offering (Lev. X. 17ff.). This flesh was a thing 'most holy.' . . . By eating this flesh, and that in the holy place, the priests themselves effected the removal of evil. They were appointed to do this in order, as mediators, 'to bear the iniquity of the community' and [thereby] to make expiation for them before Jahweh (Lev. X.17)."[44]

This priestly meal is the foundation for the messianic banquet, where, according to Jewish tradition, the Leviathan was served up to the righteous (2 Bar. 29:3ff.; Ps. 74:14). It is only natural, then, to search for this trait in Daniel 7, when the fourth monstrous beast is put to death. Nothing of the sort happens, however. The beast is not eaten, but given to be burned. At this point we are sent back to another tradition, that of "the goat of the sin offering" in Leviticus 10:16ff. There, counter to Moses' expectation that they would "eat" the sin of the people, the priests burned up their sins, according to Aaron's interpretation, who then convinces Moses. Daniel 7:11 echoes Leviticus 10:16ff., in that the "people of the saints" do not take the place of the sinners, and the historic monster, Antiochus IV, is not a proper sacrificial victim for the sins of Israel. This corresponds to the general idea of Daniel, for which the division set up between saints and apostates is now established definitively (see 12:1-3).

2. The setting: There is, as we have seen, an *épokhè* (reduction) of the notion of the king that returns it to its base in Adam, or, similarly, of the Messiah that touches its deepest meaning as the opposition of man to beast.[45] The same is true concerning the temple—a bridgehead from which the cosmos can emerge into eternity. The apocalypse thus returns us to the model, to the eternal and celestial *tabnit* of which the temple is merely the copy (See Exod. 25:9, 40; 2 Kgs. 16:10; 1 Chr. 28:11-12, 18-19; Wis. 9:8; and esp. 2 Bar. 4:3-7, in which God says that the temple "was prepared beforehand here from the time when I took counsel to make Paradise, and showed it to Adam").[46]

It is clear in these texts that the temple was considered the center of the cosmos. Pseudepigraphic and rabbinic literature was to take up this theme. The temple was the *omphalos* of the world (See 1 Enoch 26:1-2; Jub. 8:12, 14; b. *Yoma* 54b; b. *Sanh.* 37a). Underlying this concept is the extremely ancient principle of analogy. According to the inscription of "statue B" of Gudea at Lagash (ca. 2400 B.C.E.) for example, the plan of the temple of Gudea consecrated to Ningirsu was cosmic and in the image of heaven.[47] Toward the end of the pre-Christian era the Scroll of the Temple at Qumran also conceived of Jerusalem as a Sinai continuum. The divine Presence had descended from Mount Sinai and had alighted on the tabernacle, which was brought to Jerusalem by David.

The importance of the principle of analogy has no need to be stressed. It is the very foundation of apocalyptic thought, and it manifests itself in a thousand and one guises. Even the language best suited to apocalyptic reflects it; symbol, metaphor, and metonymy crowd every page. As in the book of Ezekiel in particular, the referent is directly celestial, and even political struggles and wars find their parallels in angelic combats (Dan. 10:20–11:1). But, above all, sacred things are, sacramentally speaking, the presence of eternity in time. Thus the son of man is both celestial and terrestrial. He could be said (in somewhat anachronistic terms) to be "preexistent"—as could everything that concerns the eschaton, for that matter. Rabbis were later to establish lists of "things that preceded the creation," such as "the Torah, repentance, paradise, hell, the Throne of glory, the [celestial] Temple, and the name of the Messiah" (cf. *Pes.* 54a and *Ned.* 39b; *Gen. Rab.* 1.4; *Tanhuma*, S. Buber, ed., *Naso* par. 19, etc.). We might also compare the declaration of Rabbi Simai (ca. 200): "The creatures that were created from the heavens have all their souls and their bodies from the heavens, except man, whose soul is of heaven and whose body is of the earth. This is why, if man fulfills the Torah and the will of his Father in heaven, he is like the creatures on high (Ps. 82:6); if he does not do so, he is like the creatures here below (Ps. 82:7)."[48]

Thus it is clear that the profanation of the temple by the representatives of Antiochus not only made it improper for divine service, but also corrupted the heart of the cosmos. It is just as evident that, according to the apocalyptist, God is not going to permit this "monstrous thing," this "abomination of desolation" to triumph. The visionary, in an inspired flight that makes an obviously polemical point, places the temple of Jerusalem on the level of the contingent, and recalls that it was but the "shadow" of the real temple in God's presence. That was where the thrones were installed and where the cloud accompanied God's glory.[49]

Pharisaism, representing an eschatology of restoration, was later to provide a transcendent use of the temple in the terrestrial sense by the spiritualization of rite.[50] The apocalypse, for its part, transcends the temple in a celestial direction; apocalypse was an eschatology of rupture that no longer pinned its hopes on improvement through historical process. As a consequence, even when the material profanation of the temple ended (in 164), criticism of the "temple made by the hand of man" remained valid. Phenomena had begun a process of radical relativization that was never to be reversed. For although the same problems were posed for both the apocalyptists and these Pharisees before the fact, the solutions of the two groups were very different. The Pharisees were to keep patient watch to guarantee that institutions lasted; the apocalyptist made a virtue of their impatience to see the end of terrestrial institutions and their replacement by their divine model.[51] To speak of Pharisaic optimism and apocalyptic pessimism in this connection is misleading. It is not with death in its heart that apocalypse expected no further historical transformation in Israelite institutions.

Any restoration of things as they had been would only slow the coming of the "new things"—of the "new heaven and new earth" that Third Isaiah spoke of (Isa. 65: 16*b*-17; 66:22). Then would the provisory cede to the definitive; then would what had been subject to human "hardness of heart" in the law of Moses give way to what was "at the beginning" and will be at the end of time (*Urzeit-Endzeit*; cf. Matt. 19:8). Then would the temple be transformed, in the image of its essential—that is, celestial—identity.

3. Temporality: The connection between the scene described in Daniel 7 and the Festival of Jerusalem, with its mythopoeic language, has been mentioned. The ceremony of enthronement had its *Sitz im Leben* in this context, and the festival coincided with Succoth and probably also with the New Year (see the so-called "coronation" psalms: 47; 93; 96–99, among others). It was modeled on similar festivals, notably in Babylon and Ugarit. In general, the ceremony began with a ritual combat, during which the king was saved *in extremis* by God himself (cf. Ps. 18:43). We find a parallel to this motif in Daniel 7 with the victory over the monster. But here victory is delegated by "the One-who-endures" to "one like a son of man," and this profoundly transforms the fabric of the ritual. It is no longer the king figure who is saved; to the contrary, he becomes the savior of his "people of the saints."[52] The festival takes on a shift in meaning that is important to evaluate correctly, for it becomes significantly different from its Israelite original. What happened, and why?

Apocalypse borrowed the categories of mythopoeic language, as we have seen. The result is that it remythologized in formal terms what ritual in Jerusalem had found it so difficult to demythologize (and which it did only imperfectly, what is more). Thus, by a sort of backtracking, apocalypse returned to the paradigm of Near Eastern religions (before the "prophetic" transformation of that paradigm) and the king once more played the role of the divinity in the ritual. Does this become pure myth, then? Hardly, for what is true on the formal plane is not necessarily true on the level of meaning, as we shall soon see. In reality, the message in the apocalypse is different from that of the myth of origins, because the apocalypse envisages, not mythical beginnings, but the eschatological resolution of history.[53]

As for the priestly function discussed above, investigation of this question should not be limited to Daniel 7. The fact is that Daniel B in its entirety follows a rhythm like that of the liturgical year. From Succoth in chapters 7–8 we pass on to Yom Kippur (and the Jubilee year) in 9:24; then to a "Kippurized" Passover in 10:3-4, 12; to return to Succoth in chapter 12 (vv. 1-3 speak, as in ch. 7, of the enthronement of YHWH). I might note in passing that the religious calendar itself is revised in terms of the current situation and its spiritual import (as in Dan. 9). What is considered contingent is in the process of relativization in the name of its transcendent or pleromatic dimension.

In a context that is so decidedly liturgical, one might expect to find a matching temporality. The time scheme that is the proper of ritual language is "now and every time" (that the rite is accomplished). Underlying this scheme is the desire to ensure durability—to which the Pharisees were to remain faithful in their hermeneutics. In the apocalypse, however, nothing of the sort takes place. To the contrary, we pass here from a temporality of the repetitive to a temporality of the definitive, with an emphasis on the notion of *kairos* or "concentrated time"— that is, eternity. As Johannes Pedersen has so well put it,

> Concentrated time . . . is called eternity, *olam*. Eternity is not the sum of all the individual periods, nor even this sum with something added to it; it is "time" without subdivision, that which lies behind it; and which displays itself through all times. That the throne of David is to remain eternally means that it must be raised above or, rather, pervade changing periods, in that it has its foot in primeval time itself, the stock from which all time flows. Primeval time absorbs in it the substance of all time, and is therefore the beginning of all time.[54]

It should not be necessary to point out that it is this primordial time that serves as a chronological coordinate in Daniel 7, combined with the primordial spatial coordinate, the celestial sanctuary. This represents a profound transformation of cultic temporality.

4. The central personage: The son of man of Daniel is thus, among other things, priestly. Priesthood in Israel belonged, not to a caste, but to the man *qua* man. Before it is particular, priesthood is here universal. This is recalled by P (e.g. Gen. 1; Num. 3:40ff.) or again by the literary level that is present in Exodus 19:4-6 and that resembles D, but was probably independent.[55]

The apocalypse returns to this Adamic basis for priesthood. The one who is enthroned with God in Daniel 7 is a "man." Hence there is a "democratization" of the high priesthood. This is what the remainder of chapter 7 emphasizes when it speaks of the people of the saints, the collective dimension of the son of man.

The figure of the son of man is the fruit of a hermeneutic of a radical type, the obvious prolongation of which can be seen in the documents of the primitive Christian church. This hermeneutic is characterized by its teleological nature. It is in light of the pleroma that one can and one must envisage historical phenomena, which are merely "the shadow of things to come." We need to place ourselves in the perspective of pleromatic reality in order to appreciate the shadows cast by that reality. In other terms, it is only with a consciousness of the "already" that the "not yet" has meaning and significance.[56]

Clearly, the son of man is a figure, not a title, and even less reality itself. The comparative, "like a son of man," clearly shows the metaphorical nature of the vision. H. R. Balz judiciously notes that we should translate the term, not by "son of man," but by *Menschenähnlich*, the one who resembles a man.[57] This is what distinguishes second century B.C.E. apocalypse from the Christianity of the first centuries C.E. The first had a vision of ultimate reality; the second bears witness to its incarnation. Put differently, the first had at its disposal only a new symbol with which to evaluate the meaning of historical phenomena; the second claims to have seen with its own eyes the signified itself, so that the pleroma is no longer like a son of man but is the Son of man in person.

This remarkable promotion of a metaphor to the level of messianic title is an extraordinarily interesting phenomenon, but it is not unique.[58] It is of such decisive importance that it is only natural to turn toward the origins of the notion to attempt to discover the secret of an ideological promotion of the sort. All critics of the apocalypse and of New Testament literature have given it a try; the most recent development has been an expert exploration of the linguistic substratum of the expression.[59]

I have no intention of taking up this aspect of the problem here. It has been demonstrated beyond reasonable doubt that the expression "son of man" was a way of speaking of "someone," or, on occasion, of replacing the personal pronoun.[60] With this as background, I prefer to turn to an examination of literary criticism. On the literary level it is evident that the origin of the formula is to be found in the book of Ezekiel. The expression "son of man" is frequent there, appearing a hundred times or more to designate the prophet himself, especially in contrast to the glory of the Lord. In short, it had become a stereotype. That this notion is repeated in Daniel indicates at least that we need to add the prophetic to the messianic, kingly, priestly, and angelic meanings that we have already encountered.[61] This is because the author of Daniel does not create any new raw materials; the apocalyptist spun together scattered threads that already existed. It is the genius of the book of Daniel to have united differing tendencies with such lapidary concision. Its expression uses the forms of common language, but Daniel adds a content so enriched as to suggest a connection between heaven and earth.

We need to take this question one step further. Otto Procksch has called attention to the *Versichtbarung* of God in Ezekiel 1:26. This divine "visibility" shows through in Daniel 7:13.[62] Balz pursues this argument: the figure of "one like a son of man" is "the result of a 'doubling' of the apparition of divine majesty in Ezekiel 1."[63] On the other hand, in Ezekiel 8–11 and 43 we find a messianic and priestly personage called "man." He is sent by God, whose appearance is also described as human, which establishes a close relation between him and the anthropomorphic God of Ezekiel 1:26. Daniel 7:9 places these human semblances on two (or perhaps more) thrones to indicate that there is a duality of functions. He attributes to the quasi-hypostasis son of man the role of supreme judge, because of the designation of an angel for functions of the sort in Ezekiel 8–11 and 43.[64]

Balz has thus taken Procksch's intuition and given it a more scientifically distinct form. It must be admitted, however, that so far the matter has gone no further than a preparatory stage. The invitation to reread Ezekiel 8–11 and 43 is a pressing one, and it will permit us to pursue the lines sketched out by those German scholars.

1. Ezekiel 8: In this chapter the prophet is transported by something with the appearance of a man into the temple of Jerusalem. It turns out that this "man" is the *ruah* (Spirit) of God. The prophet is between heaven and earth, a motif that takes on its full value in parallel with Daniel 7 when we remember that here and elsewhere Ezekiel is called "son of man."

The temple contains divine glory, as the prophet has seen it in chapter 1. The entire scene takes place within the sanctuary. The holy place is polluted, however, by a particularly repulsive idol. God is about to intervene in some radical manner, but the agents of this action are described variously, as man, spirit, or YHWH himself. Abominations occur six times here,[65] and they invariably call to mind the *šiquz mešomém* of Daniel (8:13; 9:27; 11:31; 12:11). Moreover, the term *šeqez* is used in Ezekiel in 8:6, but also in 11:18 and 21. Impure and monstrous beasts are mentioned (8:10).

The parallels with Daniel 7 are impressive. Moreover, we must remember that the profanation of the temple, which appears to Ezekiel as the ultimate violation of everything most sacred in this world, occurs during the exile in Babylon, and this chronology fits in perfectly with the historical fiction presented in Daniel. Even more interesting for our purposes, there is a real *Verspaltung* ("merging together of the subjects of the action") in this chapter of Ezekiel, as Walther Zimmerli has correctly noted:[66] the "man" of verse 2 is YHWH, but later there is a shift to a "heavenly messenger."

2. Ezekiel 9: The *ruah* of chapter 8 is now a man "clothed in linen"—that is, a priestly figure.[67] To my surprise, however, Zimmerli says that Daniel 10:5 and 12:6-7 are unrelated to this passage.[68] Be that as it may, the angel of Ezekiel is also a scribe, and it should be noted that in Israel there was a close connection between this function and that of the priesthood. "The man" is accompanied by six angels, who are also called "men."

Some of the people remain apart and "marked": the parallel with the "saints" in Daniel 7 is clear. On the other hand, those who served the abomination are put to death, and it is even decreed that the temple must be profaned and filled with corpses (9:7). Daniel 7 is the counterpart of this: there is purification by judgment of the monsters and transfiguration of the temple into the kingdom of God. In a similar comparison Ezekiel sees the temple as the point in which the sins of *Israel* are concentrated and from which they spread; Daniel sees the corruption of the *nations* as progressing from the periphery to the center of life (which may be the temple, or it may be heaven). That is where judgment takes place and the universe is transformed.

3. Ezekiel 10 returns to the elements of the vision in chapter 1 (the throne, the divine glory, the cloud, the wheels, the cherubim bearing the four faces of an angel, a man, a lion, and an eagle). Aside from the juxtaposition of the angelic, the human, and the animal, as in Daniel 7, one should also note the mention of a cherub with the "form of a human hand" (cf. Dan. 5).

In this chapter of Ezekiel the man clothed in linen now has to accomplish the further task of taking fire from the altar. Zimmerli says in this connection: "Who other than a priest could undertake to take hold of the holy fire of God!"[69] The priestly action described here goes beyond human capacities, however, for in order to do so, he has to mingle with the cherubim of the Holy of Holies. The text seems to say that the one true priest is a celestial or angelic being. After marking some people for salvation, he destroys the others with the fire of judgment.

4. Ezekiel 11: Once again we find familiar motifs such as the *ruaḥ*. The glory of God leaves the temple (v. 23) and, by implication, returns to the celestial spheres. Verse 24 underlines the fact that the prophet is describing a vision (cf. Dan. 7:1*a*), and verse 25 shows that this vision must be told (cf. Dan. 7:1*b*).

5. Ezekiel 43 teaches us nothing new. It pursues the theme of the prophet going everywhere in the new city, which has become one large temple and its dependencies. Once again we meet the glory of God, the *ruaḥ*, the pollution of the temple, and abominations. In verse 7 the throne of God is mentioned once more. God announces that this is "the place of the soles of my feet" and that he will "dwell in the midst of the people of Israel for ever," for there will be no more profanation of the temple by the hand of Israel or its kings. There is a connection between the heavens, where God sits, and the earth, where he rests his feet.

In conclusion, it is clear that these passages from Ezekiel were a source of inspiration par excellence for Daniel B. Like those of Ezekiel in a land far from home, Daniel's visions are set in Babylon. But what the prophet, the son of Buzi, saw happening in a more or less distant future, Daniel sees as imminent or already in course. The glory of God could once again be seen, if not in Jerusalem, at least in the heavens, which is where all was to be consummated. This is why Daniel introduces clouds and other celestial elements to indicate that the ultimate act of God is at hand. All apocalypse, moreover, "is nothing but the contemplation of celestial designs concerning what is to come to pass on earth"[70] (cf. 2 Bar. 81:4; 1 Enoch 103:2; 51:2; etc.).

Thus my analysis for the most part confirms the opinions of Procksch and Balz. Now let us see where this discovery leads us. To return to the thread of the argument: Ezekiel sketched an extremely complex figure that combined, under the label of "man," elements as varied as God in his visibility, the angel, the Spirit, the priest, the scribe, and the prophet. The richness of a combination of this sort can be credited to the Exile prophet and was not, consequently, originated by the second-century apocalyptist. It is obviously of primary importance that human semblance is the common denominator among all these aspects of the complex figure presented in Ezekiel. The angel or the Spirit, for example, are "men." God is visible in human guise. In point of fact, we can find "man" at the two poles of heaven and earth, of divine glory and derisory humanity. At the base of the mysticism in Ezekiel—which Jewish tradition calls the *ma'assè ha-merkabah*—there is ubiquitous humanity. As Ezekiel says, God on his heavenly throne has a footrest "amidst his people"; human resemblance has its head in the clouds and its feet on the earth. To be sure, God in his seemingly human manifestation and man are in no way confused, but there is between them close "family" connections, we might say, that are difficult to describe in anything but anthropomorphic terms, as almost all of biblical revelation attests. Not only is anthropomorphism a concession that theological language makes to our limited human comprehension; this metaphorical language is consecrated from the start by the priestly affirmation that the human is the image of God. When Ezekiel—followed by Daniel—reverses the order of this proposition, he is backed up by the ample tradition of his people, who conceived of its God with decidedly human features, having once and for all resolved to understand divine transcendence in terms of relation with Israel and not of essence.

The anthropomorphic personage in Ezekiel, then in Daniel, is a bridge between two worlds, the celestial and the terrestrial. In Genesis 28 Jacob sees "a ladder set up on the earth, and the top of it reached to heaven; and behold, the angels of God were ascending and descending on it!" (v. 12). Hugo Odeberg has written interestingly on this text—or rather on John 1:51, which repeats these terms and applies them to the Son of man.[71] He cites *Genesis Rabbah* 68.18 (*Yal.* 119), according to which the angels were ascending and descending on Jacob himself, and not on the ladder. At the top they found the graven image of the patriarch; at the bottom they found him asleep. Odeberg comments: the celestial apparition is the true Jacob—that is, Israel. There is between him and the sleeper an "identity in essence." The angels "symbolize the connexion of the earthly man with his celestial counterpart." In John 1:51 the angels ascend and descend on the Son of man, and the disciples are thus witnesses to the unity of Christ humiliated and glorified. As it happens, according to Isaiah 49:3, man glorified is also the glorification of God (see also John 13:31). This is because the movement of God toward man and the movement of man toward God coincide, even though in contrary directions. It is a descent, a καταβασις of God and an ascent, αναβασις of man (see John 14:9-10).

Odeberg's development sheds light, retrospectively, on the meaning of Genesis 28 and on its use—explicit or implicit—in later passages on the son of man in Ezekiel and Daniel, then in the New Testament. The idea of a correspondence between heaven and earth, of a bilateral communication between the divine and the human, of a *coincidentia oppositorum*, is already expressed in the JE text of Genesis. There is a connection between God and his elect. This time the connection is expressed by the metaphor of the angels—that is, by those half-human, half-divine beings that originally were cosmic forces, personalized and deified by the Canaanites, which the Israelites subordinated to God and made into vehicles for the divine Presence.[72] It was normal for Ezekiel and then Daniel to take up this metaphor of the angels and combine it with the human metaphor. As we have seen in Ezekiel, the prophet consistently presents angelic beings as men. The same situation can be found in Daniel (8:15; 9:21; 10:5, 18; 12:6–7; see also Ezek. 1:26; Zech. 1:10; 1 Enoch 87:2; 90:14, 17, 22; Rev. 14:14–20; 21:17). It was precisely on this basis that Nathaniel Schmidt correctly intuited, as early as 1900, that the son of man in Daniel 7 is none other than the archangel Michael.[73] After Schmidt's article, the manuscripts of the desert of Judea confirmed this identification. The clearest passage in this connection can be found in 1QM 17.6–8, which says in one breath that God "exalts the authority of Michael among the angels and the domination of Israel over all flesh." It is understandable, in retrospect, why the Apocalypse of the Animals in 1 Enoch 83–90 shows the archangel Michael not as an animal but in human guise (90:14, 17, 22). On a more general plane I note, with George W. E. Nickelsburg, that designations such as the heavenly children in 2 Maccabees 7:34 and the sons of God in 3 Maccabees 6:28 originally referred to angels.[74] Nickelsburg adds that these texts were separated from their apocalyptic context, and the titles were then applied to the righteous.[75]

Ulrich Müller was correct in reacting against the hypothesis of Balz that the figure of the son of man is a hypostasis of God. Müller says, "One should describe him as a celestial hypostasis of the people ... rather than of God,"[76] for he must first be introduced into God's presence, since he comes from elsewhere (see Dan. 7:13). The angel Michael is also a counterindication of Balz's views. Müller concludes, "The idea of correspondence between the terrestrial and the celestial can also be found in the representation of the *Völkerarchonten* [the archons, leaders of the nations]. It explains the relationship between the visionary and celestial figure in Daniel 7:13f., on the one hand, and the saints of the Most High—eschatological Israel—on the other. The archon is an angel of particular eminence in the council of the Throne of God. Michael, for example, represents the people of Israel."[77]

Müller's objection leads me to my last topic: the collective dimension of the son of man in Daniel 7. The idea is not new here; we have met it at every turn. By turning to it again briefly we can perhaps arrive at a more concise definition of the figure of the son of man.

Placed in its immediate context, the vision of the son of man in Daniel 7 leads us to the level of world empires, consequently to the level of authority and royal dominion. Jean de Fraine is certainly correct when he declares, "The term 'son of man' (in Daniel, and perhaps in the New Testament as well) sometimes symbolizes the kingdom, sometimes the individual who represents it."[78] We might compare it to the amphibolic symbolism of the servant of YHWH, which, as we have seen, is far from absent in Daniel B. In the context of the "songs" in Isaiah, the expression designates all of Israel, but in the songs proper he is an individual. Following Aage Bentzen, John McKenzie, for example, says that we must think of a Mosaic model, for "the Servant appears with some of the traits of a new Moses."[80] He adds this reflection, valid concerning the son of man and the servant of YHWH alike: "The actions of an ideal figure are not historical actions; they are traits in the portrayal of the idea. The ideal figure gathers together the history of the past and the hopes of the future."[81] This is why we feel a certain fluidity in the apocalyptist's presentation of the scene in Daniel B.

McKenzie is a great help to our comprehension. But his insistence on the "idea" and the "ideal" is unfortunate. We can do better concerning the relationship between the son of man and those whom he represents. Ulrich Müller spoke of the *Völkerarchontenvorstellung*. He saw in the son of man an "imaginary celestial figure representing the people of the saints of the Most High—that is, Israel—in the sense of the notion of the archons of the nations."[82]

It is probably impossible to avoid learned approximations such as the *Völkerarchont* in defining the son of man, or such as "anthropomorph" in describing him. That is not the major problem. It seems to me, however, that we get closer to the meaning of the metaphor of the son of man if we comprehend it as designating the pleromatic personality of Israel, if not of humanity in general (the one does not exclude the other, but supposes it). With the son of man on the throne, it is humanity that is made divine according to its destiny.[83]

Thus, at any event, we avoid misconstruing the Adamic notion in Daniel B as a Platonic essence. The term *pleromatic* indicates that this is not the case, for it supposes a historical Israel, not an Israel "separated from its body"; it is transfigured, not idealized.[84]

RESURRECTION

Daniel 12 is the one text of the Old Testament that clearly announces individual resurrection. When critics express their surprise at having to wait until the second century B.C.E. for a statement of a doctrine that was immediately to become of such enormous importance, they usually point, first, to the collective nature of expectation in Israel before the second century and, second, to the dramatic historical evolution under Antiochus Epiphanes that led apocalypse to imagine a compensation/retribution after this life for the martyrdom of the pious Jews.

These two remarks are perfectly apt, but they are incomplete. In particular, it is true that the pressure of events had always been the one real motivation for the elaboration of Israel's credo. Everything that Israel proclaimed as worthy of belief is based in the events of history. Philosophical or theological speculation came after. Without Antiochus' persecution of 167 there would have been no reason for Daniel 12. We might ask, however, whether the individual Israelite really took no interest in what might happen to him after death and was for some eleven centuries content with the loose and often vague ideas found scattered in Scripture.[85]

Furthermore, the problem is perhaps somewhat different. When Mitchell Dahood, for example, attempts to find expressions of an ancient Israelite belief in survival after death, similar to that of the Canaanites, his attempt is, in my opinion, a failure.[86] It has the merit of attracting attention to the root of the problem, however, which is exactly how Canaan's and Israel's paths crossed. Dahood, like many others before him, failed to take sufficiently seriously the ascetic thoroughness of anti-Canaanite sentiment in Israel. When traces of ancient Western Semitic cultures are found in Israelite literature, it does not prove dependence but contact. And if we can speak of heritage, that heritage is far from remaining intact in the hands of the heirs. At the other end of the chronological scale, in polemic anti-Hellenistic Jewish literature, the same phenomenon occurs. The vocabulary used necessarily takes on some of the color of the adversary's vocabulary. At the risk of appearing to set up a circular argument, I will say that the lasting reluctance to speculate about individual resurrection, an existential problem if ever there was one, and one that has always troubled men everywhere,[87] is the best possible proof that Israelite resistance to Canaanite culture was fierce and effective.

Perhaps the common people had somewhat unorthodox views on the question. It is not surprising to find biblical evidence of popular idolatry (e.g., Isa. 17:10; Ezek. 8:14). These are, precisely, indications of the popular chthonian religions that provoked the stern prophetic resistance. If by now the Yahwists can relax their vigilance, it is proof that the danger must have passed. This was true in the second century B.C.E.; but only for a while, however, and only among the Hasidim.[88] This is what explains the apocalyptic return to a mythopoeic language.

In other words, the announcement of individual resurrection in Daniel 12 is not to be explained solely by the martyrdom of the pious. This proclamation has its place in the particular logic of the apocalypse, in its symbolism, and in its temporality.

To justify this three-part affirmation of logic, symbolism, and temporality, let me begin by recalling some of the elements basic to the interpretation of death in Israel. In doing so, I may for the moment give the impression that the problem goes no further than the enigma of Hasidic martyrdom. It was, in point of fact, this martyrdom that raised the problem of death to its point of maximum tension. Hence this is where we must begin, if not also end up. The discussion needs to be enlarged, however, to embrace much vaster horizons. We need to begin by explaining why the doctrine of resurrection became, seemingly overnight, one of the basic principles of Judaism, and later of Christianity.

Death is a sign of the fundamental weakness of the human creature before God, and even of humanity's sinful state.[89] Put differently, nothing can subsist before divine justice, and death is, consequently, no matter how it is regarded, "the wages of sin," the fruit of a curse that weighs on all created things. In this sense, death is not "normal." Above all, it is not an element in an immutable natural cycle. This is why YHWH is absent from Sheol, the place of the dead, unlike the agrarian divinities for whom death is their kingdom just as much as life.[90]

MAJOR THEOLOGICAL LESSONS

This entire concept was questioned radically in the second century. The martyrdom of innocent people under persecution gave rise to scandal, for their death not only failed to fall under the definition of deserved punishment; it was in contradiction to it.

Here, in fact, divine malediction was out of the question. Death was by no means seen as negative and sterile, the end of a fragile and ephemeral creature ("The years of our life are threescore and ten, or even by reason of strength fourscore," Ps. 90:10). That death was its own definition, as factual and brutal as it was apodictic and stupid. But what was there to say of death as an offering, le-šem ha-šamayim (for the love of heaven)? This was not the pitiful result of the confrontation of mankind with being, but the sign of the choice of being over nothingness. These were totally different givens. From a deserved punishment for the guilty, death became the undeserved fate of the innocent.

This was, then, an exceptional situation, created by Antiochus' persecution of the Hasidim. A similar problem had been envisaged in poetic terms in the fifth century by the book of Job. The rule (or the law) is applicable in the general, but it runs into difficulty in the particular. It ceases to be a factor of order and life within the community and becomes scandalous when it claims the right to mow down anyone whose head rises above the norm. In the case that interests us, the limits of the normal were reached when history prompted death of an unforeseen kind—an innocent, hence a positive and a creative, death. There is one sort of death that is no longer a sign of the pathetic weakness of human beings but of their transcendence. It is the supreme offering one can make to God; in it one surpasses oneself infinitely. Faced with the option of "saving" his life by rejecting the Source of life—by denying God—the martyr "loses" his life and descends into hell. In doing so, he sterilizes death's negative nature and blunts its sting. The martyr's death is thus not episodic, and its import not merely accidental. Second Isaiah understood the utterly revolutionary originality of this, as seen in his celebration of the oblation of the Servant.[91]

Death as punishment is an end; death as oblation requires an aftermath, else "who knows whether the spirit of man goes upward and the spirit of the beast goes down to the earth?" (Eccl. 3:21). Death as punishment was its own justification; death as oblation is not justified without a divine response to consecrate it. This response, according to Daniel 12, is resurrection.

What have we learned from this phenomenological approach?

a) Resurrection is part of theodicy. It is a problem of retribution and of justice.

b) A latecomer in Yahwist thought, the notion of resurrection arose from the need to make a distinction between two sorts of death: death as chastisement (the "wages of sin," and the finitude of a creature marked by weakness) and death as the martyr's oblation.

c) In a sense, death as oblation was a new historical phenomenon. It was prompted by the first pogrom in history, the anti-Judaic persecution of Antiochus IV in 167–164.

d) The external conditions necessary to the emergence of the doctrine of the resurrection of the dead came together at that time. First, there was the exercise of violence with the aim of stifling faith and the ancestral customs of the faithful Jews. Second, there was the distinction in Israel, drawn by the traditionalists, between the pious and the apostates, which put the Hasidim on one side and those who collaborated with the Hellenization of Judea on the other. The refusal of any compromise on the part of the *maskilim* and the *maṣdikim*—categories of individuals distinguished by a determination to keep the faith unto death—created a new situation that endowed death with a positive rather than negative charge.[92]

e) To be sure, one cannot speak of novelty in absolute terms. The martyrs of the second century were not the first to have ever given their lives in a supreme sacrifice. As there is a prehistory for the apocalypse, there is a prehistory for the formal proclamation of individual resurrection in Daniel 12.[93] The songs of the Servant in the book of Deutero-Isaiah are the first milestones of a continuing evolution (see Isa. 53:12 in particular).

f) According to these prolegomena, it is clear that initially, at least, it was the martyrs who earned resurrection. Not only is resurrection in Daniel 12 not general; it does not even include all the people of Israel. The term *maskilim* in verse 3 is explicit: no category other than the one mentioned in verse 2 is concerned. Similarly, the *maṣdikim* are the *maskilim*. The two terms designate martyrs for the faith. They alone are concerned in resurrection, for their death is unjust and untimely. It was only later that this restrictive category was to be extended to all of Israel, then to all of humanity. As Robert Martin-Achard writes, "Resurrection concerns here [2 Macc. 7] only the righteous, and perhaps only matyrs; 2 Macc. 7 thus seems to confirm the doubly restrictive interpretation of Daniel 12:2 proposed by B. Alfrink."[94] Paul Volz had already insisted on the limited scope of resurrection in Daniel 12:3. There are, Volz says, classes of the righteous for whom resurrection is reserved: the wise, martyrs, and ascetics. Here, it is the spiritual leaders of Israel. These wise men are probably scholars of the Torah, as in ʾAbot 11.7, 16; 1 Enoch 98:9; 2 Baruch 46:5; 66:2. Or they are apocalyptists, as in 1 Enoch 48:1; 100:6; 104:12, and so forth.[95] Thus, he continues, those who are resuscitated tend to be:

a) some of the personages of ancient history; e.g., Moses, Elijah, David, Hezekiah, Daniel (Dan. 12:13);

b) martyrs from a more recent past (Dan. 12:1; 2 Macc. [e.g., 7:9]; 1 Enoch 90:33; Jos. C. Apion. 2. 218, and B.J. 2. 152–53;

c) the righteous in general (Pss. Sol. 3:10ff.; 1 Enoch 91–92; 100:5);

d) all men (Dan. 12:2 [sic]; 1 Enoch 22 and, esp., 51:1).[96]

Reflection on the two sorts of death, one to no purpose,[97] the other a sacrifice agreeable to God, is typically Israelite. The enigma created by the second sort of death is also a Jewish problem. Solving it through a recompense after death may, of course, have been influenced by Iran, and even by Canaanite and other agrarian cults. But the so-called "history of religions" approach leads us off the track. Martin-Achard says, correctly, "The determinant element came from Israel itself."[98] This is why resurrection was not universal and cosmic (at least at the beginning), as in Iran. Its setting is here juridical,[99] creational,[100] and communal (or "affective," as Martin-Achard puts it).[101]

Anyone who examines the means of expression chosen by Jewish literature after Daniel 12 to speak of resurrection is struck by the variety of opinions reflected. Paraphrasing H. C. C. Cavallin, Martin-Achard concludes: "Their authors, and perhaps also their first audience, did not attach any decisive importance to these very diverse expressions; they were more interested in the message that they were trying to transmit. In order to comprehend them, they had to be 'demythologized.'"[102] Thus we return to the images themselves, which must be interpreted with a good margin for maneuvering, as one would read a poem.

The germ of the idea of resurrection of the dead (or of some of the dead) is already discreetly present in the images involved in the son of man theme in Daniel 7. Not only can we find the model for this in the Canaanite Baal coming to life after every winter, but the scene of the enthronement of the son of man must be seen as an ascension from the sea (hell) up to heaven, as, for example, in 4 Ezra 13, a reinterpretation of Daniel 7.[103] In short, keeping in mind the collective dimension of the son of man, Daniel 12 further clarifies, in comparison to Daniel 7–8, that the eschaton brings redemption/creation or re-creation/resurrection to the "people of the saints."[104]

The only truly "new" element here is resurrection. Deutero-Isaiah had already, in the sixth century, organized his entire message of comfort by articulating one to the other redemption and creation. Similarly, Ezekiel, in chapter 37 in particular, emphasized the same intimate connection. Resurrection was a supplementary aspect of this complex. This aspect arose because events made it imperative to take thought of the individual fate of the righteous, since their death could not be—as in death as punishment—a separation from God.

In this perspective of the correspondence of the terms *creation*, *redemption*, and *resurrection*, we need to take quite seriously the introduction, in verse 1, of the announcement of the resurrection of the dead found in Daniel 12:2. Verse 1, in point of fact, places this announcement in a context typical of the final catastrophe. As we have seen before, the *Urzeit* reflected in the *Endzeit* repeats—in reverse, of course—the sequence Eden/flood. The point of arrival is, as Ezekiel 47 had announced, the transformation of the land into paradise. Daniel 12:1 thus recalls the universal setting within which the action of verses 2ff. will take place. The correspondence in the context establishes that what is to happen on the cosmic plane at the end of time will be reflected, by rights, on the individual level: the ultimate crisis of humanity—the triumph of the greatest enemy, death—will not be less amphibologic than the universal eschatological cataclysm.[105] Just as the latter leads not only to destruction but also to the victory of life in the midst of death, so the death of the righteous contains a germ of eternity.[106]

It is, furthermore, perfectly logical to add resurrection to the complex of creation and redemption. The central idea of the apocalypse is that there is a concomitance of the final cataclysm and the coming of the kingdom of God. This is an application in an absolute sense of the principle of *coincidentia oppositorum*. It was normal that the apocalyptist turn toward Sheol[107] as a "vestige of chaos"[108] in order to point to its defeat. In this perspective, the doctrine of resurrection is a particular case of a general conception of the eschaton as a repeat of creation.[109]

Apocalyptical logic in this domain applies from another point of view as well. I have mentioned, following other critics, the influence that the songs of the Servant of YHWH had on the formulation of Daniel 12. The Servant's exaltation after his death is "presented as an extraordinary phenomenon which could happen to an individual only in very exceptional circumstances. But in the Old Testament all God's extraordinary interventions, such as prophetic utterance, the priesthood, election in general, are called to pass in scope from the particular to the universal, so that the hope of resurrection will spread from these indications through the mass."[110] If the death of the righteous contains a germ of eternity, with death anyone can attain this glorious level. It will only depend on an existential choice (see Deut. 30:19).

Eternity, and not a simple return to life ending once more in a second death.[111] For the first time, Jewish apocalypse envisages a final omega to history, not to be followed by a new development toward another omega, as in the political eschatology of the prophets. At this point there is no further speculation on "new things" to come in this world. This world is destined to disappear, not to be converted and live. All will be swallowed up in the final deluge of fire. Nothing will remain of this world under malediction, corruptible and corrupting. At the end of the first century C.E., 4 Ezra 7 was to say that even the Messiah must die, as if to sweep things clean for an entirely new world. There is already a trace of this conviction in Daniel 12, for unlike Noah, who survived the flood of origins and thus assured the continuity of the two worlds (cf. 4 Ezra 9:21), the apocalyptical antitypes of Noah die, dragged into the tomb in the last shudders of a universe on its way to annihilation. What they do not share with this world is *dera'on*—horror (cf. Isa. 66:24 and Dan. 12:2*b*). There is thus a discontinuity between the two worlds and, in like fashion, between this existence, based on death, and "eternal life."

The dichotomy between "now" and "then" is even more accentuated by the astral glorification of the risen.[112] This point will permit us to get closer to the question of discontinuity. First, we need to see the connection between the elevation of the righteous to the stars and their association with the angels. This is an affirmation, in terms of images, that the life to come will be transcendent and celestial (see, e.g., 1 Enoch 92:4; 104:2; 2 Bar. 51:10; Wis. 3:7; 7:3*a*; Pss. Sol. 3:12; *Bib. Ant.* 33.5).[113] Stars and angels are side by side. They both burn with a divine flame, and it is not surprising that the seraphim ("the burning ones") of Isaiah 6 grasp burning coals and "angelize" the prophet, so to speak, through contact with the altar fire.[114] Similarly, to be under the protection of a tutelary angel (as were Israel and the nations, according to Daniel) was equivalent to having a lucky star.

Pseudepigraphic and rabbinic texts lead us in another direction, however, or perhaps in several other directions. Thus, 1 Enoch 43:4; 4 Ezra 7:97, 125; 4 Maccabees 17:5; Assumption of Moses 10:9; *Sifré Parasha Debarim* 10 or *Leviticus Rabbah* 20.2; *Targum of Isaiah* 14.13[115] all see in the stars and in their immutability a symbol of perfect obedience to God. The righteous are compared to them for that reason. In contrast to the stars, men in general are in desperate rebellion (see 1 Enoch 2–5:3; 5:4ff.; 43:1–4; 69:16–21, 25; T. Naph. 3:2).

Finally, we must not forget that the angels were for Daniel "awake" (or "vigilant"; 4:13 [10], 17 [14], 23 [20]), and, for Qumran, "knowledgeable" (1QH 11.14). Being associated with angels meant, for the pious, sharing their mysteries (1QH 3.22–23; 13.13–14). Is it fair to say that the cosmic position of the stars permitted them a global view of the universe, hence superior knowledge? In any event, "their immutable order proceeds from the mouth of God and is a testimony to being" (1QH 12.9).

But the stars have always been among the *stoikheia tou kosmou* (the cosmic forces; cf. Gal. 4:3, 9; Col. 2:8) of which Saint Paul speaks and before which man feels so small that he is willing to worship them. The mention of them in Daniel 12 is therefore an audaciously mythopoeic trait, like so many others in Jewish apocalypse. Here again, however, the motif of the stellar glorification of the blessed is no exception to the rule: it is also a means of demythologization of the "heavenly bodies." There is no reason to adore them or to fear them. The stars are merely signs of the postmortem glorification of the elect.

Once again, there is a correspondence here with the creation myths, for, evidently, the demythologization of celestial "luminaries" began as early as Genesis 1:15–18. In reality, what Genesis 1 did with the myth of creation, Daniel 12 does with the Canaanite myth of the seasonal return to life of the god Baal. The two themes are united, moreover. The *Weltanschauung* dominant in mythopoesis, as we have seen concerning the son of man in Daniel 7, is the tension between chaos and cosmos. That is, in anthropological terms, between death and life.

On this and other levels it would be prudent to avoid drawing hasty conclusions separating apocalypse from the rest of Scripture. To speak, for example, of transcendence and universalism concerning the fate of the dead according to Daniel 12 risks not doing justice to Israelite eschatology, which was still at this stage, and for some time to come, national and terrestrial.[116] Here, as in Isaiah 26, what is at stake is the continuation of the nation or, to be more precise, the continuation through eternity of the faithful faction of Israel.[117] The kingdom of God is inaugurated on this earth, where it annihilates and replaces historical kingdoms marked by the beast (Dan. 2:34, 44; 7:14).[118] Wilhelm Rudolph fell victim to an a priori dogmatics when he declared that Isaiah 24–27 could not be apocalyptic because the separation with history is not complete. There, Rudoplh says, eschatology is *nationalistisch-particularistisch*.[119] But where in the Bible is this not so? To be sure, the kingdom of God extends throughout the globe in Daniel as well (7:14, 18, 27), but this adds nothing in particular to ancient prophecy or the messianic expectation attached to the person and the dynasty of David.[120]

"Transcendent" should not be opposed to "terrestrial" in this connection. As Paul Hanson writes, Sigmund Mowinckel himself must admit that in Jewish sources the two types fused.[121] I believe that the tension set up in Jewish thought on the future liberator between an accentuation of the terrestrial and national, on the one hand, and the transcendental and cosmic, on the other, can best be explained in dialectic terms. The entire postexilic period was characterized by this tension between a "pragmatic" concept that recognized the order of history as being the sphere of divine activity and a "visionary" concept of divine activity as taking place on the cosmic plane. The circles that held the visionary conception tended to describe the future liberator in cosmic terms (e.g., in Dan. 7; 4 Ezra 13). On the other hand, those of the pragmatic turn of mind spoke of this event in terrestrial or national terms (Hag., Zech., the Tgs., Pss. Sol., T. 12 Patr.). This is another way of putting the distinction that Paul Tillich made between "essence" and "existence."[122]

Israelite eschatology is an upshot of theology and anthropology. The doctrine of resurrection that followed from it was tied to the notion of people (of Israel or of the saints) and is comprehensible only in the framework of the communitarian covenant. Thus it is a historic fact, in contrast to the Canaanite naturistic formulation.[123] In conformity with apocalyptic thought in general, the doctrine of resurrection is an event that reveals a secret that human history has done everything possible to obscure. This secret is the transcendent dimension of man (his *Sôma pneumatikon*, as 1 Cor. 15:44 says). It is the divine purpose that man be transformed ultimately into a son of man, according to Daniel 7–8, or be raised to the rank of the angels or of the stars, according to Daniel 12, which amounts to the same thing.[124]

The problem of knowing whether apocalyptic eschatology is a break with history or whether it is itself a chapter of history loses much of its urgency, for the best answer is that it is both.[125] When the eschaton comes—which is itself an event in history, like death of the individual—history will tip over into the utterly other, which is governed by its own laws and criteria. But those laws have been exactly the same as those of real history—of *Heilsgeschichte*, if you prefer—from the very beginning. History triumphs with the eschaton, as does the being designated by the Creator to "name" it: man.

Cavallin is thus in part justified when he emphasizes the incoherence of the descriptions of the resurrection of the body (at the end of time and in an instant) and of spiritual immortality (which means that when a righteous man dies, he is immediately welcomed into the kingdom of God) between 100 B.C.E. and 100 C.E.[126] Our Occidental thought has great difficulty in conceiving that the transition from one world to another is not spatial—we might say quantitative—but qualitative, spiritual, existential. The "other world" is present here and now, concealed by "this world." Similarly, eternal life is here and now, stifled by the life we live, which is merely the sign of eternal life.[127] We shall return to this point.

It should be noted in passing that the New Testament is totally faithful to this apocalyptic vision when it proclaims that the Messiah reconciles terrestrial and celestial things and, so to speak, "recapitulates," i.e., renders its head to, a history that up to that point had been "decapitated" (see 1 Cor. 15:20, 23; Eph. 1:10, 22–23; Col. 1:15–18). As it happens, the messianic act penetrates all of human time ("the true light that enlightens every man," John 1:9). History is never deprived nor emptied of its accomplishment. But, up to the ultimate moment of the apocalyptic intervention of God, we see this crowning event only "through a glass darkly." That does not prevent the eschaton from being, as Eliane Amado Lévy-Valensi writes, "immediately, or in a deferred time that my present will prepares with all its vigilance."[128]

This involves a historical dialectic. The eternity of the world to come is not absence of time (as we tell it), but the structure of a different time. In reality, there is no "geometric" end to history. There is a passage from one world to another world; from one economy to another. It is of course logical, but fundamentally inadequate, to speak of this transition as an end followed by a beginning. There is only one world, but it necessarily is presented in the form of two economies, the historical and the eternal.[129] Israel (or, in Daniel's terms, the "people of the saints") stands at the focal point of this tensional duality. It performs the act par excellence (the liturgy) at the culminant moment in history (the sabbath),[130] at the center of space (the temple).[131] Jewish eschatology—unlike Iranian eschatology—is the explosion of this moment, of this *kairos*, which henceforth totally fills the horizon.

This explosive breaking apart put an end to a world that was, as we have seen, in constant suspension between life and death, good and evil, hot and cold, the cosmos and the chaos (cf. Gen. 8:22). It was a postlapsarian and postcataclysmic world, torn between heaven and hell, the tree of life and the forbidden tree, the garden of delights and the dust of eternal horror. The apocalyptic end brings resolution to this ontic ambiguity.[132] In this perspective, resurrection constitutes what Northrop Frye has called "a metamorphosis upward to a new beginning that is now present."[133]

Consequently, we are introduced into a new ambivalence; in fact, into a dialectic of a temporal sort. A bridge is thrown up between present and future that makes eternity contemporary with now. Resurrection in Daniel 12 is "for that time," which is the end of time. But a vision of this sort is possible only to the extent that what it evokes is expressible and comprehensible within our temporal categories. In order to speak of resurrection the author must know what he is talking about; he must have had a foretaste or a gage of it, as the New Testament says. The end of time must not merely put us off with a future uncertain ever to arrive. The justice that applied to Antiochus' martyrized victims is also the justice to be dealt out in the world to come.[134] Here and now there are *qaddišin*; there are *maskilim* and *maṣdikim*. These saints, these sages, and these righteous men are the presence of eternity in this current and fallen history that is destined to perdition. They are the authentic dimension of the human, as eternity is the true meaning of history.[135] In order to understand that it has been thus since the beginning, we need to return once more to Daniel 7. "The one like a son of man" was the *ruaḥ* of the origins (vv. 2ff.), crowned and seated at God's side. In this meaning, he was preexistent, as life overflows the domain of finitude in every direction. Collins saw clearly when he wrote, "Daniel 7, Daniel 8 and 10–12 all deal with the same events in somewhat different language, because no one formulation is adequate."[136]

Now that we have arrived at the end of these reflections on resurrection in Daniel 12, we can, I think, add it all up and make sure that the task assigned at the beginning has been accomplished. The announcement of resurrection in the second century B.C.E. responds to the internal logic of apocalyptic. The glorification of the martyrs for the faith signified the concomitance of Easter and Good Friday.[137] "Whoever loses his life for my sake will find it," the Nazarene would later say, building on the forward thrust of apocalyptic, which had championed a logic of extravagance that proved a real stumbling block for all Aristotelian logic.

There is also a symbolic correspondence with the rest of apocalypse. By that I mean that the *fact* of the resurrection overflows all its limits as a fact and becomes the symbol of the transcendence of death here and now as well as there and then.[138] This symbolism runs throughout apocalypse, and in particular through the book of Daniel.

This leads to my third point, that of the temporality of the apocalypse. This temporality, as we have seen, organizes around the notion that *Urzeit wird Endzeit* (primal time becomes end time). The schema of the beginning (prehistory/catastrophe/*Heilsgeschichte*) is repeated in reverse order (*Heilsgeschichte*/catastrophe/posthistory). This is true in the life of the individual, whose fate after death is not a return to the uterus (corresponding to prehistory), as in nature religions or in psychological disorders. The destiny of the saints *transcends* death. Thus the temporal scheme of the apocalypse makes that of the cult absolute. For to the "now and every time" that is true of the cultic celebration, a permanent "now" of access to divine glory has been substituted. "All things have been brought to their fulfillment." Since they were an apocalyptical community, the sectarians of Qumran, for example, were conscious of participating here and now in the angelic life (1QM 12.7ff.; 1QH 3.19–23; 11.3–14; 1QSa 2.3–11; cf. 1 Cor. 11:10). The parenetic aim of the apocalyptic writings is precisely to exhort their readers to "live their lives *sub specie aeternitatis*, with the heavenly life in mind."[139]

NOTES

1. Northrop Frye, *The Anatomy of Criticism*, 315.

2. It is well known that the Deuteronomist school edited prophetic books of the preexilic period. Influenced by the punishment the Jews underwent during their exile in Babylon, Deuteronomy blunted the cutting edge of the original catastrophe and turned the message toward a promise of restoration. The best example is in the book of Isaiah,

which was retouched over a five-hundred-year period. The Deuteronomist, for one, added chs. 36–39. See also Amos 9:11–15; Hos. 3:5 (?); Mic. 4–5; 7:8–20; Zeph. 3:8; Nah. 2:1.

3. John Milton remarked the correspondence between the apocalypse and the flood in *Paradise Lost* in the prophecy of the archangel Michael, which turns around the apocalypse, on the one hand, and the flood, on the other; see Frye, *Anatomy of Criticism*, 324.

4. Claus Westermann, *Genesis*, 70.

5. Carl Kraeling, *John the Baptist*, 117

6. The same theme of the flood can be found in 1 Enoch 14:22, where it serves as a cosmic judgment of the bad angels and as a paradigm for the last judgment.

7. See Rev. 20:4–7; 2 Bar. 39–40; 4 Ezra 5:2–7:4.

8. The same telescoping can be found in the "time of grace" after the flood and in the "paradisiac time" after the cataclysm, in 1 Enoch 10:17ff., a point that Christopher Rowland unfortunately missed (*The Open Heaven*, 161).

9. *Traduction Oecuménique de la Bible* adds, in a note, "Human perversity will not trouble the permanence of the laws of nature, which are a gift of God." Cf. Matt. 5:45 and, much earlier, Jer. 33:25.

10. Although then it belongs to the *Urzeit*.

11. The natural or climatic conditions only reflect a moral or historical situation as it is now defined by the revolt of man and the patience of God.

12. Cf. my Commentary on Second Zechariah in Amsler et al., *Aggée, Zacharie, Malachie*.

13. This is the mistake even of scholars such as Martin Buber and Gerhard von Rad.

14. The Epistle to the Hebrews seems to have interpreted the meeting of Abraham and Melchizedek along similar lines in Gen. 14. See LaCocque, *But as For Me*.

15. Or at least "the durable." Note the title of God in Dan. 7:13, "The One Who Lasts," generally translated as "the Ancient of Days." Cf. Mal. 3:6; Num. 23:19; Rom. 11:29.

16. Frye, *Anatomy of Criticism*, 316.

17. The New Testament also reflects a preoccupation with this question. Thus Jesus is reported as saying, "I am the alpha and the omega"; "Before Abraham, I am." Christ is identified with the primordial Word; he is the life of all the living, their nourishment, and their substance.

18. He is identified with the Davidic Messiah in 1 Enoch 46 and 4 Ezra 13, among other texts.

19. See D. S. Russell, *The Method and Message of Jewish Apocalyptic*, 231.

20. For the mythic dimensions of Davidic kingship, see 2 Sam. 21:1, 17; 23:3–5; Lam. 4:20; Pss. 72; 89:19; 84:10; 110.

21. To the extent that Yahwism found authorized expression in the canonical texts of the Hebrew Scriptures, which were gathered together and produced by the Jewish community of the Second Temple.

22. Although some people in Israel did not hesitate to judge kingship severely, see source E, Hosea, etc.

23. As the heir of Judaism, Christianity does not really need water in order to baptize, nor bread and wine to hold Communion.

24. This notion is enormously important to hermeneutics. The things the apocalyptist says about the son of man, the resurrection of the dead, or the eschaton in general always have an immediate meaning *plus* a meaning relating to a referent. It is precisely its surplus of meaning that makes this literature so rich, as is true of all biblical literature. Paul Ricoeur had the merit of insisting on this point; see *Interpretation Theory: Discourse and the Surplus of Meaning.*

25. This is what set off the apocalyptic movement, with its particular hermeneutic, in the second century.

26. See my Commentary on Daniel (8:11 and 9:24); cf 1 Chr. 23:13.

27. An entire school of Old Testament hermeneutics has received the evocative name of "Myth and Ritual," which is also the title of the work by S. H. Hooke that has become a classic.

28. B. Otzen, H. Gottlieb, K. Jeppesen, eds., *Myths in the Old Testament,* 11. Otzen cites Widengren, Mowinckel, Hooke, and Childs in support of his theses. On the cultic model for apocalyptic language and thought, see below.

29. Such as the alternation of day and night, knowledge of things, the division of the sexes, human labor, death, etc.

30. See Mircea Eliade, *The Sacred and the Profane,* 39–40, and *Patterns in Comparative Religions.*

31. See Ps. 33:4ff. Thus, in Babylon, the marine monster Tiamat revived annually and annihilated the cosmos, so that Marduk had to vanquish it anew and re-create the world.

32. See Pss. 95:3–5; 96:5; 93:1–2; 74:12–14; 89:9–12.

33. U. B. Müller, *Messias und Menschensohn in jüdischen Apokalypsen und in der Offenbarung des Johannes,* 23ff.

34. Otzen et al., eds., *Myths in the Old Testament,* 52.

35. See S. Mowinckel, *He That Cometh,* 21–95; H. Ringgren, *The Messiah in the Old Testament,* 41–46. Cf. H. Gottlieb, "Myth in the Psalms: The Enthronement of Yhwh."

36. See W. Schmidt, *Die Schöpfungsgeschichte der Priesterschrift,* 127–49.

37. Once again, Sinai is bypassed toward *Urzeit.*

38. "Die Vorstellung vom Menschensohn hat wohl nie eine so klar begrenzte Bedeutung gehabt, dass eine Vermischung mit anderen Ideen ausgeschlossen blieb" (The Son of Man representation was never so precisely defined that it eschewed any influence of other ideas). Müller, *Messias und Menschensohn,* 217. Similarly, H. R. Balz writes, "Die Apokalyptik ist als Konglomerat A.T.er Heilstraditionen zu verstehen. Es werden oft stark divergierende Motive aufgenommen und ohne Rücksicht auf ihren systematischen Zusammenhang kompiliert" (Apocalyptic must be understood as the mix of traditions of salvation. Often it happens that conflicting motifs are present and compiled without regard for their systematic contexts). *(Methodische Probleme der neutestamentlichen Christologie,* 61). Later in the same book Balz judiciously recalls that it is a vision in which all "wird rein bildhaft geredet. Durchgängige Eindeutigkeit kann deshalb gerade nicht erwartet werden" (All is spoken of in a purely figurative language. Therefore, a straightforward clarity cannot be expected).

39. In Daniel A the situation is just as clear. Cf. 1:4 and Lev. 21:17–23; 22:17–25; also 1:8 and, for the cultic ring of this verse, Isa. 59:3; 63:3; Lam. 4:14; Zech. 3:1; Mal. 1:7,

12; Ezra 2:62; Neh. 7:64. Dan. 2:46 presents a priestly vocabulary parallel to the one in Lev. 1–7; the structure of Dan. 3 resembles a liturgical text; and so forth.

40.   See my Commentary on Daniel, 121. The same combination of meanings can be found concerning the eschatological *nuntius* (envoy) in As. Mos. 10:2ff. He is priestly (v. 2; cf. Exod. 28:41; 29:9; Lev. 8:33; 21:10; T. Levi 8:10). He has the functions of the "son of man" (the entire scene, moreover, follows the model of Dan. 7), and of the Messiah (avenger of his people). The envoy is angelic, as both his title and his protective function indicate (cf. Dan. 10:13, 21; 12:1; 1 Enoch 20.5; 1QM 9.15ff.; 17.6f.

41.   This idea is more fully developed in my Commentary on Daniel, 143–44.

42.   See also Ps. 110:1, 4; T. 12 Patr.; Jub. 31:13–23.

43.   In reality, the transition from a kingly ideology to a priestly ideology occurred earlier, in P. According to Ringgren, "It is probable that the garment of the High Priest, as described in Ex. 18, is a post-exilic copy of the royal robe" (*The Messiah*, 13). He adds that Psalm 8 should be read, "originally said to the king" (p. 20).

44.   Gerhard von Rad, *Old Testament Theology*, 1:248. I might add that Daniel takes us precisely into the sanctuary, a point to which I shall return.

45.   In a striking synthesis of meanings, *Abot R. Nat.* (A I. 14) comments on Gen. 3:17–18 as follows: "When Adam heard that the Holy One—may he be blessed—said to him: 'You will eat the grass of the fields,' his members began to tremble, and he said, 'Master of the world, will the beasts and I eat from the same trough?' The Holy One— may he be blessed—answered, 'Since your members have trembled, I will bless you. It is with the sweat of your brow that you will eat your bread.' "

46.   Translation of P. Bogaert, *Apocalypse de Baruch*, 1:464–65.

47.   *ANET* 268-69.

48.   According to *Sifré* Deut. 306; translation of J. Bonsirven, *Textes rabbiniques des deux premiers siècles chrétiens*, 79. It should be noted that one of the important consequences of this is that one should not exaggerate the difference between apocalyptic visions of an eschatological tendency, on the one hand, and beatific visions of the celestial regions, on the other. The latter, even when eschatology seems absent from them (e.g. 1 Enoch, in part; Apoc. of Abr.; 2 Enoch; 3 Bar.,), are not totally unfamiliar with "last things." To have a vision of the divine model of all terrestrial things also belongs, in a larger sense, to the "apocalyptic eschatology," in that the vision invites us to turn our eyes away from the contingent to fix them on the absolute (2 Bar. 4:2–6). This can be achieved either on a temporal axis or on a spatial axis (2 Bar. 59:4, 5–11). One serious weakness in Christopher Rowland's *The Open Heaven* is that he goes much too far in opposing these two sorts of vision. The narrations of mystic ascensions into heavenly places are as proleptic as they are purely beatific (See 1 Enoch 91:10; 43:1–4, etc.).

49.   On the terrestrial temple, destined to be replaced by its celestial model, see 1 Enoch 90:28; 83:8 (E ms.); 91:13.

50.   See above, the reflection of R. Yohanan ben Zaccai on the ruins of the temple after the catastrophe of 70.

51.   One can see something of a parallel with the old and modern rifts in Islam between the Sunnites and the Shi'ites. Religio–social phenomena are surprisingly similar under all latitudes.

52.   The important role played by the motif of the Suffering Servant in Daniel is well known. Ch. 10–12, which use this symbol, have been called by H. L. Ginsberg "the oldest

interpretation of the suffering servant" (in his article of that title). See in particular 11:35, which is an expansion (midrash) on Isaiah 53; see also 12:2–3 whose vocabulary comes from Isa. 53:10f.; and so forth. Nevertheless, between Isa. 53 and Dan., there is an intermediary stage that transforms the motif of the substituted suffering of the Servant into royal and messianic traits. This is Zech. 9:9–10 (cf. my Commentary on Second Zechariah, 153ff.). There, on the model of Isa. 45:21–25, Zechariah describes a monarch who is "justified and saved . . . poor and riding on an ass" (and not on a horse), in the image of the oppressed party in Jerusalem in the fifth century, for whom the prophet is spokesman. As a consequence, this "Messiah" is entitled to bring to all a justice and a salvation that he himself has experienced. It is in this perspective that we now understand that in the middle of the worst persecution, "one like a son of man" is the qualified representative of the people of holy martyrs. He is the first (the New Testament says he is the head) to be glorified and victorious before—but also for and with—the faithful people (the body). Dan. 7 could thus be read as a midrash of Isa. 53:10–12, "he shall see his offspring." The same is true of Daniel 12:2–3. See the discussion of resurrection below.

53. "Une interprétation philosophique de Freud," (Paul Ricoeur, *The Conflict of Interpretations*, 160ff.)

54. J. Pedersen, *Israel: Its Life and Culture*, 1:491. See Dan. 4:3 [3:33]; 4:34ff. [31ff.]; 6:26[27]: "His kingdom is an everlasting kingdom and his dominion is from generation to generation."

55. See also Gen. 14, in which Abraham prostrates himself before Melchizedek. Lacocque, *But as For Me* is a loose commentary on Exod. 19:4–6.

56. See 1 Enoch 90:37–38 (all the animals become white bulls in imitation of the Messiah, a white bull). Rowland *(The Open Heaven*, 163), comments: "The whole community is gradually transformed into perfect humanity as God intended . . . to reflect the glory of the first man."

57. Balz, *Methodische Probleme*, 68.

58. One earlier parallel can be found, e.g., in the transition from the metaphor Ṣemaḥ (sprout, branch) in Jer. 23:5; 33:15, (cf. Isa. 11:1–2) to a messianic title in Zech. 3:8; 6:12. This was of much more limited scope than in the case of the "son of man."

59. See C. Colpe, "Son of Man"; G. Vermes, "Son of Man"; J. A. Fitzmyer, *A Wandering Aramean: Collected Aramaic Essays*.

60. LaCocque, *The Book of Daniel*, 145 n. 116.

61. In Dan. 8:17 the expression is used, as in Ezekiel, to designate the prophet or the seer. This usage, overly mimetic, should be distinguished from the one found elsewhere in Daniel, particularly, in ch. 7.

62. O. Procksch, *Theologie des Alten Testaments*, 416–17. Procksch's argument is largely based on intuition, however.

63. Balz, *Methodische Probleme*, 94.

64. Rowland, *The Open Heaven*, 96–97, reproaches Balz for not having paid sufficient attention to the parallel between Ezek. 1:26-27 and Ezek. 8:2. Here there is a separation between the human figure and the throne. Rowland adds that it is not, as Balz says, that there is a "splitting up of divine functions among various angelic figures." Ezekiel is showing rather that the form of God acts "as a quasi-angelic mediator." A confirmation of this interpretation is given by the Septuagint text of Dan. 7:13: "And he [the son of man] came as being [*hōs*], the Ancient of days." Cf. Rev. 1:13; Apoc. Abr. 11.

MAJOR THEOLOGICAL LESSONS

65. The sixth time is in ch. 9.

66. W. Zimmerli, *Ezekiel: A Commentary on the Book of the Prophet Ezekiel*, 1:236.

67. Lev. 16:4, 23; 1 Sam. 2:18; Ezek. 9:2, 3, 11; 10:2, 6, 7. See H. Meissner, *Babylonien und Assyrien*, 2:55, 62; Babylonian priests also wore linen.

68. Zimmerli, *Ezekiel*, 246.

69. Ibid., 250, col. 1.

70. Balz, *Methodische Probleme*, 72.

71. H. Odeberg, *The Fourth Gospel*, 35-36.

72. "The figure of Man must be seen as a development of the prince of the host of YHWH who apears to Joshua in Josh. 5:13 and of the angel of the Exodus. We should note that the tendency to substitute this figure for YHWH met with some opposition in Israel. Isa. 63:9 denies that any 'prince' or angel led Israel—YHWH himself did so" (J. J. Collins, "The Mythology of Holy War in Daniel and the Qumran War Scroll: A Point of Transition in Jewish Apocalyptic," 601 n. 20).

73. N. Schmidt, "The Son of Man in the Book of Daniel."

74. G. W. E. Nickelsburg, *Resurrection, Immortality, and Eternal Life in Intertestamental Judaism*, 104 n. 53.

75. The speculations on Christ as an angel, in which Christ was identified as the archangel Michael, should be noted. This doctrine is attested in Christian patristic in Rome, although with some qualification, and later, in the second and third centuries, in the works of Arius. See Mircea Eliade, *A History of Religious Ideas*, 409.

76. U. Müller, *Messias und Menschensohn*, 35.

77. Ibid., 28.

78. J. de Fraine, *Adam et son lignage*, 177. De Fraine refers to John 11:52, among other passages, and his book bears an epigraph from Kierkegaard: "Adam, c'est lui-même et son lignage."

79. Sigmund Mowinckel sees in this individual the person of Second Isaiah, and John McKenzie, in AB commentary *The Second Isaiah*, thinks that the songs come from Third Isaiah.

80. McKenzie, *Second Isaiah*, 20-21: "The second Exodus, like the first, was in need of its Moses." See Aage Bentzen, *King and Messiah*.

81. *Second Isaiah*, lii.

82. Müller, *Messias und Menchensohn*, 217.

83. This explains the manifest ambiguity in the book of Enoch, where the seer speaks of the son of man (71:17), and is simply identified with him (71:14). We are evidently at the threshold of a theology of incarnation. Cf. 1 Enoch 105, which should not be attributed hastily to a Christian hand as is shown by texts like 4 Ezra 7:28–29; 13:32, 37, 52; 14:9).

84. For Paul, the glorified Christ must "take form" within us, and we already have, right now, the earnest of the Holy Ghost.

85. I have no intention of studying the pertinent texts in detail here. Citation and commentary can be found in a work that has become a classic: Robert Martin-Achard, *De la mort à la résurrection*, and in his article "Résurrection dans l'Ancien Testament et le judaisme."

86. M. Dahood, *Psalms*. In my Commentary on Daniel, see the introduction to ch. 12, esp. pp. 236–38.

87. Cf. the Egyptian "daring valorization of death, henceforth accepted as a sort of exalting transmutation of incarnate existence. Death accomplishes passage from the sphere of the meaningless to the sphere of the meaningful" (Eliade, *A History of Religious Ideas*, 1:99).

88. According to Bentzen, mythological language no longer represented a danger in the age of Daniel: "Monotheism was now so firmly rooted that mythology could not imperil Israel's religion," (*King and Messiah*, 74–75).

89. Edmond Jacob writes, "By this definitive nature [of death, due to man's disobedience], death takes on the appearance of a punishment." He expresses surprise, however, that this aspect is so little expressed in many of the texts that speak of death (*Theology of the Old Testament*, 300).

90. See Pss. 6:5; 30:18; 31:17; 88:13; 115:17; e.g. Pertinent texts can be found in Martin-Achard, "Resurrection," col. 442.

91. No matter what objective model of the prophet is involved, collective or individual, it is clear that the poet *chooses* this death-oblation for himself in the future—unless the songs of the Servant were composed by the so-called Third Isaiah school. In this case, the disciples of the poet celebrate his sacrifice and adopt it as the crowning of their own lives. The death of the martyr is fecund: "He shall see his offspring" (See Isa. 53:10–12).

92. There are two sorts of life and two sorts of death (see 4 Ezra 9:22).

93. The conjunction of the two is not accidental. According to Collins, the apocalypse has as a kerygma the transcendence of death. ("Apocalyptic Eschatology as the Transcendence of Death." Collins writes elsewhere, "[The] hope for the transcendence of death is what decisively distinguishes apocalyptic from earlier prophecy. . . . The novelty of apocalyptic lies in the fact that humans have access to this higher life . . . permanently" ("The Symbolism of Transcendence in Jewish Apocalyptic," 10-11).

94. Martin-Achard, "Résurrection," col. 462. On Alfrink's interpretation, See my Commentary on Daniel, esp. 243-44.

95. P. Volz, *Die Eschatologie der jüdischen Gemeinde im neutestamentlichen Zeitalter*, 352.

96. Ibid., 231–32. See also T. Judah 23:1–4.

97. According to 4 Ezra 9:22, the lot of the "multitude that was born in vain" is to die in vain.

98. Martin-Achard, "Résurrection," col. 468.

99. Nickelsburg, *Resurrection, Immortality, and Eternal Life*, 23: "For Daniel, resurrection has a juridical function" (See also p. 27).

100. 2 Macc. 7:28; *Mid. Ps.* 25.2: Resurrection can be founded in the fact that God re-creates mankind every morning (cf. *Gen. Rab.* 78.1 on Gen. 32:27).

101. Pss. 16:10-11; 23:4; 49:10ff.; 73:23ff.; Martin-Achard, "Résurrection," cols. 470–72.

102. Martin-Achard, "Résurrection," col. 473.

103. The same reading can be found, e.g., in Tg. (of Jerusalem) Exod. 12:42:

Moses will come out of the desert
And the King Messiah will come out of Rome (or out of high places)
One will be transferred to the summit of the clouds
And the other will be transferred to the summit of the clouds.

When the rabbis speak of the messianic son of man "coming on the clouds" they reflect another reading of Dan. 7, dictated by the delay in the Messiah's coming. Or perhaps the rabbis add to the enthronement of the Messiah (going from low to high) the motif of his coming (from high to low) among men. Cf. Mark 8:38; 13:26; 14:62.

104. Cf. 1QH 3.7–12, 19–36, where "the eschatological reference serves as a metaphor for the psalmist's experience" (Collins, *The Apocalyptic Imagination*, 137).

105. Individual death is put in parallel with final cataclysm in 4 Ezra 3:9–12.

106. Cf. 4 Ezra 9:31: the seed of eternity here is the Torah.

107. See J. Pedersen, *Israel*, 1, 462: "All graves have certain common characteristics constituting the nature of the grave, and that is Sheol. The 'Ur-grave' we might call Sheol . . . manifests itself in every single grave, as *mo'ab* manifests itself in every single moabite." (A negative criticism of this can be found in James Barr, *The Semantics of Biblical Language*.)

108. Jacob, *Theology of the Old Testament*, 304.

109. See Isa. 65:17; 66:22; also the impressive passage in 4 Ezra 7:31ff., where resurrection (general or dualist) is also presented as a creation and as a reward.

110. See Jacob, *Theology of the Old Testament*, 312.

111. As was still the case with the passages from the book of Kings or with the resurrection of individuals by Jesus in the Gospels. Resurrection is in this case a supreme sort of cure.

112. This dichotomy is mitigated, however, by the fact that the eschatological cataclysm is historical (as is human death), and that the "righteous" belong to both worlds. The sectarians of Qumran were to exploit this last point thoroughly, as we shall see below.

113. See H. C. C. Cavallin, *Life After Death: Paul's Argument for the Resurrection of the Dead in I Cor. XV*, 27, 203ff. Volz, *Die Eschatologie*, 354–55, also cites 1 Enoch 43; Pss. Sol. 18:9ff.; Jub. 19:25; As. Mos. 10:9. E. M. Laperrousaz, "Le Testament de Moïse." But Dan. 8:10ff. also makes an association between stars and angels (See my Commentary on Daniel, 161-62) and, even earlier, Isa. 52:13 certainly serves as a model. The oldest text to enter into the dossier is Num. 24:17. In Parsiism (see ch. 4 above, under "Angelology") the *fravashis* are both angels and stars.

114. With classic prophecy the prophets take the place of the angels (Hag. 1:13).

115. These texts and the ones that follow are cited in M. Stone, "Revealed Things in Apocalyptical Literature," 430-31.

116. In fact, until the destruction of the temple in 70 C.E.; see 4 Ezra 7:30-31.

117. See Russell, *The Method and Message*, 297ff.

118. See the discussion of the *Urzeit-Endzeit*, above; also O. S. Rankin, *Israel's Wisdom Literature*, 130.

119. Wilheim Rudolph, *Jesaja 24–27*, 63. His lead is followed by J. Lindblom, *Die Jesaja-Apokalypse in der neuen Jesajahandschrift*, 102, and E. Kissane, *The Book of Isaiah*, 267, among others, who share this initial misunderstanding.

120. Paul Volz seems to oversimplify the problem when he declares, "Es ist ganz gleich, ob es sich um das nationale Heil oder um das Weltende handelt; überall weiss der Glaube, dass das Ende herbeigekommen ist." ("It is indifferent whether it is a question of national or of universal salvation; the main thing that faith knows is that the end has come"). *Die Eschatologie*, 137.

121. Paul Hanson, "Prolegomena to the Study of Jewish Apocalypse," 412.

122. Paul Tillich, *Systematic Theology* (Chicago, 1957), 2:29–44.

123. For O. S. Rankin, "The first principal cause of the retarded development and late appearance in Hebrew religion of a doctrine of personal existence after death was the tenacious endurance of the conception of YHWH as a sky- or heaven-god." *Israel's Wisdom Literature*, 137. This means a God dissociated from the forces of nature and, consequently, as far as possible from a Baal alternatively dying and coming back to life.

124. Nils Messel insists on the profound unity of Jewish eschatology; see *Die Einheitlichkeit der jüdischen Eschatologie*.

125. "The idea that two contradictory formulations . . . such as elevation to the stars or resurrection on earth . . . could be simultaneously affirmed runs counter to Aristotelian logic but is fundamental to mythical thinking." (Collins, "The Symbolism of Transcendence in Jewish Apocalyptic," 19).

126. Cavallin, *Life After Death*, 199ff.

127. Collins in particular insists on this point: "I mean that there is another sphere of life parallel to this. In the words of *4 Ezra*, 'the Most High made not one world but two.' [7:40] These two, however, are not only in temporal succession, as envisaged by *4 Ezra* and often thought to be typical of all Jewish apocalyptic. They are also contemporaneous, as envisaged by Daniel, 1 Enoch, and Qumran. . . . It is clear from the example of Qumran that the transition to the higher form of life was essentially a depth experience in the present. Death was transcended by an intensity in this life." ("Apocalyptic Eschatology as the Transcendence of Death," 21–43, 41). See also Collins, *The Apocalyptic Vision of the Book of Daniel*, 176.

128. E. Amado Lévy-Valensi, *Le temps dans la vie morale*.

129. See 4 Ezra 7:26, which announces the eschatological manifestation of the "city that now is invisible" and the "land which is now concealed," and 7:50, already cited: "The Most High has made not one world but two." See also the fine passage in Wis. 19:18–21: "For the elements changed their order one with another, just as the notes of a psaltery vary the character of the rhythm, continuing always the same each in its several sounds." (v. 18; see *APOT* 1:568). Neither is death a space that succeeds another space called life. As Jacob rightly insists, there is "a realm of death which breaks into the realm of life in such a way that man may be involved in it without ceasing for that reason to live. . . . [it includes] the desert, the sea, sin, disease, chaos, or darkness," (*Theology of the Old Testament*, 299).

130. The *shabbat*, or the feast. For Zech. 14, e.g., the culminating point in history is the last feast of Succoth (Dan. 12:1 is a scene of the enthronement of YHWH at the feast of Succoth). On the relationship between the apocalypse and the cult see below.

131. The temple, as we have seen, is the bridgehead from which the cosmos can be born into eternity.

132. See the powerful passages in Zech. 14:6–7; 4 Ezra 7:38c–42; Sib. Or. 8. 89–92; 2 Enoch 10:2; Sir. 12:2; and Isa. 30:26.

133. Northrop Frye, *The Great Code: The Bible and Literature*, 137. See also Karl Rahner, "The Hermeneutics of Eschatological Assertions," 4:331; and J. Pedersen, *Israel*, 1:491.

134. See 4 Ezra 9:6: "The beginnings are [visible] in portents and secret signs, and the end in effects and marvels."

135. Transposed into hermeneutics, analogical interpretation gives the deep meaning of Scripture. See Volz, *Die Eschatologie*, 128: "überall hat ein Ding erst seinen vollen Wert und seine wahre Gestalt, wenn es den Abschluss erreicht hat."

136. Collins, "The Symbolism of Transcendence," 19. Collins refers to Paul Ricoeur *The Symbolism of Evil*, 168: "There does not exist, in fact, any act of signifying that is equal to its aim."

137. See Lacocque, *But as for Me*, 79ff.

138. "The literal can also be symbolic." (Collins, "The Symbolism of Transcendence," 19).

139. Ibid., 11. Collins' citation of Col. 3:1–4 is much to the point.

SEVEN

The Figure of Daniel

The figure of Daniel, as it can be drawn from the different literary pieces sewn together into the canonical and extracanonical book that bears his name, is a complex one. As established in chapter 3 above, Daniel A is much older than Daniel B, and they belong to vastly different genres. In Daniel A the hero is a wise counselor in a foreign court; in Daniel B he is a visionary. The former is composed of six tales concerning Daniel or his companions and is written in the third person; the latter reports in the first person visionary experiences of Daniel. Only the second is apocalyptic. Moreover, a short time after the Semitic composition of the book, other stories were added that are present in the Greek extended versions of Septuagint and Theodotion. These accretions are of still another date, and their literary texture is a far cry from the artistic achievement of Daniel A with which they are kindred. Here Daniel is much more of a *theos anēr* (Divine Man), and he has meanwhile lost much of his modesty. The Additions to Daniel are, to some extent, what the apocryphal gospels are to the Four Evangels.

What brings together such disparate elements is, first, the sewing together of all or part of them into one literary unit. Daniel A's material, antedating Daniel B as it does, has been reused and reshaped by the apocalyptist. The tales, originating probably from the Jewish Diaspora, are no longer what they used to be. Whatever may be their positive attitude vis-à-vis the Mesopotamian kings—an attitude that evolves toward more severity as the chapters progress—the reader cannot forget the ominous shadow of Antiochus IV cast upon Nebuchadnezzar and his successors. Consequently, the personality of "Daniel" begins to be shaped by Daniel A, even though in the author's mind it is only one side of his hero's character.

Such a literary mixture in the book, however, is not accidental. J. J. Collins is right when he states, "We must conclude that the group which identified with Daniel the visionary also identified with Daniel the wise courtier."[1] This is the cement between all parts of the composition and for all aspects of the figure of Daniel. This figure is complex because it represents a sociologically multifaceted group.[2] Our endeavor in this chapter is thus justified. By analyzing the different elements that shape the hero's personality, we contribute, with the original author, to the profile of the sect to which the latter belonged.

The role of narratives in Daniel A is much debated.[3] It is not the place here to summarize that discussion (see my Commentary on Daniel and ch. 3 above). Be that as it may, the figure of Daniel is shaped in a most characteristic way. Had we only Daniel B, Daniel would appear unremarkably pale, almost totally disappearing behind a message that he would merely record for our instruction. This in itself is not insignificant, but, whether infelicitous or felicitous, the Additions to Daniel A considerably enhance Daniel's figure.[4] True, nothing is said about his origins or genealogy, but we learn that Daniel was a young man when deported by Nebuchadnezzar to Babylon, where he became a courtier for nearly seventy years (from the reign of Nebuchadnezzar to the reign of Cyrus; i.e., exactly from one end of the Exile to the other). The author's silence on his hero's origins is purposeful. It leaves them in the dark and thus confirms the legendary character stressed already by Ezekiel 14:14; 28:3, where Daniel is an ancient holy man associated with the patriarchs Noah and Job.[5]

In other words, the focus is definitely on Daniel's person, and the aura of mystery that surrounds him only increases the reader's interest and desire to know more about him. In fact, the tales of Daniel A are literary compositions close to the prophetic legenda, and more particularly, to the didactic aretalogies which, as Alexander Rofé notes, may center on a nonprophetic hero.[6] Those stories insist on the miraculous. One example is provided by 2 Kings 5 (Elisha and Naaman), where the leprous Syrian ambassador is healed, but the healing is told, not for itself, but to make a point. That is why, although the prophet generally accepts gifts, here Elisha refuses all remuneration for his services (v. 16), so that "the miracle . . . be enacted in a way that will prove its godly origin and differentiate it unequivocally from the sorcerous practices of the heathens."[7] The parallel in Daniel 5:17 is striking.

Among the legenda, let us further note 2 Kings 20:1-11, the healing of king Hezekiah through the mediation of the prophet Isaiah and the performance of a "magic" act. The parallel of the healing of King Nebuchadnezzar in Daniel 4 leaves the human intervention totally out of the picture. Daniel's role is a passive one: he forecasts the future but he does not mold it.[8] This is an important point that needs to be stressed. N. Habel, for example, has insisted upon the fact that the prophet is called to participate actively in the divine shaping of history. "The herald of YHWH must therefore be more than a messenger. He must be the agent of his Lord."[9] The contrast with the apocalyptist is remarkable. There is here no "call narrative" involving, as in the case of the prophet—and more generally of a messenger (e.g., Gen. 24:3, 4 ff.; Judg. 6:11-17)— "1. divine confrontation, 2. introductory word, 3. commission, 4. objection, 5. reassurance, 6. sign."[10] True, it may be said that the frequent statement in the call-narratives (*Berufungsberichten*) that God is *with* the prophet is also valid in the case of the apocalyptist (see Dan. 9:23). But, besides the fact of the absence of such a formula here, God's election of Daniel is for a different purpose. The holy man must "understand the word and have the intelligence of the vision." There is reflected here almost the same idealism that some Greek philosophers displayed in thinking that a correct understanding brings about a correct action and behavior.

Even if this parallel with Greek philosophy appears to some overdrawn, it remains clear that the book of Daniel leans toward universalism. Since it is a matter of understanding—even though here of a transcendent character—the archenemy of Israel, Nebuchadnezzar himself, can be made privy to a secret that can save him from being debased to the rank of an animal. And here again lies another point of contrast with the prophetic calling. The sign, given by God as a signature to his reassurance to the prophet, does always involve Israel as a whole. "The call of the prophet or mediator establishes a historical connection between YHWH's past and present involvement in Israel's history."[11] This element crucial for the prophetic ministry is missing in apocalyptic literature.

THE FIGURE OF DANIEL

This is not to say, however, that deeds of power beyond words were not expected from the holy man. Indeed, Daniel A is a succession of such deeds, and it is legitimate to regard the "court contests" in which Daniel and his companions are enmeshed as examples of those competitions between shamans for power and recognition illustrated almost everywhere in the world. But there, the nature of the "signs," if one insists on so calling them, is very different. They are as it were self-serving. The person of Daniel becomes through them more and more awesome; the foreign king elevates the Jewish magician higher and higher. Meanwhile, however, Israel as a whole remains absent. Parallels in Jewish literature are not found among the prophets but among popular hero tales such as the Joseph novella, the book of Esther, the story of Ahikar, and so forth.

As can be expected in a literature that does not display the soberness of the prophetic books, Daniel's deeds surpass anything that had been seen before. In fact, as the authority of the prophet rested on the twin pillars of his transcendent communion and his acts of power,[12] so Daniel is also said to enjoy "the spirit of the holy gods" and "light and understanding and an excellent wisdom" (5:14). On both scores, therefore, Daniel is superior to all others, and it is without surprise that we see him having private access to kings, like prophets before him. But, while the latter were recognized as God-sent by Judean and Israelite leaders, Daniel is acknowledged by heathen monarchs, and they must more than once confess that Israel's God is the only God. The point is not that Daniel would be more diplomatic in his approach, for no less than the prophets who confronted Israel's kings did Daniel speak without flattery or compromise to the world's potentates. To every one of those dictators before whom the whole earth trembled with fear, Daniel denounced his corruption and wickedness (Dan. 2; 4; 5; see also 2 Sam. 12:1-15; 1 Kgs. 20:41-42; Isa. 7:13-14; 38:1-8; Jer. 37:16-17; 38:14-15). Many of the prophets who confronted their nation's kings with defiance remained unheeded and were even persecuted (see 1 Kgs. 22), but Daniel's authority was such that foreign kings—cruel and inhuman kings—never willingly harmed him (Dan. 6).

The shamanic dimensions of Daniel's personality strike an important root in mantic widsom, from which, as we shall see below, the figure of Daniel has received much of its color. But when we consider the prophetic influence on the shaping of the holy man's profile, it is undoubtedly to Ezekiel that we must turn as the model for the subsequent Jewish literature of visions and celestial raptures. There for the first time a prophet is presented by tradition as a quasi-psychotic person, stricken by inability to speak or by bodily paralysis, catalepsy or trance, translation to other places, and fantastic visions. Some scholars speak, in connection with Ezekiel, of pathological phenomena.[13] More to the point, however, is the analysis of Johannes Lindblom, who prefers to subsume prophetic psychic phenomena under the term *ecstasy*. Ecstasy, says Lindblom, is "an abnormal state of consciousness in which one is so intensely absorbed by one single idea or one single feeling, or by a group of ideas and feelings, that the normal stream of psychological life is more or less arrested."[14]

This definition is certainly applicable to Ezekiel's behavior as described above. It is also relevant as far as Daniel's experiences as a visionary are concerned (see 7:15; 10:9-10, 16-17). In 7:28 Daniel says, "My thoughts frightened me greatly and my color changed." In 8:27 he adds, "then I, Daniel, fainted and was sick for days. . . . I was appalled by the vision." In 8:18 he falls into lethargy—a condition of total receptivity that the Testament of Reuben calls an eighth human sense, a *pneûma toû húpnou meth' hoû ektísthē ékstasîs phúseōs* (3:1; see also Gen. 15:12: *thardemah*, Hebrew; *ékstasis*, Septuagint; see the Septuagint of Num. 24:4, 16). Then, says the same text, the visionary has the appearance of a corpse (*eikōn toû thanátou*; see also Rev. 1:17).[15]

In short, Daniel's visions are no fictional constructions; they are the fruit of mystical experiences. Such experiences were not unknown by prophets (see Isa. 21; Hab. 3:16; Ezek. 3:14-15). They also forecast events in the lives of individuals (see Jer. 28:16-17; 32:6-7; Ezek. 24:1-2; 32:21-22). They also had revelatory dreams (Num. 12:6; Deut. 13:2; Jer. 23:25ff.), but those vehicles of prophecy are the exception rather than the rule. Classical prophecy censured dreams (Jer. 23:27-28, 32; 27:9; 29:8; see also Sir. 34:1-8; Joel 3:1ff. is an exception). In any case, there is no question of hallucinations—that is, visions without perception of an object. Prophetic and apocalyptic visions are internal visions, as imaginative as art or music. The Testament of Reuben, quoted above, insisted on that. In other words, the actual world and its sensations are left behind, and another world is unveiled—the world of ultimate reality. The visions are eidetic. They perfectly fit the apocalyptic disaffection with history. If we call direct revelation the dialogue that God initiates with those whom he chooses without favoring anyone in particular, the phenomenon of ecstasy emphasizes the absence of direct revelation that was so deeply felt by the returnees from exile. An intermediary between God and people has become indispensable. In what eventually became orthodox Judaism that intermediary is the scribe transmitting to the ignorant populace the demands of the Torah recognized as the unique source of revelation and direction. In the party of opposition the mediator is a holy man, a visionary who transmits the mystic revelation of a transcendent reality superseding history.[16] In the former group the dangers menacing the scribe are all too clear. In the latter group it happened time and again that technique substituted for charisma.

The way to fend off phoniness is indicated by the book of Daniel. It is a combination of wisdom and righteousness that enables Daniel to be a holy man and a visionary. He is ascetic (Dan. 1), law abiding (1; 6), pious (4; 9), and so forth. In sum, Daniel is a Hasid. His main motivation is the fear of God. His asceticism is exercised not only in the dietetic realm but, if I may be allowed to offer an argument *e silentio*, in sexual life as well. There is in the book no mention of or allusion to women.[17] This is not fortuitous. In the parallel literature the exhortations to keep away from women are frequent (see 1 Enoch 15:4; T. Reub. 6:1-2; T. Iss. 1; 2; T. Judah 16:1-3 (α); see also 1 Cor. 7:1-9). Sometimes the texts' attitude becomes outright mysogynic (T.Reub. 5:1-5). Asceticism had become an important act of devotion because of the increased difficulty, in the second century B.C.E., of offering sacrifices. Sacrifice was thus replaced by exercises of penance and atonement. Fasting as well as prayer became highly regarded, as shown, for example, in Daniel 9.[18] Both of these devotional practices are conducive to visionary receptivity.[19] It is thus not in the same spirit as that of the legalistic party in Judaism that we find among the visionaries a scrupulous respect of Torah. One should keep in mind that the Hasidim's aim was to serve as a model for the rest of their compatriots. They formed a *synagoge asidaiôn* (1 Macc. 2:42; Ps. 149). Their opposition to the conservative party was surely not in terms of a greater laxity. They practiced the Levitical rites (Dan. 1; 6:11; 10:3). Indeed, in Daniel B they are in dialogue with angels, with whom they are associated (e.g., 7:27; 10:12ff.; 12:3). This idea found later expression in Wisdom of Solomon (5:5) and a remarkable development at Qumran.[20]

As with dreams, classical prophets (Zechariah excepted) attempted to purge their trade of all mention of angelic intermediaries. In this the prophets were backed up by the Deuteronomist reform. A.

Rofé states that "the figure of the angel, leader of Israel in the desert and in Canaan, which is so prominent in Exodus, has completely disappeared from Deuteronomy."[21] . . . "No different is the attitude of the Priestly Code."[22] Y. Kaufmann contrasted the prophetic disinterest in the unseen world, on the one hand, and the apocalyptic speculations, on the other.[23] Indeed, as in the case of dreams and visions, angelology came back in apocalypticism with a vengeance. And, with both, there was a return to myth and to mythopoeic formulations.[24]

In order to understand what all this means one must remember that the pattern ABA is typical of the apocalyptic approach to reality—and to history. The End time is a return of the primal time that has been interrupted by postdiluvian human history.[25] Not surprisingly, such a negative judgment on *Geschichte* results in the apocalyptists' return to archaic forms and ways of expression that had been painstakingly suppressed by the prophets, whose effort to strip the preaching of the Word of all fantastic and magical elements was fundamentally dictated by their option for *history* against cyclical recurrence. Anything that would abstract man from the actual, the earthly, the this-wordly, was condemned as a kind of drunkenness (see Isa. 29:9-10; Jer. 51:7). That is why there is a prophetic repudiation of magic. God responds to prayer (1 Kgs. 17:21-22), to repentance (Jonah 3:10; 4:2), to confession of sin or of faith (2 Kgs. 5:15), but not to hocus-pocus formulas. But prophetic religion is the fruit of a long process of refinement, for in the remote past to which the "simple legenda" (Rofé) send us back, the ancient prophets did not shy away from performing miracles through magical means. One need think only of Elijah and Elisha (e.g. 2 Kgs. 2:21, 24; 4:4-7, 41; 6:6).

The resurgence of magic in Daniel and other apocalyptic books belongs thus to the same return to origins. However, other phenomena that recurred in the apocalypse after a long eclipse were not fraught with so great a danger for the Israelite faith as this one. True, the use of mythology, dreams, or angelology is risky, but their harmfulness can be to a large extent dampened by a sophisticated interpretation. Miracles, for example, can be a cheap way to quench the popular thirst for the fantastic and the sensational (1 Kgs. 18), but they may also channel human religiosity toward praising the Living God (1 Kgs. 17:24; 2 Kgs. 5:15). But magic is not part of God's intervention in history and it has no theological meaning.

188

Therefore, there must have been compelling reasons why the apocalyptist resorted to the fantastic and to magic. These reasons are the particular relationship between apocalypticism and wisdom, more specifically, mantic wisdom. This extremely important aspect of apocalypticism is so far from cutting loose from its moorings in prophetism that it takes us back, on the contrary, to the latter's oldest forms, and even to a certain kind of shamanism; that is, to a stage in religion where the wise man and the oracular diviner were not distinguished, for both aspects were joined in the clairvoyant who *knows* and *forecasts*. As far as Daniel is concerned, as an avatar of the formidable perfect men of old—with Job and Noah, according to Ezekiel[26]—he is the point of convergence of old prophetism and mantic wisdom.[27] As K. Koch says, Daniel's wisdom is paradoxically exercised in revealing mysteries of the End (2:22; 11:35, 40; 12:4, 9, 13). He also solves riddles, and prophecies of old are among the riddles whose meaning he unveils (2:18-19, 27-30; 9), along with heavenly mysteries. There is, therefore, according to the apocalyptist, a first-stage revelation with the prophets and a second-stage revelation with Daniel.[28]

But if Daniel is "also among the prophets," he is nonetheless among the sages. Koch objects that the attribution of Daniel to wisdom literature has to confront the fact that wisdom literature presents no form-critical parallel to Daniel. There is, furthermore, no eschatological interest in wisdom of the second century B.C.E. But Koch's objection is the outcome of a confusion between two types of wisdom, one ancient and "primitive," the other more sophisticated. The former type is mantic; the latter is aphoristic. In the biblical writings gathered under the classification of Israelite wisdom literature, only aphoristic wisdom is represented. In the same way that early prophetism—or, if you prefer, shamanic prophetism—has been progressively replaced by oracular prophetism—or logoic prophetism—so early wisdom, mantic wisdom, was in Israel to make way for a wisdom of ethics and of theodicy. Daniel, however, is a perfect man, a holy man of old, who allegedly came before that shift occurred. Already the Canaanites knew of him and celebrated his wisdom in their literature. He is with Job and Noah an ancient universal patriarch. Second, Daniel in the book that bears his name is the representative of a group calling themselves *maskilim*, or wise (1:4; 11:33-35; 12:3), whose vocation it is to make others wise and just (11:33; 12:3). Last but not least, Daniel is put by circumstances in the midst of Chaldean courtiers and counselors whose activity belongs precisely to mantic wisdom. Like Moses and Aaron, who outwitted Egyptian soothsayers and magicians (Exod. 7ff.), like Joseph, who surpassed in clairvoyance later members of the same Egyptian groups, Daniel beats the Chaldeans at their own game. J. J. Collins as well speaks of the idealization of Chaldean wisdom in Jewish Eastern Diaspora.[29]

Hans Peter Müller has emphasized the relations of apocalyptic with mantic wisdom. For Müller also such a wisdom came to the knowledge of the Jews of Mesopotamia. Five characteristics of apocalyptic literature are thus explained: its eschatological orientation; its determinism; the seers' claim to special authorization; the encodement in symbols; and, possibly, its pseudonymity.[30] Also emphasizing mantic wisdom's influence upon the apocalyptic part of Daniel's book, Paul A. Porter has shown that the old Mesopotamian lists called *šumma izbu* ("if an anomaly . . .") —some twenty-four tablets from ca. 1600 to ca. 100 B.C.E., served as a model.[31] Although Israel came in contact with Mesopotamian mantic wisdom traditions rather late, a formula such as "like" (*kima*) plus an animal comparison, characteristic of the *šumma izbu*, is strikingly similar to Daniel's own visionary expressions (e.g. 7:4, 6; 8:15; these two chapters are particularly close to their Mesopotamian model). 1 Enoch 85–90 (the Animal Apocalypse, written slightly later than Daniel) provides another example.

Adopting Müller's conclusions, James C. VanderKam has written a monograph on Enoch that is of particular interest to us, not only because it shores up so convincingly the theory of apocalyptic dependence upon the mantic wisdom of Mesopotamia, but because of the kinship that some texts establish between Enoch and Daniel (see ch. 1, above: Daniel is Enoch's father-in-law; Jub. 4:20), evidently a literary device used to emphasize an ideological parallel between the two characters and their respective traditions. VanderKam's thesis is that "Enoch was a Jewish literary crystallization of Sumero-Akkadian lore about the seventh antedeluvian king Enmeduranki."[32] The latter is the mythical founder of the guild of Mesopotamian diviners (*bārûs*). Jewish traditions (e.g. Jub. 4:17, 19, 21) place Enoch among those diviners. He has the knowledge of everything on earth and in heaven, and he writes down "all the deeds of the generations until the day of condemnation" (v. 24), thus making him the scribe in heaven (v. 23) and the prosecutor of the fallen angels (v. 22). P. Grelot has shown that Jewish tradition transferred traits of Enmeduranki and of the hero of the flood to Enoch.[33]

According to fragments in cuneiform writing, Enmeduranki was appointed by the gods Shamash and Adad and granted "the tablet of the gods . . . a secret of heaven."[34] What this "secret" was is exposed in the fields of interest covered by Mesopotamian divination; namely, astronomical divination and oneiromancy, which include reports on other wordly travels. Of particular interest is the fact that the gods encode their intentions in *symbols*. The sage decodes them by using the *pašaru* ([science of] interpretation). The equivalence with the term *pešer* in Daniel 4:3; 5:12 and in Genesis 40:5; 41:13, about Joseph's wisdom, is striking.

Regarding the eschatological component of Jewish apocalypses, however, VanderKam has a more restricted understanding of that notion than had Müller. For VanderKam, the Mesopotamian sources do not provide any firm ground for apocalyptic eschatology, which, for him, depended essentially upon biblical prophetic eschatology. He writes concerning 1 Enoch 1–5, the first part of the "Book of the Watchers" (1 Enoch 1–36), "Enoch is, for the first time in surviving literature, brought into relation with the *eschaton*."[35] Indeed, Enoch's functions, like those of Enmeduranki, are those of a heavenly scribe. His revelations are the antipode of and the antidote to those that the fallen angels abusively shared with the "daughters of man." Those secrets were stolen from heaven and they corrupted human beings. But Enoch (and Daniel and the sages) impart a transcendent knowledge unveiling the meaning of life and the world.[36]

In this respect it is striking how, beside other "signs" in the cosmic realm, prophecy also had become, as VanderKam says, "another cryptic indication of the future" (p. 167). Daniel 9 is a perfect illustration of this. This explains once more the convergence of mantic wisdom and prophetic eschatology in apocalyptic literature. All the omens, be they cosmic signs or prophetic divinations, are written on "tablets" or "books," much like the inscription on the wall in Daniel 5. As a scribe (*sōpher*), Daniel or Enoch can read and understand what for others remains cryptic and mysterious. Both are *bārûs*—something like shamans—with a specialty, the reading of signs. The interpretation of dreams belongs to the same expertise.

Dreams permeate Daniel A and Daniel B. So far, I have insisted upon the influence of mantic wisdom on the apocalyptic section of

Daniel B. I can now turn back to Daniel A, thus completing this chapter as it had started.[37] Those narratives, as a matter of fact, are, among other things, expressions of practical wisdom (again, the story of Joseph provides a good parallel). Now, in conformity with Daniel B, the personage of Daniel is also presented in the first part less as someone who *practices* wisdom than as one who *originates* wisdom—that is, a revealer, like Enoch, and like him with roots in primordial times.

The coexistence of the sophisticated apocalyptic world view (*Weltanschauung*), on the one hand, and of the narrative stream meant to stir the masses' admiration for the hero Daniel, on the other, may appear conflictual. The key to the dilemma is that wisdom provides an intercultural and international perspective that permeates, in different ways, both Daniel A and Daniel B. The apocalyptists are sages writing for the populace. They are the *maskilim* among the populace and are *maṣdikim* (turning into righteous) the *rabbim* (the masses). This point has been well understood by Collins when he states that the message of Daniel is "a political manifesto, produced by one section of the intelligentsia but designed to affect the populace."[38] To do just that, "the *masdikim* formulated their ideal of mantic wisdom by using a collection of tales set in the Diaspora."[39]

Daniel A is, one could say with Susan Niditch and Robert Doran, "the success story of a wise courtier."[40] The literary type in question is the type 922, "Clever Acts and Words" of A. Aarne and S. Thompson,[41] exemplified in biblical texts also by Genesis 41–45 and by the intertestamental Ahikar Syr. 5–7.23. There are four parts to the tale: 1) a person of lower status is called before a person of higher status to answer/solve a problem; 2) the problem is exposed; 3) the servant solves the problem; 4) he is rewarded greatly.

As far as the Daniel tales are concerned, however, other subdivisions of the material can be made that are particularly useful. Furthermore, the hero is not just mastering "clever acts and words," but the tales, at some point, take off from type 922. First, the subdivisions: a decisive contribution comes from W. Lee Humphreys, who uses the nomenclature "court tales of conflict" to designate, e.g., Daniel 3 and 6; Esther; Ahikar; and "court tales of contest" to characterize, e.g., Daniel 2; 4; 5; Genesis 40–41.[42] The former is called "conflict" because one faction is shown seeking the ruin of the other, but to no avail. Faction A is punished, and faction B is rewarded. In the court "contest" the hero succeeds where all others have failed.

Collins, to the contrary, sees three categories of tale in Daniel A:

1. "The tale may emphasize the wisdom and ability of the court-ier."[43] One example is Daniel 2. One recognizes here Humphreys' "contest." Daniel outshines foreign sages (as do Joseph and Esther) in a realm that was the Chaldeans' glory: the interpretation of dreams (see Isa. 44:25; 47:13; Dan. 2:27).[44] In fact, for Collins, Daniel 2 is probably originally "a Babylonian prophecy which recalls the reign of Nebu-chadnezzar as a golden age and looks for the establishment of a lasting Babylonian kingdom."[45] The tale of Daniel 2 has built on that outline a totally different picture, leading to the king's confession: "Your god is indeed God of gods and Master of kings, a revealer of mysteries, since you could reveal this mystery" (2:47).

2. "The tale may focus on the drama of danger and humiliation fol-lowed by salvation." Examples are in Daniel 3; 6. It is Humphreys' "conflict" tale. Here the story follows a pattern already set up by the novella of Joseph, the tale of Ahikar, and the book of Esther. W. Sibley Towner summarizes the plot thus: "The heroes move from a state of prosperity to one of danger, usually because of a conspiracy; then, in the moment of direst straits, the heroes are released, their greatness is rec-ognized, and they are given even higher standing than before."[46]

3. "The tale may be used as a vehicle for the message of the court-ier." Examples are in Daniel 4 and 5. The foreign king has dreams he cannot understand. His courtiers fail to give the explanation, but Daniel succeeds and is exalted.

Clearly, the tales in Daniel A propose to present Daniel as the ideal wise courtier at a foreign court. He is a new Joseph. But Collins is cer-tainly right to emphasize, more than did Humphreys, fidelity to YHWH as the key to wisdom and success. Rather, Humphreys had thought of the tales' motif being the possibility of a Jewish *modus vivendi* among Gentiles. It is precisely Daniel's insistence on God as the source of all wisdom that constitutes an original nuance distancing Daniel A from type 922. Niditch and Doran saw this well, and elements foreign to type 922 are taken in Daniel 2 as examples: the prayer of supplication, the divine answer to the prayer, and the presence of the divine helper. More than a panegyric, Daniel A is a commentary on Isaiah 44:25-26: God is the one who makes diviners mad, turns wise men backward and makes their knowledge foolish.

It is thus not surprising to find the courtier in an attitude of relative passivity. He is confident of a divine miraculous intervention. It is not the same passivity as the king's, for the latter is a stock figure, led by event, counselors, and dreams, more than a real leader of his people. Daniel, like Joseph, effaces himself in success, glorifying the only one who deserves gratitude, the God of Israel. True, at one point "King Nebuchadnezzar fell on his face and worshipped Daniel. He commanded that an oblation and perfumes be offered to him" (Dan. 2:46). But this is another way for the author to scoff at the foolishness of a king before whom, ironically, the world trembled. From his perspective, the colossus has clay feet. Confronted by a true greatness embodied in Daniel, it crumbles. Nebuchadnezzar appears almost benign, and the much-feared Chaldeans are "paper tigers." They are put in a reasonably favorable light because there is nothing to fear from them when one is a man of God.

All the more so since, from the wisdom point of view, the truth heralded by Daniel is convincing by nature and truly irresistible. Even the revelation of a bleak future and his personal death brings about the king's confession of the Living God and praises for the messenger of ominous tidings. This recurrent theme in Daniel A is really striking. Many scholars have put too much emphasis on the absence of hostility between the foreigners and the Jews *qua* Jews in Daniel A, in stark contrast with Daniel B. But the optimism expressed there is not about human potential, especially among heathens.[47] It is about transcendent truth and its irrevocability. No Babylonian, Median, Persian, or Greek potentate can resist truth. And it does not need to be pushed down the throats of people by coercion. In that respect the Maccabean successes are only "a little help" (Dan. 11:34). The sage is calm; when threatened with death, he quietly continues his devotions three times a day in his room (6:10).

This is how the author of Daniel responded to the Stoic definition of the wise man as in full possession of virtue in all his dealings with the world and with society. Daniel's patience in a hostile environment, his prudence, and his modesty are not Stoic virtues, but rather confidence in his God. Furthermore, all his wisdom is not aimed at Stoic individual happiness but at Hasidic fidelity. All the same, there is in Daniel a certain imperturbability that is not without kinship with Stoicism.[48] He sometimes behaves "as if not," according to the famous dictum that Paul later was to adopt (1 Cor. 7:29-31). One need only recall Daniel's unswerving piety while the whole Babylonian empire worships Nebuchadnezzar's statue. Daniel's wisdom, however, is no longer based on observation of nature, but exclusively on divine revelation. Such wisdom cannot be taught as a philosophical doctrine, but is reception (*qabbala*) of secrets that can be shared only with infinite prudence and wrapped in a symbolic language for the masses.

We would be gravely mistaken if we concluded from this that the author of Daniel and his religious group opted out of the political situation. The heavenly secrets, emphasizing as they do transcendent values and the sacrality of life, have a direct and decisive impact on daily reality. The transcendent Kingdom to come from on high is to crush to pieces the existing empires. "It will pulverize and wipe out all the other kingdoms and it will be set up for ever" (Dan. 2:44). In other words, the relative irenism of Daniel A should not mislead us. True, the holy man here does not spit fire (cf. Rev. 11:5), but all the same his message is revolutionary. "Daniel works within the traditions of holy war," says Collins.[49] The atmosphere in Daniel 1–6 is deceptive on more than one occasion. Kings are brought to their knees and must confess that Daniel's God is the only God. But this conclusion is only the miraculous outcome of a tense conflict in which the saint is about to lose his life. The tales play on the theme—well known in comedy—of sudden relief after tension has almost reached its breaking point. Daniel and his companions are led to (interrupted) martyrdom.[50] In the reflective part of the book (Daniel B), the *maśkil* is not only to make many understand (11:33), but also to suffer persecution in order to purify others (11:35; see also T. Moses). His vocation is thus a double one, of teaching and of suffering. As in the somewhat later Wisdom of Solomon (between 50 B.C.E. and 10 C.E.), the righteous "is able to withstand persecution because he understands the eschatological mysteries."[51]

This is why, at certain points, the tales in Daniel A border on the genre of the martyr legend, without, however, displaying many of the flaws that blemish that kind of writing.[52] Characteristic of the legend is that it starts with a date (see Dan. 2:1), and its ending must be moral. But the book of Daniel goes much deeper than just teaching a moral lesson with the figure of its hero. The suffering of the *maśkil* is here definitely propitiatory. The legend explodes, so to speak, and martyrdom is no display of religious heroism. The backdrop is the deeply moving song of the Suffering Servant in Isaiah 53. In my Commentary on Daniel 11 I have adopted H. L. Ginsberg's thesis that Daniel 10–12 is an interpretation of that Isaianic tradition. The time has come to expand that conclusion to encompass the whole tradition about Daniel's figure. As a matter of fact, the Servant furnished a model for the conception of the righteous man that became so important in the second century B.C.E. and throughout the intertestamental period.[53] Prepared by Isaiah 53 and Psalm 22, the notion of a substitutive suffering developed after Antiochus' persecutions of the faithful (Hasidim). As I have insisted above in chapter 6, the martyrs' death could not be in vain and still less in retribution for sin. Hence, besides the book of Daniel, texts of that period state that the martyrs' blood was expiatory, the supreme act of piety of the faithful, whose "merit" is so overflowing that it saves not only the victims but also the *rabbim*. The fidelity of the latter is the echo of the martyrs' faith, although not commensurate with it. Suffice it here to refer to 2 Maccabees 7:38; 4 Maccabees 1:11 (see also 17:21-22.); Assumption of Moses 9 (Taxo), for example.[54]

Daniel personally is a type and figure of Hasidic perfection. It is fitting, therefore, that he exemplify the glorious resurrection that awaits the righteous. To him it is said in the last sentence of the book: "You, go until the end. You will have rest and you will arise to receive your lot in the end of the days."

NOTES

1. J. J. Collins, "The Court-Tales in Daniel and the Development of Apocalyptic."

2. See ch. 2 above on the Hasidim/*maskilim*.

3. See H. L. Ginsberg, *Studies in Daniel*; H. H. Rowley, "The Unity of the Book of Daniel"; Ginsberg, "In Re My Studies in Daniel"; Rowley, "A Rejoinder"; Ginsberg, "The Composition of the Book of Daniel."

4. W. L. Humphreys, emphasizes the infelicity of the Additions; "The reader must stretch his credulity to the breaking point in being asked to accept that the Daniel who is both completely loyal to his Jewish heritage and God and is able to function as a skilled and loyal courtier . . . is also the Daniel whose visions in the latter part of the book reveal those same monarchs and nations as oppressive and completely condemned in the divine plan" ("A Life-Style for Diaspora: A Study of the Tales of Esther and Daniel," 223).

5. See ch. 1 above.

6. A. Rofé, "Classes in the Prophetical Stories: Didactic Legenda and Parable."

7. Ibid., 146.

8. This passivity is all the more striking when contrasted with the active intervention of the Jewish healer in 4QPrNab.

9. N. Habel, "The Form and Significance of the Call Narratives," 315.

10. Ibid., 298.

11. Ibid., 318.

12. See B. O. Long, "Prophetic Authority as Social Reality," 3-20.

THE FIGURE OF DANIEL

13. See the analysis of such opinions in Walther Zimmerli, *Ezekiel*. Zimmerli mentions in particular B. Baentsch, E. C. Broome, and K. Jaspers (p. 16-17). On Ezekiel's aphasia, see 3:26; 24:27; 33:22; on neurotic paralysis, 4:4ff.

14. J. Lindblom, *Prophecy in Ancient Israel*, 4. This obsession with one single idea or feeling Lindblom calls also "monoideism" (p. 5).

15. See my development in ch. 5 above.

16. Mircea Eliade writes, "Shamans are of the elect," and as such they have access to a region of the sacred inaccessible to other members of the community." They "serve as mediators between [peoples] and their gods. . . . This small elite not only directs the community's religious life but, as it were, guards its 'soul'" (*Shamanism: Archaic Techniques of Ecstasy*, 7-8, 136).

17. The only exception is the queen mother in 5:10.

18. See Ps. 35:13; Joel 2:12; 1 Bar. 1:5; Tob. 12:8; Jud. 8:5-6; Luke 2:37; Mark 2:18; T. Reub. 1:10; T. Judah 15:4; T. Simeon 3:4; Pss. Sol. 3:9. "Asceticism" is to be taken here in a broad sense. In ch. 1 Daniel, as says Josephus, "had resolved to live austerely (*sklérogogein*)." As a result, he "readily mastered all the learning which was found among the Hebrews and the Chaldeans" (*Ant.* 10.10. 2; cf. Dan. 1:8, 17). In ch. 9 he fasts and mortifies himself. In 10:2-3 he mourns and eats "no pleasant bread . . . flesh or wine" and he does not anoint himself. In short, "he humiliates himself" (v. 12).

19. See LaCocque, "The Liturgical Prayer in Daniel 9." See 4 Ezra 5:20; 6:35; 9:23-27; 12:49-51; 2 Bar. 9:2; 12:5; 21:1; 47:2; Apoc. Abr. 9.

20. See my development on Daniel and Qumran in ch. 2 above. On the angel as "extension of the personality of God," see A. R. Johnson, *The One and the Many in the Israelite Conception of God*, 32ff.

21. See esp. Deut. 6–7, quoting extensively Exod. 23:20-33.

22. Rofé, "Classes in the Prophetical Stories," 162.

23. Y. Kaufmann: *Toldot* 3:15ff.; 547ff.

24. See Dan. 7 and my Commentary; also ch. 5 above.

25. See ch. 4 above.

26. All three happen to be non-Jews. Daniel, for one, was annexed by Israel's tradition as a Jewish sage. For John Day ("The Daniel of Ugarit and Ezekiel and the Hero of the Book of Daniel") the evolution may have been the following: a) The Ugaritic Daniel is called "man of Rp'u"; b) Rp'u is none other than El; c) El is currently identified with YHWH by Israel; d) Daniel, being "man of YHWH," is thereby Israelitized.

27. There is an expansion of this aspect in an older witness of the Daniel cycle, namely in 4QPrNab, where the Jewish "shaman" is a seer, a sage, and a healer. At the other chronological extreme, the pseudo-Epiphanes' *Vitae Prophetarum* (4:3-9) draws a parallel between King Nebuchadnezzar's "diet" in Dan. 4:32-33 [29-30] and Daniel's regimen in ch. 1. For *Vit.Proph.*, as for the ancient rabbis in general, the Babylonian king was advised by Daniel to "eat grass as oxen." But, while for the former this act is to the credit of Daniel, who then appears as a powerful adviser, knowing and forecasting, for the latter it was a sinful move to save Nebuchadnezzar, and Daniel was punished by being thrown into the lions' den (*B. Bat.* 4a).

28. K. Koch, "Is Daniel Also Among the Prophets?" *Interpretation* 39 (April 1985).

29. Collins, *The Apocalyptic Vision*, 55.

30. H. P. Müller, "Mantische Weisheit und Apokalyptik" and "Magisch-mantische Weisheit und die Gestalt Daniels."

31. P. A. Porter, *Metaphors and Monsters: A Literary-Critical Study of Daniel 7 and 8.*

32. J. C. VanderKam, *Enoch and the Growth of an Apocalyptic Tradition*, 8.

33. P. Grelot; "La légende d'Hénoch dans les apocryphes et dans la Bible: origine et signification." He refers to Berossus' *Babylomiaca* 6-13.

34. See Gen. 5:22, 24a (Source P). Enoch "walks with the Elohim," i.e., with the angels, while "Elohim" in v. 24b designates God.

35. VanderKam, *Enoch*, 119.

36. See 1 Enoch 14:2-3; 17–36; 72–82. Perhaps it is permissible, within that perspective, to see in the fallen angel Danel/Danjal of 1 Enoch 6:7; 69:2 a counterpart to the wise Daniel of whom Ezekiel speaks and who was already known in Ugaritic literature (Aqht). There is, also a good angel Daniel mentioned on an Aramaic incantation bowl: see C. D. Isbell, *Corpus of the Aramaic Incantation Bowls*, 102-3, no. 43, l. 4-5. This parallel was first drawn by Day "The Daniel of Ugarit," 183.

37. The pattern ABA, as I have indicated above, is favored by apocalyptists. It has been theorized that the Greek versions of Daniel add legends at the end (Susanna, Bel), so that such a pattern on a literary plane could be observed in the book.

38. Collins, *The Apocalyptic Vision*, 213.

39. Ibid., 57.

40. See S. Niditch and R. Doran, "The Success Story of the Wise Courtier."

41. A. Aarne and S.Thompson, *The Types of the Folktale.*

42. Humphreys, "A Life-Style for Diaspora," 211-23.

43. Collins, "The Court-Tales in Daniel," 218-34.

44. Dan. 2:44 originally referred to Babylon.

45. P. 222. See Diodorus Siculus 2.29: The Chaldeans' expertise was in astrology, "predictions about future events," and interpretation of dreams.

46. W. S. Towner, *Daniel*, 48

47. In the words of J. L. Crenshaw, wisdom narrative "is sparing in reference to divine activity, recognizes an opposition between human intentions and divine economy, and appreciates the nature of humanity" (IDB Sup 956).

48. For Josephus, quite expectedly, "the disciplined pursuit of purification has brought Daniel to the supreme achievement of the Graeco-Roman sage—the movement from human to divine wisdom," says D. Satran ("Daniel, Seer, Philosopher, Holy Man," 38). Satran calls attention to the Josephus addition of dried figs to Daniel's diet, an essential staple in a Pythagorean diet.

49. Collins, *The Apocalyptic Vision*, 207.

50. See A. Bentzen, "Daniel 6: Ein Versuch zur Vorgeschichte der Märtyrerlegende."

51. Collins, *The Apocalyptic Vision*, 211.

52. See H. Gunkel, "Sagen und Legenden." (The story has something of the fabricated about it, and there is an absence of freshness. The characters are stereotyped; the miracles tend to become grotesque, and so forth.)

53. See G. W. E. Nickelsburg and M. E. Stone, *Faith and Piety in Early Judaism.*

54. Interestingly enough, in the perspective of the parallelism between the patriarch Joseph and Daniel, for T. Benj. 3:8a, Joseph is the Suffering Servant of whom Second Isaiah wrote.

Bibliography

Aarne, A., and S. Thompson, *The Types of the Folktale*. Folklore Fellows Communications 184. Helsinki, 1964.

Ackroyd, Peter R. "Israel Under Babylon and Persia." New Clarendon Bible, Old Testament, 4: 340ff. Oxford, 1970.

Albright, W. F. "The Seal of Eliakim and the Latest Preexilic History of Judah, with Some Observations on Ezekiel," *JBL*, 51 (1932): 77–106.

_____."New Light on Early Canaanite Language and Literature," *BASOR* 46 (1932): 15–20.

_____."New Canaanite Historical and Mythological Data," *BASOR* 63 (1936): 23–32.

Altheim, Franz. *Alexander und Asien: Geschichte eines geistigen Erbes*. Tübingen, 1953.

Amado Lévy-Valensi, E. *Le temps dans la vie morale*. Paris, 1968.

Amsler, S., A. Lacocque, and R. Vuilleumier. *Aggée, Zacharie, Malachie*. CAT 11c, Neuchâtel and Paris, 1981.

Anderson, Bernhard W. *Understanding the Old Testament*. Englewood Cliffs, NJ, 1957.

Askenazi, Léon, *Anges, démons, et êtres intermédiaires*. Colloquy of the Alliance mondiale des religions, 13–14 January 1968. Paris, 1969.

Baillet, M., J.T. Milik, and R. de Vaux. *Discoveries in the Judaean Desert*, vol. 3: *Les petites grottes de Qumran*. Oxford, 1962.

Baldwin, J. G. "Ṣemaḥ as a Technical Term in the Prophets." *VT* 14 (1964): 93–97.

Baltzer, K. *Das Bundesformular*. Neukirchen-Vluyn, 1964.

Balz, Horst R. *Methodische Probleme der neutestamentlichen Christologie*. WMANT 24. Neukirchen-Vluyn, 1967.

Baron, S. W. *A Social and Religious History of the Jews*. 2d ed. New York, 1952.

Barr, James. *The Semantics of Biblical Language*. London, 1961.

Barthélemy, D., and J. T. Milik. *Discoveries in the Judaean Desert*, vol. 1: *Qumran Cave I*. Oxford, 1955.

Baumgartner, W. "Das Aramäische im Buche Daniel." *ZAW* 45 (1927): 81–133.

_____. "Ein Vierteljahrhundert Daniel forschung." *TRu*, n.f. 2, (1939): 136ff.

Bentwich, Norman, *Hellenism*. Philadelphia, 1919.

Bentzen, Aage. "Daniel 6: Ein Versuch zur Vorgeschichte der Märtyrerlegende." In *Festschrift for A. Bertholet*. Tübingen, 1950: 58–64.

_____. *Daniel*. HAT Erste Reihe 19. Tübingen, 1952.

_____. *Messias, Moses redivivus, und Menschensohn*. Zurich, 1948. ET *King and Messiah*, ed. G. W. Anderson. Oxford, 1970.

Betz, Otto. *What Do We Know About Jesus?* London, 1968.

Bevan, Edwyn R., and Charles Singer. "Hellenistic Judaism." In *The Legacy of Israel*, ed. Bevan and Singer. Oxford, 1927.

Bickerman, Elias. "Notes on Hellenistic and Parthian Chronology." *Berytus* 8, fasc. 2 (1944): 73–83.

_____. *The Maccabees*, trans. by M. Hadas. New York, 1947.

_____. *Der Gott der Makkabäer*. Berlin, 1937. ET *The God of the Maccabees*, trans. by H. R. Moehring. Studies in Judaism in Late Antiquity 32. Leiden 1979.

_____. *Four Strange Books of the Bible*. New York, 1967.

Blenkinsopp, Joseph. *Prophecy and Canon*. Notre Dame, 1977.

DANIEL IN HIS TIME

Bogaert, Pierre. *Apocalypse de Baruch*, 2 vols. Sources chrétiennes 144, 145. Paris, 1969.
Bonsirven, Joseph. *Textes rabbiniques des deux premiers siècles chrétiens*. Rome, 1955.
Bouché-Leclercq, Auguste. *Histoire des Séleucides*. Paris, 1913.
Bousset, William. *Die Religion des Judentums*. 2d ed. Berlin, 1906.
Box, G. H. "IV Esdras." In *Apocrypha and Pseudepigrapha of the Old Testament*. Oxford, 1913.
———. *Judaism in the Greek Period*. Oxford, 1932.
Bright, John. *A History of Israel*. London, 1960.
Buber, Martin. *I and Thou*, trans. by R. G. Smith. 2d ed. New York, 1958.

Caquot, A. "Les songes et leur interprétation." *Sources Orientales* 2. Paris, 1959.
Cavallin, H. C. C. *Life After Death: Paul's Argument for the Resurrection of the Dead in I Cor. XV.* Part I: *An Inquiry into the Jewish Background*. Coniactanea biblica, New Testament, Series 7.1. Lund, 1974.
Cerfaux, L., and J. Tondriau. *Le culte des souverains dans la civilisation gréco-romaine*. Tournai, 1957.
Charles, R. H., ed. *The Apocrypha and Pseudepigrapha of the Old Testament*. Oxford, 1913.
———. *A Critical and Exegetical Commentary on the Book of Daniel*. Oxford, 1929.
Charlesworth, J., ed. *The Pseudepigrapha of the Old Testament*. Garden City, NY, 1983.
Childs, B. *Introduction to the Old Testament as Scripture*. Philadelphia, 1979.
Clements, R. *Abraham and David: Genesis 15 and Its Meaning for Israelite Tradition*. Studies in Biblical Theology, 2nd series 2. Naperville, IL, 1967.
Cloché, Paul. *Alexandre le Grand*. Neuchâtel, 1953.
Collins, John J. "Apocalyptic Eschatology as the Transcendence of Death" *CBQ* 36 (1974): 21–43.
———. "The Symbolism of Transcendence in Jewish Apocalyptic." *BR* 19 (1974): 5–22.
———. "The Mythology of Holy War in Daniel and the Qumran War Scroll: A Point of Transition in Jewish Apocalyptic." *VT* 25 (1975): 596–612.
———. "The Court-Tales in Daniel and the Development of Apocalyptic." *JBL* 94 (1975): 218.
———. "Pseudonymity, Historical Reviews and the Genre of the Revelation of John." *CBQ* 39 (1977): 329–43.
———. *The Apocalyptic Vision of the Book of Daniel*. Cambridge, 1977.
———. "Apocalypse: Toward the Morphology of a Genre." *Semeia* 14 (1979): 1–20.
———. "The Jewish Apocalypses." *Semeia* 14 (1979): 26, 38.
———. *The Apocalyptic Imagination*. New York, 1984.
———. "Daniel and His Social World." *Interpretation* 39 (April 1985).
Colpe, C. "Son of Man." *TWNT* 8.
Cornford, F. M. *The Origin of Attic Comedy*. New York, 1961.
Crenshaw, J. L. "Wisdom in the Old Testament," *IDB Sup*.
Cross, F. M., Jr. *The Ancient Library of Qumran*. Garden City, NY, 1958.

Dahood, M. *Psalms*, 3 vols. AB 16, 17, 17a. New York, 1965–1970.
Davies, W. D. *The Setting of the Sermon on the Mount*. 2d ed. Cambridge, 1977.
———. *Torah in the Messianic Age and/or the Age to Come*. JBL Monograph Series 7. Philadelphia, 1952.
Day, John. "The Daniel of Ugarit and Ezekiel and the Hero of the Book of Daniel." *VT* 30 (1980): 174–84.

BIBLIOGRAPHY

Delcor, M. "Le milieu d'origine et le développement de l'apocalyptique juive." In *La littérature juive entre Tenach et Mischna*, ed. W. C. Van Unnik. Leiden, 1974.
Dennefeld, L. *La Sainte Bible*, vol. 7, ed. L. Pirot and A. Clamer. Paris. 1947.
Dheilly, J. "Daniel." In *Dictionnaire biblique*. Tournai, 1964.
Dodds, E. R. *The Greeks and the Irrational*. Berkeley, CA, 1951.
Doeve, J. W. "Le domaine du Temple de Jérusalem." In *La littérature juive entre Tenach et Mischna*, ed. W. C. Van Unnik, Leiden, 1974.
Dreyfus, T. "Comprendre le Maharal de Prague." *Les Nouveaux Cahiers* 6. Paris, 1966.
Driver, G. R. "The Aramaic of the Book of Daniel." *JBL* 45 (1926): 110–19.
Driver, S. R. *An Introduction to the Literature of the Old Testament*. Rev. ed. New York, 1914.
Dupont-Sommer, A. *Les écrits esséniens découverts près de la Mer Morte*. 2d ed. Paris, 1964.
Durant, Will. *The Story of Civilization*, vol. 2. New York, 1935.

Eddy, S. K. *The King Is Dead*. Lincoln, NB, 1961.
Eissfeldt, Otto. *Einleitung in das Alte Testament*. 3d ed. 1964. ET *The Old Testament: An Introduction*, trans. by P. R. Ackroyd. Oxford, 1965.
Eliade, M. *Le sacré et le profane*. Paris, 1965; 2d ed. 1976. ET *The Sacred and the Profane*, trans. by W. R. Trask. New York, 1961.
———. *Aspects du mythe*. Paris, 1963. ET *Myth and Reality*, trans. by W. R. Trask. New York, 1963.
———. *Traité d'histoire des Religions*. Paris, 1959. ET *Patterns in Comparative Religions*, trans. by R. Sheed. Cleveland, 1966.
———. *Shamanism: Archaic Techniques of Ecstasy*. Bollingen Series 76. Princeton, 1972.
———. *Histoire des croyances et des idées religieuses*. Paris, 1978. ET *A History of Religious Ideas*, trans. by W. R. Trask. Chicago, 1978.

Fackenheim, Emil. *God's Presence in History*. New York, 1970.
Finkel, A. "The Pesher of Dreams and Scriptures." *RevQ* 15 (1963): 357–70.
Finkelstein, L. *The Pharisees and the Men of the Great Assembly* (in Hebrew). Tel Aviv, 1950.
Fitzmyer, J. A. *The Genesis Apocryphon: A Commentary*. Bib. Or 18A. 2d ed. Rome, 1971.
———. *A Wandering Aramean: Collected Aramaic Essays*. Missoula, MT, 1979.
de Fraine, J. *VD* 25 (1947).
———. *Adam et son lignage: Etudes sur la notion de "personnalité corporative" dans la Bible*. Tournai, 1959.
Frankfort, Henri. *Before Philosophy*. Baltimore, 1963.
Freedman, D. N. "The Prayer of Nabonide." *BASOR* 145 (1957): 31–32.
Freud, S. *The Interpretation of Dreams*, trans. by A. A. Brill. New York, 1913.
Frey, J. B. "Apocalyptique." *DBSup* 1. Paris, 1928.
Frost, S. B. *Old Testament Apocalyptic: Its Origin and Growth*. London, 1952.
Frye, Northrop. *The Anatomy of Criticism: Four Essays*. Princeton, 1957.
———. *The Great Code: The Bible and Literature*. New York and London, 1982.

Gadd, C. J. *Anatolian Studies* 8 (1958): 35–92.
Gammie, J. "Spatial and Ethical Dualism in Jewish Wisdom and Apocalyptic Literature." *JBL* 93 (1974): 356ff.
———. "The Classification, Stages of Growth, and Changing Intentions in the Book of Daniel." *JBL* 95, (1976): 191–204.

DANIEL IN HIS TIME

Gehman, H. S. "Dream" and "Visions." In *New Westminster Dictionary of the Bible*.

Geiger, A. *Urschrift und Übersetzungen der Bibel in ihrer Abhängigkeit von der innern Entwicklung des Judentums*. Frankfurt, 1928.

Ginsberg, H. L. *Studies in Daniel*. New York, 1948.

_____. "In Re My Studies in Daniel." *JBL* 68 (1949): 402–7.

_____. "The Oldest Interpretation of the Suffering Servant." *VT* 3 (1953): 400–404.

_____. "The Composition of the Book of Daniel." *VT* 4 (1954): 246–75.

Ginsburg, C. D. *Introduction to the Massoretico-Critical Edition of the Hebrew Bible*. New York, 1966.

Goldstein, J. A. *I Maccabees*. AB 41. Garden City, NY, 1976.

_____. *II Maccabees*. AB 41A. Garden City, NY, 1983.

Gottlieb, H. "Myth in the Psalms: The Enthronement of Yhwh." In *Myths in the Old Testament*, ed. B. Otzen et al. London, 1980.

Grelot, P. "La légende d'Hénoch dans les apocryphes et dans la Bible: origine et signification." *RSR* (1958): 5–26, 181–210.

Gressmann, H. *Die hellenistische Gestirnreligion*. Beiheft zu der Alten Orient 5, 1925.

_____. *Der Ursprung der israelitisch-jüdischen Eschatologie*. Göttingen, 1905.

Guillaume, A. *Prophecy and Divination Among the Hebrews and Other Semites*. New York and London, 1938.

Gunkel, Hermann. *Schöpfung und Chaos*. Göttingen, 1895.

_____. "Sagen und Legenden." *RGG* 5 (1913): 194ff.

_____. *Einleitung in die Psalmen*. Supplement to HKAT. Göttingen, 1928.

Habel, N. "The Form and Significance of the Call Narratives." *ZAW* 77 (1965): 297–323.

Haller, M. *Das Judentum Geschichtsschreibung, Prophetie und Gesetzgebung nach dem Exil*. 2d ed., Göttingen, 1925.

Hanson, Paul. "Prolegomena to the Study of Jewish Apocalypse." In *Magnalia Dei: The Mighty Acts of God*, ed. F. M. Cross et al., New York, 1976.

_____. *The Dawn of Apocalyptic: The Historical and Sociological Roots of Jewish Apocalyptic Eschatology*. 2d ed. Philadelphia, 1980.

Hartman, L. *Prophecy Interpreted: The Formation of Some Jewish Apocalyptic Texts and of the Eschatological Discourse in Mark*. Lund, 1966.

Heaton, E. W. *The Old Testament Prophets*. Atlanta, 1977.

Hengel, Martin. *Judentum und Hellenismus, Studien zu ihrer Begegnung unter besonderer Berücksichtigung Palästinas bis zur Mitte des 2. Jhr. v. Chr*. Tübingen, 1973. ET *Judaism and Hellenism*, trans. by J. Bowden. London and Philadelphia, 1974.

Heschel, A. *The Prophets*. New York, 1962.

Hilgenfeld, A. *Die jüdische Apocalyptik in ihrer geschichtlichen Entwicklung*. Jena, 1857.

Holm-Nielsen, S. *Hodayot: Psalms from Qumran*. Aarhus, 1960.

Hölscher, G. "Die Entstehung des Buches Daniel." *TSK* 92 (1919): 113ff.

Hooke, S. H. *Middle Eastern Mythology*. Baltimore, 1963.

Humphreys, W. L. "A Life-Style for Diaspora: A Study of the Tales of Esther and Daniel." *JBL*. 92 (1973): 211–23.

van Imschoot, P. *Théologie de l'Ancien Testament*. Tournai, 1954.

Isbell, C. D. *Corpus of the Aramaic Incantation Bowls*. Missoula, MT, 1975.

BIBLIOGRAPHY

Jacob, Edmond. *Les thèmes essentiels d'une théologie de l'Ancien Testament.* Neuchâtel, 1955. ET *Theology of the Old Testament,* trans. by A. W. Heathcote and P. J. Allcock. New York, 1958.

Jahn, G. *Das Buch Daniel nach LXX.* Leipzig, 1904.

Jaubert, Annie. *La notion d'Alliance dans le Judaïsme.* Paris, 1963.

Jeppesen, Knud. "Myth in the Prophetic Literature." In *Myths in the Old Testament.* ed. B. Otzen et al. London, 1980.

Jepsen, Alfred "Bemerkungen zum Daniel-Buch." *VT.* 11 (1961): 386–91.

Johnson, A. R. *The One and the Many in the Israelite Conception of God.* Cardiff, 1942.

Jouguet, Pierre. *L'impérialisme macédonien et l'hellénisation de l'Orient.* Paris, 1961.

Jung, Carl. *Memories, Dreams, Reflections.* New York, 1961.

Junker, H. *Untersuchungen über Literarische und Exegetische Probleme des Buches Daniel.* Bonn, 1932.

Kaufmann, Y. *Toldot haEmunah HaYisraelit* (History of Israel's Faith). Tel Aviv, 1937–47. ET *The Religion of Israel, from its Beginnings to the Babylonian Exile,* trans. and abridged by M. Greenberg. Chicago, 1960.

Kermode, Frank. *The Sense of an Ending: Studies in the Theory of Fiction.* London, 1966.

Kissane, Edward J. *The Book of Isaiah,* 2 vols. Dublin, 1941 and 1943.

Klausner, Joseph. *History of the Second Temple Period* (in Hebrew). Tel Aviv, 1949.

Koch, Klaus "Is Daniel Also Among the Prophets?" *Interpretation* 39 (April 1985).

Kraeling, Carl. "Myth in the Psalms: The Enthronement of Yhwh." In *Myths in the Old Testament,* ed. B. Otzen et al. London, 1980.

————. *John the Baptist.* New York, 1951.

Kraeling, Emil. *Commentary on the Prophets.* Camden, NJ, 1966.

Kuhl, Curt *Altorientalische Texte zum Alten Testament,* 2d ed. ed. H. Gressmann. Berlin, 1965.

Kuhn, H. K. *Enderwartung und gegenwärtiges Heil, Untersuchungen zu den Gemeindeliedern von Qumran.* Göttingen, 1966.

Kuhn, Karl G. "Die Sektenschrift und die Iranische Religion." *ZTK* 49 (1953).

————. *Konkordanz zu den Qumrantexten.* Göttingen, 1960.

LaCocque, André. "The Liturgical Prayer in Daniel 9." *HUCA* 47 (1976): 119–42.

————. *Le livre de Daniel.* CAT 15b. Geneva, 1976. ET *The Book of Daniel,* trans. by D. Pellauer. London and Atlanta, 1979.

————. *But as for Me.* Atlanta, 1979.

————. "Job and the Problem of Evil," *BR* 24–25, (1979–80), 7–19.

————. Article on 4 Esdras. *SBL 1981 Seminar Papers.* Chicago, 1981.

————. "Job or the Impotence of Religion and Philosophy." *Semeia* 19 (1981) 33–52.

————. *Daniel et son temps* Geneva, 1983.

Lagrange, M.-J. *Le Judaïsme avant Jésus-Christ.* Paris, 1931.

Lambert, W. G. *The Background of Jewish Apocalyptic.* London, 1978.

Laperrousaz, E. M. "Le Testament de Moïse." *Semitica* 19 (1970).

Lindblom, J. *Die Jesaja-Apokalypse in der neuen Jesajahandschrift.* Lund, 1938.

————. *Prophecy in Ancient Israel.* Philadelphia, 1962.

Lods, A. *Histoire de la littérature hébraïque et juive.* Paris, 1950.

Loewenstamm, S. E. "Mal'ach." *Biblical Encyclopedia* 4, cols. 975–990 (in Hebrew).

DANIEL IN HIS TIME

Long, B. O. "Prophetic Authority as Social Reality." In *Canon and Authority*, ed. G. W. Coats and B. O. Long. Philadelphia, 1977.
Lord, A. *The Singer of Tales*. New York, 1968.

Maimonides. *The Guide for the Perplexed*, trans. by M. Friedlander. 2d ed. New York, 1956.
Marrou, H.I. *Histoire de l'éducation dans l'antiquité*. Paris, 1948.
Martin, F. *Le livre d'Hénoch traduit sur le texte éthiopien*. Paris, 1906.
Martin-Achard, R. *De la mort à la résurrection*. Neuchâtel and Paris, 1956.
——. "Résurrection dans l'Ancien Testament et le judaïsme." *DBSup* 55 (1981): cols. 437–84.
McGinn, B. *Apocalyptic Spirituality*. New York, 1979.
——. *Visions of the End: Apocalyptic Traditions in the Middle Ages*. New York, 1979.
McKenzie, John. *The Second Isaiah*. AB 20. Garden City, NY, 1968.
McNamara, Martin. "Daniel." In *Old Testament, A New Catholic Commentary on Holy Scripture*, ed. L. Johnston. London, 1953, 1969.
Meissner, H. *Babylonien und Assyrien*. 2 vols. Heidelberg, 1920.
de Menasce, J. "Daniel." In *Bible de Jérusalem*. Paris, 1954.
Messel, Nils. *Die Einheitlichkeit der jüdischen Eschatologie*. Giessen, 1915.
——. *Der Menschensohn in den Bilderreden des Henoch*. Giessen, 1922.
Meyer, Eduard. *Ursprung und Anfäng des Christentums*. Stuttgart, 1921; Berlin, 1923.
Milik, J. T. "Prayer of Nabonidus and Other Writings of a Daniel Cycle." *RB* 63 (1956): 407ff.
Moltmann, Jürgen. *Theologie der Hoffnung*. Munich, 1964. ET *Theology of Hope*, trans. by J. W. Leitch. London, 1967.
Montgomery, J. A. *A Critical and Exegetical Commentary on the Book of Daniel*. New York, 1927.
Moore, G. F. *Judaism in the First Centuries of the Christian Era*. Cambridge, 1958.
Morgenstern, Julian. "The King-God Among the Western Semites and the Meaning of Epiphanes." *VT* 10 (1960): 138–97.
Mowinckel, Sigmund. *He That Cometh*, trans. by G. W. Anderson. 2d ed. New York, 1959.
——."Psalms and Wisdom." In "Wisdom in Israel and the Ancient Near East," ed M. Noth and D. W. Thomas. *VTSup* 3 (1960).
Müller, H.-P. "Magisch-mantische Weisheit und die Gestalt Daniels." *UF* 1 (1969): 79–94.
——. "Märchen, Legende und Enderwartung." *VT* 26 (1976): 338–50.
——. "Der Begriff 'Rätsel' im Alten Testament." *VT* 20 (1970): 475ff.
——. "Mantische Weisheit und Apokalyptik," *VTSup* 22 (1972), 268–93.
Müller, U. B. *Messias und Menschensohn in jüdischen Apokalypsen und in der Offenbarung des Johannes*. Gütersloh, 1972.

Neher, A. *Jérémie*. Paris, 1960.
——. *Le puits de l'exil*. Paris, 1966.
Nickelsburg, G. W. E. *Resurrection, Immortality, and Eternal Life in Intertestamental Judaism*. Harvard Theological Series 21. Cambridge, MA, and London, 1972.
——. "The Apocalyptic Message in 1 Enoch 92–105." *CBQ* 39 (1977): 309–28.
Nickelsburg, G. W. E., and M. E. Stone. *Faith and Piety in Early Judaism*. Philadelphia, 1983.

BIBLIOGRAPHY

Nicolas, M. *Les doctrines religieuses des Juifs pendant les deux siècles antérieurs à l'ère chrétienne.* Paris, 1860.

Niditch, S., and R. Doran. "The Success Story of the Wise Courtier: A Formal Approach." *JBL* 96 (1977): 179–93.

Noth, Martin. "Zur Komposition des Buches Daniel." *TSK* 98–99 (1926): 143–63

———. "Noah, Daniel und Hiob in Ezekiel XIV." *VT* 4 (1951): 251–60.

———. *The Laws in the Pentateuch and Other Essays*, trans. by D. R. Ap-Thomas. Philadelphia, 1967.

Odeberg, H. *The Fourth Gospel.* Uppsala, 1929; Chicago, 1968.

Otto, Rudolf. *The Kingdom of God and the Son of Man*, trans. by F. F. Filson and B. L. Woolf. Grand Rapids, 1943.

Otzen, B., H. Gottlieb, and K. Jeppesen, eds. *Myths in the Old Testament.* London, 1980.

Pedersen, J. *Israel: Its Life and Culture.* 2 vols. London, 1926.

Perrin, Norman. "Wisdom and Apocalyptic in the Message of Jesus." *Proceedings of the Society of Biblical Literature* 2 (1972): 543–72.

Pfeiffer, R. H. *Introduction to the Old Testament.* New York, 1941.

van der Ploeg, J. *Le Targum de Job de la grotte 11 de Qumran (11 Qtg Job), Première Communication.* Amsterdam, 1962.

Plöger, Otto. *Theokratie und Eschatologie.* Göttingen, 1959. ET *Theocracy and Eschatology*, trans. by S. Rudman. Richmond, 1968.

———. *Das Buch Daniel.* Gütersloh, 1965.

Porteous, Norman W. *Daniel.* Philadelphia, 1965.

Porter, P. A. *Metaphors and Monsters: A Literary-Critical Study of Daniel 7 and 8.* Lund, 1983.

Pritchard, J. B., ed. *The Ancient Near Eastern Texts Relating to the Old Testament.* Princeton, 1950.

Procksch, O. *Theologie des Alten Testaments.* Gütersloh, 1950.

Propp, V. *The Morphology of the Folktale.* Austin, 1973.

Rabin, C. *Qumran Studies.* Oxford, 1957; New York, 1975.

von Rad, Gerhard. *Die Theologie des Alten Testaments.* Munich, 1957–1960. 4th ed., Munich, 1965. ET by D. M. G. Stalker. *Old Testament Theology*, 9 vols. New York, 1965.

———. *The Message of the Prophets*, ET by same, 1967.

Rahner, Karl. "The Hermeneutics of Eschatalogical Assertions." *Theological Investigations*, 4. Baltimore, 1966.

Rankin, O. S. "The Festival of Hanukkah." In *The Labyrinth*, ed. S. H. Hooke, London, 1935.

———. *Israel's Wisdom Literature, Its Bearing on Theology and the History of Religion.* Edinburgh, 1936.

Reicke, Bo, and Leonard Rost. *Biblisch-historisches Handwörterbuch.* Göttingen, 1962.

Reitzenstein, R. *Die hellenistischen Mysterien-Religionen.* Stuttgart, 1912. ET *Hellenistic Mystery Religions, Their Basic Ideas and Significance*, trans. by J. E. Steely. Pittsburgh, 1978.

Ricciotti, G. *Histoire d'Israël.* Paris, 1948.

Ricoeur, Paul. *Le conflit des interprétations: Essais d'herméneutique.* Paris, 1969. ET *The Conflict of Interpretations*, ed. and trans. by D. Ihde. Evanston, 1974.

———. *The Symbolism of Evil*, trans. by E. Buchanan. Boston, 1972.

———. *Interpretation Theory: Discourse and the Surplus of Meaning.* Fort Worth, 1976.

Ringgren, H. *The Messiah in the Old Testament.* Chicago, 1956.

Rivkin, Ellis. *The Shaping of Jewish History.* New York, 1971.

Robberechts, Ludovick. *Husserl.* Paris, 1964.

Rofé, Alexander. "Classes in the Prophetical Stories: Didactic Legenda and Parable." *VT Sup* 26 (1974): 143–164.

Rössler, Dietrich. *Gesetz und Geschichte.* Neukirchen, 1960.

Rostovtsev, Mikhail. *Social and Economic History of the Hellenistic World.* Oxford, 1941.

Rowland, Christopher. *The Open Heaven.* New York, 1982.

Rowley, H. H. *The Aramaic of the Old Testament.* London, 1929.

———. "The Bilingual Problem of Daniel." *ZAW* 9 (1932): 256–68.

———. "A Rejoinder." *JBL* 70 (1950): 201–3.

———. "The Unity of the Book of Daniel." *HUCA* 23, 1 (1951): 233–73; reprinted in *The Servant of the Lord and Other Essays.* London, 1952.

———. "The Composition of the Book of Daniel." *VT* 5 (1955): 272–76.

———. *Darius the Mede and the Four World Empires in the Book of Daniel.* Cardiff, 1959.

———. *The Relevance of Apocalyptic.* New York, 1964. 3d ed., London, 1968.

Rudolph, W. *Jesaja 24–27.* BWANT 55. Stuttgart, 1933.

———. *Chronikbücher.* HAT Reihe 1, 21. Tübingen, 1955.

Russell, D. S. *The Method and Message of Jewish Apocalyptic, 200 BC – AD 100.* London and Philadelphia, 1964.

Rutten, Marguerite. *"La Science des Chaldeens," Que sais-je?* Paris, 1960.

Sachs, A. J., and D. J. Wiseman. "A Babylonian King-list of the Hellenistic Period." *Iraq* 16 (1954): 202–12.

Sanders, E. P. *Paul and Palestinian Judaism.* London, 1977.

———, ed. *Jewish and Christian Self-Definition.* Philadelphia, 1981.

Sanders, J. A. *Discoveries in the Judaean Desert of Jordan,* vol. 4: *The Psalms Scroll of Qumran Cave 11 (11 QPsᵃ).* Oxford, 1965.

Satran, D. "Daniel, Seer, Philosopher, Holy Man." In *Ideal Figures in Ancient Judaism.* LXX and Cognate Studies 12. Chico, CA, 1980.

Schaeder, H. H. *Iranische Beiträge* 1. Halle, 1930.

Schechter, S. *Documents of Jewish Sectaries.* Cambridge, 1910.

———. *Fragments of a Zadokite Work.* Documents of Jewish Sectaries, vol. 1. New York, 1970.

Schmidt, N. "The Son of Man in the Book of Daniel." *JBL* 19 (1900): 22–28.

Schmidt, W. *Die Schöpfungsgeschichte der Priesterschrift.* Neukirchen, 1967.

Schmithals, W. *The Apocalyptic Movement: Introduction and Interpretation,* trans. by J. E. Steely. Nashville, 1975.

Scholem, G. *The Messianic Idea in Judaism and Other Essays on Jewish Spirituality.* New York, 1971.

Schürer, Emil. *A History of the Jewish People in the Time of Jesus,* ed. N. Glatzberg. New York, 1961.

———. *The History of the Jewish People in the Age of Jesus Christ (175 B.C.-135 A.D.): A New English Edition,* ed. G. Vermes, F. Millar, and M. Black. 2 vols. Edinburgh, 1973, 1979.

BIBLIOGRAPHY

Schüssler Fiorenza, Elisabeth. "Composition and Structure of the Book of Revelation." *CBQ* 39, (1977): 365–66.

Scott, Robert B. Y. "I Daniel, the Original Apocalypse" *AJSL* 47 (1930–31): 289–96.

Seeligmann, J.-L. "Voraussetzungen der Midraschexegese." *VTSup* 1 (1953): 150–81.

Sellin, E. *Einleitung in das Alte Testament.* 9th ed. Heidelberg, 1959.

Silberman, Lou H. "Unriddle the Riddle: A Study in the Structure and Language of the Habakkuk Pesher." *RevQ* 11 (1961): 323–64.

Smith, Jonathan Z. "Wisdom and Apocalyptic." In *Religious Syncretism in Antiquity.* ed. B. A. Pearson. Missoula, MT, 1975.

Smith, Morton. *Palestinian Parties and Politics That Shaped the Old Testament.* New York, 1971.

Snaith, N. *The Jews from Cyrus to Herod.* New York, 1956.

Soederblom, N. *La vie future d'après le mazdéisme.* Paris, 1901.

Steinmann, Jean. *Daniel.* Paris, 1961.

Stone, M. "Revealed Things in Apocalyptical Literature." In *Magnalia Dei: The Mighty Acts of God,* ed. F. M. Cross, W. E. Lemke, and P. D. Miller, Jr., New York, 1976.

――――. *Scriptures, Sects and Visions.* Cleveland, 1980.

Tcherikover, Victor. *Hellenistic Civilization and the Jews,* trans. by S. Appelbaum. Philadelphia, 1959.

Testuz, Michel. *Les idées religieuses du Livre des Jubilés.* Geneva, 1960.

Thompson, Alden L. *Responsibility for Evil in the Theodicy of IV Ezra, A Study Illustrating the Significance of Form and Structure for the Meaning of the Book.* SBL Dissertation Series 29. Missoula, MT, 1977.

Thomson, J. E. H. "Apocalyptic Literature." In *International Standard Bible Encyclopaedia* 1: 161–78. Chicago, 1915.

Tillich, Paul. *Systematic Theology.* Chicago, 1957.

Towner, W. Sibley. "Poetic Passages of Daniel 1–6." *CBQ* 31 (1969): 317–26.

――――. *Daniel.* Atlanta, 1984.

Tresmontant, Claude. *Etudes de métaphysique biblique.* Paris, 1955.

――――. *La doctrine morale des prophètes d'Israël.* Paris, 1958.

van Unnik, W. C., ed. *La Littérature Juive entre Tenach et Mischna.* Leiden, 1974.

VanderKam, James C. *Enoch and the Growth of an Apocalyptic Tradition.* CBQ Monograph Series 16. Washington, 1984.

de Vaux, R. *La Genèse.* Paris, 1961.

Vermes, G. "Son of Man." Appendix E in M. Black, *An Aramaic Approach to the Gospels and Acts.* Oxford, 1968.

Volz, P. *Die Eschatologie der jüdischen Gemeinde im neutestamentlichen Zeitalter.* Tübingen, 1934.

Weinberg, M. "The Covenant of Grant in the Old Testament and in the Ancient Near East." *JAOS* 90 (1970): 184–203.

Weissbach, F. H. *Die Keilschriften der Achämeniden.* Leipzig, 1911.

Welch, Adam C. *Visions of the End.* London, 1958.

Westermann, C. *The Old Testament and Christian Faith,* ed. B. W. Anderson. New York, 1963.

――――. *Genesis.* BKAT 1. Neukirchen-Vluyn, 1966–1968.

_____. *Genesis 1–11: A Commentary.* trans. by J. J. Scullion. Minneapolis, 1984.

Wheelwright, P. *The Burning Fountain.* Bloomington, IN, 1954.

Wilder, A. N. *Eschatology and Ethics in the Teaching of Jesus.* New York, 1939.

Wilson, R. D. "The Aramaic of Daniel." *Biblical and Theological Studies,* ed. Members of the Faculty of Princeton Theol. Sem. New York, 1912, 261–305.

Winter, Paul. Review of J. van der Ploeg, *Le Targum de Job* (Amsterdam, 1962), in *Rev Q* 4:441.

Wyngarden. *The Syriac Version of the Book of Daniel.* Leipzig, 1923.

Zevit, Z. "The Structure and Individual Elements of Daniel 7." *ZAW* 80 (1968): 385ff.

Zimmerli, W. *Ezekiel: A Commentary on the Book of the Prophet Ezekiel,* vol. 1 trans. by R. Clements; ed. by F. M. Cross and K. Baltzer. Philadelphia, 1979.

INDEXES

I. Index of References to Ancient Texts

1. THE OLD TESTAMENT

209

2. THE OLD TESTAMENT APOCRYPHA

3. THE OLD TESTAMENT PSEUDEPIGRAPHA

4. THE QUMRAN LITERATURE

5. RABBINIC LITERATURE

Mishnah

Babylonian Talmud

Jerusalem Talmud

Tosefta

6. THE NEW TESTAMENT

7. EARLY CHRISTIAN LITERATURE

8. CLASSICAL LITERATURE

INDEXES

II. Index of References to Modern Authors

INDEXES

III. Index of References to Subjects

SUBJECTS

SUBJECTS

INDEX OF REFERENCES